THE JUNIOR MANUAL

A HANDBOOK OF METHODS FOR JUNIOR CHRISTIAN ENDEAVOR WORKERS

BY

AMOS R. WELLS

MANAGING EDITOR OF THE GOLDEN RULE AND THE JUNIOR GOLDEN RULE, AUTHOR OF "WAYS OF WORKING SERIES," "SOCIAL EVENINGS," "GOLDEN RULE MEDITATIONS," ETC.

First Fruits Press
Wilmore, Kentucky
c2015

The junior manual : a handbook of methods for junior Christian Endeavor workers, by Amos R. Wells.

First Fruits Press, ©2015
Previously published: Boston and Chicago: United Society of Christian Endeavor, ©1895.

ISBN: 9781621713883 (print), 9781621713890 (digital)

Digital version at http://place.asburyseminary.edu/christianendeavorbooks/13/

For all other uses, contact:

First Fruits Press
B.L. Fisher Library
Asbury Theological Seminary
204 N. Lexington Ave.
Wilmore, KY 40390
http://place.asburyseminary.edu/firstfruits

Wells, Amos R. (Amos Russel), 1862-1933.
    The junior manual : a handbook of methods for junior Christian Endeavor workers / by Amos R. Wells.
    vi, 304 pages ; 21 cm.
    Wilmore, Ky. : First Fruits Press, ©2015.
    Reprint. Previously published: Boston : United Society of Christian Endeavor, ©1895.
    ISBN: 9781621713883 (pbk.)
    1. International Society of Christian Endeavor. 2. Christian education of young people -- Handbooks, manuals, etc. I. Title.
BV1426 .W47 2015

Cover design by Jonathan Ramsay

asburyseminary.edu
800.2ASBURY
204 North Lexington Avenue
Wilmore, Kentucky 40390

First Fruits
THE ACADEMIC OPEN PRESS OF ASBURY SEMINARY

First Fruits Press
The Academic Open Press of Asbury Theological Seminary
204 N. Lexington Ave., Wilmore, KY 40390
859-858-2236
first.fruits@asburyseminary.edu
asbury.to/firstfruits

THE JUNIOR MANUAL.

A HANDBOOK OF METHODS

FOR

JUNIOR CHRISTIAN ENDEAVOR WORKERS.

BY

AMOS R. WELLS,

MANAGING EDITOR OF THE GOLDEN RULE AND THE JUNIOR GOLDEN RULE,
AUTHOR OF "WAYS OF WORKING SERIES," "SOCIAL EVENINGS,"
"GOLDEN RULE MEDITATIONS," ETC.

———

BOSTON AND CHICAGO:
UNITED SOCIETY OF CHRISTIAN ENDEAVOR.

PREFACE.

THE preparation of this Manual would have been quite impossible for me had I not received the most cordial assistance from Junior workers all over the world. In response to a request printed in *The Golden Rule*, letters from Junior superintendents fairly rained down upon me, each expressing the great need of a manual of Junior methods, and the desire of the writer to co-operate. I wish it were possible to print here the names of these kind friends, who are more the authors of this book than I am. I can at least express thus publicly my sense of obligation to them, and my sincere gratitude.

Will not all Junior workers take up and continue this partnership? New and useful ways of working are constantly devised by Junior superintendents. If you will send to me, at the office of *The Golden Rule*, Boston, Mass., an account of any helpful plan not incorporated in these pages, it will be published at once in the international Christian Endeavor organ, and be inserted in future editions of the Junior Manual.

It is too much to hope that this book, even though a large amount of labor has been spent upon it, will prove entirely satisfactory to every one, and in all of its forty chapters. I have done my best, however, to make it straightforward, practical, and to the point; and I shall be richly rewarded if the noble Junior Christian Endeavor workers, whom I so much honor, are in any way inspired and helped by these pages.

AMOS R. WELLS.

BOSTON, March 22, 1895.

CONTENTS.

CONTENTS.

THE JUNIOR MANUAL.

CHAPTER I.

HISTORY OF THE JUNIOR SOCIETY OF CHRISTIAN ENDEAVOR.

The Mizpah Circle. — One of the immediate precursors of the Christian Endeavor Society may be said to have been a little missionary society organized by the wife of the founder of Christian Endeavor, Mrs. Francis E. Clark. The Williston Mizpah Circle consisted of girls and boys, who met once a week on Saturday afternoons in Portland, Me., earned money for home and foreign missions, and studied about them.

Another forerunner of the Christian Endeavor Society was the pastor's class connected with the Williston Church ; a company of young people who met with the pastor each week to study the church creed, *Pilgrim's Progress*, and other books. Especially was this class a forerunner of the Junior society, for its members signed a pledge in many respects like the Junior pledge of to-day.

On that eventful day, February 2, 1881, the first society of Christian Endeavor was formed, which included some boys and girls, as well as many older young people.

The First Junior Society. — Christian Endeavor went on for three years before a distinctively Junior society was formed. In southwestern Iowa, in the college town of Tabor, was an earnest pastor, J. W. Cowan by name. There were no older Christian Endeavor societies in town, because the Young Men's and Young Women's Christian Associations of the college seemed to fill their place ; but for the children there was no Christian organization, and the idea occurred to Mr. Cowan to form them into a Junior Christian Endeavor society.

The date of the organization of this first society is March 27, 1884. There were eleven charter members, all of whom have grown up into earnest Christian manhood and womanhood. The first to sign the Junior constitution is now a young man, Mr. Raymond C. Brooks, who has graduated from Yale Divinity School, and begun a successful course as minister of the gospel.

This first society adopted the Christian Endeavor constitution, including the iron-clad pledge. Within two years after its organization, a Young People's Society of Christian Endeavor was formed from this Junior society by the graduation of its members. Moved by the example of their successful methods, the college organizations of the town changed their form, and became probably the first distinctively college Christian Endeavor society.

Early Workers. — The name of the first Junior superintendent, the leader of this Tabor society, should be held in perpetual honor. She was Miss Belle Smith. Much credit for the early spread of the movement is also due to Mrs. E. H. Slocum, the first secretary of the Iowa State Christian Endeavor Union. From this small beginning, in 1884, the society developed, until, at the Minnesota Convention of 1891, General Secretary Baer reported 855 Junior societies.

Rapid Growth. — No separate record of Junior societies was made until that date. The next year, at New York, an immense increase was announced, the number being 2,574. In 1893, at Montreal, the figures had risen to 4,136. In 1894, at Cleveland, the record stood 6,809 societies, with 365,000 members. At this writing, not long before the Boston Convention of 1895, there are about 8,000 societies, with approximately half a million members.

Just a Few of the Workers. — This growth is due to many earnest workers in addition to those already named. Probably no branch of Christian Endeavor has been so fruitful as the Junior Society in creating consecrated and zealous laborers. Among those who have been most active in promoting this movement among the children is Mrs. Francis E. Clark, who, during her Christian Endeavor journey around the world with her husband, devoted herself especially, in many addresses, to teaching pastors and their wives, and Christian Endeavor workers, the blessedness of labor for the children, and the best methods to use in establishing and carrying on Junior societies.

Another worker who has done yeoman service by tongue and pen, and in many different regions, for the promotion of the Junior cause, is Mrs. Alice May Scudder of New Jersey. Prominent also on this noble roll of honor is Miss Kate H. Haus of Missouri, Mr. Thomas Wainwright ("Uncle Tom") of Illinois, Mr. William S. Ferguson of Pennsylvania, Miss Nettie Harrington of Wisconsin, Miss Lillian A. Wilcox and Miss Grace E. Hyde of Massachusetts, Miss Belle P. Nason of California, Miss Mary C. Merritt of Ohio, Mrs. E. C. Smith of Connecticut, Rev. W. W. Sleeper of Wisconsin, Miss Bertha L. Hess of Idaho, Mrs. M. L. Hageman of Indiana, Miss Daisy Dunnington of West Virginia, Miss Laura C. Preston of Oregon, Miss Frances M. Schuyler of New York, Mrs. E. W. Darst and Mrs. George W. Coleman of Massachusetts, Mrs. O. M. Needham of Nebraska, Rev. A. W. Spooner of New Jersey, Miss Flora B. Berry of Maine, Miss Ruth Nash of Kansas, Mr. C. J. Atkinson of Ontario, and Miss Margaret C. Sutton of Quebec. The list of noble and devoted Junior workers could be almost indefinitely extended.

One of the chief features in the rapid progress of the Junior cause has been the formation of Junior city unions. The first of these was organized at Bridgeport, Conn., in 1891.

State Superintendents. — Another step in advance was the establishment of the office of State superintendent of Junior work. Nearly all State unions now have such officers, and most of the persons just named hold that honorable position.

At the Conventions. — At the International Conventions the Junior work is claiming a more and more prominent place. The New York Convention of 1892 first honored it with a separate session, which was crowded and enthusiastic. At Montreal the great Drill Hall was given up to a still more inspiring meeting, while at Cleveland, in 1894, the immense Sängerfest building was filled with more than ten thousand people, whose attention was held through the crowded programme of the Junior rally.

The Banners. — Much interest has been excited by the Junior banners awarded at the International Conventions. The first of these was given at the New York Convention to Illinois, the State that had the largest number of Junior societies. This banner was carried off by Illinois the next year; but in 1894, at Cleveland, it was surrendered to Pennsylvania.

At Montreal, two other Junior banners were awarded. One, for the largest proportionate increase in Junior societies during the preceding year, was carried off by the District of Columbia. The second, for the largest absolute gain in Junior societies, went to New York. This latter banner, for the greatest absolute gain, was also won by Pennsylvania in 1894, while the banner for the largest proportionate increase was at that same Convention turned over by the District of Columbia to the State of Delaware. These banners are made up of Junior badges contributed by societies all over the world.

Honor Books.— At the coming Boston Convention a new feature is to be introduced for the benefit of the Juniors, — immense honor books, four of them, in one of which are to be enrolled the names of all Junior societies that have contributed to missions ten dollars more during the year than during the former year; in another, the names of the societies whose members are faithful to the pledge; while the other two are for the societies whose members help their pastor in every way he wishes, and for those that help to make home happy.

Besides the importance of the Junior rallies at the International Conventions, the cause is gaining more and more attention at the annual conventions of the State unions, nearly all of which now hold enthusiastic and helpful Junior sessions.

Their Paper and Song-Book. — Important steps in the progress of the Junior movement were the founding, in January, 1893, of the Junior international organ, *The Junior Golden Rule*, and the publishing at about the same time of a Junior song-book, whose editors were Mr. Ira D. Sankey, General Secretary Baer, and Mr. William Shaw, treasurer of the United Society.

CHAPTER II.

HOW TO ORGANIZE A JUNIOR SOCIETY.

Preparation. — In forming a Junior society too much pains cannot be taken to become perfectly familiar with the best plans before the society is set on foot. Write to the Junior superintendent of your county union or of your State union, tell all about your surroundings, and ask as many questions as you can think of. Consult with the best Junior workers in your neighborhood. Send to the United Society of Christian Endeavor for their Junior helps, and read carefully the whole of them.

The Junior Committee. — Before you enter upon your work, get your assistants. Ask the Young People's Society of Christian Endeavor to appoint as a regular committee, called the "Junior committee," some of their best workers, who will aid you.

Talk It Up. — Do preliminary personal work with the boys and girls. Tell them of the good times a Junior society will bring about. Touch their noble impulses by showing them what a blessing such a society would be to the church, to the community, and to themselves. By noticing who are most interested in this talk, you will gain many valuable hints for the selection of officers.

The Constitution. — Make ready the constitution and by-laws of the new society. By far your best plan will be to adopt the Model Junior Constitution and By-Laws, which may be modified, of course, as necessity requires. Here they are:

CONSTITUTION.

ARTICLE I. NAME.

This society shall be called the JUNIOR SOCIETY OF CHRISTIAN ENDEAVOR OF...

ARTICLE II. OBJECT.

Its object shall be to promote an earnest Christian life among the boys and girls who may become members, and prepare them for the active service of Christ.

ARTICLE III. MEMBERSHIP.

1. The members shall consist of two classes, Active and Trial.

2. *Active Members.* Any boy or girl between the ages of.............. and................inclusive, who shall be approved by the superintendent and assistant, may become an active member of the society by taking the following pledge : —

JUNIOR MEMBERSHIP PLEDGE.

Trusting in the Lord Jesus Christ for strength, I promise him that I will strive to do whatever he would like to have me do ; that I will pray and read the Bible every day ; and that, just so far as I know how, I will try to lead a Christian life. I will be present at every meeting of the society when I can, and will take some part in every meeting.

Name...

I am willing that......................should sign this pledge, and will do all I can to help............keep it.

Parent's name... ....

Residence.............. ....

OPTIONAL PLEDGE.

[Form No. 2. For societies where the majority of members are under ten years.]

I promise Jesus to pray to him every day for strength to do whatever he would like to have me do. I promise Jesus to come to every meeting.

Name...

Date.. ....

3. *Trial Members* shall be those who wish to attend, and who promise to behave when at the meeting. These shall have their names on the trial roll, but shall not sign the pledge, or serve as leaders for the meetings.

ARTICLE IV. OFFICERS.

1. The officers of the society shall be superintendent, assistant superintendent, president, vice-president, secretary, and treasurer. There shall be lookout, prayer-meeting, and social committees, and such other committees as may be needed.

ARTICLE V. DUTIES OF OFFICERS.

1. The *superintendent* shall have full control of the society.

2. The *assistant superintendent* shall aid the superintendent in her work. The assistant shall take care of all funds belonging to the society, the money being turned over to her by the treasurer at the close of each meeting.

3. The *president* shall conduct the business meetings, under the direction of the superintendent.

4. The *vice-president* shall act in the absence of the president.

5. The *secretary* shall keep a correct list of the members, take the minutes of the business meetings, and call the roll at each meeting.

6. The *treasurer* shall take up the collections, enter the amount in the account-book, and turn over the money to the assistant superintendent, and also enter all expenditures as directed by the superintendent.

7. The superintendent and assistant may be appointed by the pastor, or by the senior society (if one exists), with the approval of the pastor. The other officers and committees shall be nominated by the superintendent and assistant, and elected by the society. All officers shall be chosen once in six months.

ARTICLE VI. DUTIES OF COMMITTEES.

1. The *lookout committee* shall secure the names of any who may wish to join the society, and report the same to the superintendents for action. They shall also obtain excuses from members absent from the roll call, and affectionately look after and reclaim any who seem indifferent to their pledge.

2. The *prayer-meeting committee* shall, in connection with the superintendent, select topics, assign leaders, and do what they can to secure faithfulness to the prayer-meeting pledge.

3. The *social committee* shall welcome the children to the meetings and introduce them to the other members of the society. They may also arrange for occasional sociables.

ARTICLE VII. RELATIONSHIP.

The relation of the Junior to the senior society of Christian Endeavor should be close and intimate; and it is expected that, when the members of the Junior society have reached their age limit, they will enter the Christian Endeavor society as active members.

ARTICLE VIII. MEETINGS.

1. A prayer-meeting shall be held once every week. A consecration meeting shall be held once a month, at which the pledge shall be

read and the roll called, and the responses of the members shall be considered a renewal of the pledge of the society. If any member is absent from three consecutive consecration meetings, without excuse, his name shall be dropped from the list of members.

2. Part of the hour of the weekly meeting shall, if deemed best, be used by the pastor or superintendent of the society for instruction, or for other exercises which they may approve.

BY-LAWS.

1. The society shall hold a prayer meeting on ....
of each week. The last regular meeting of each month shall be a consecration meeting. The business meeting may be held in connection with the first regular meeting of each month.

2. The officers and committees shall be chosen in..................and
...................and continue six months, beginning on the first of the month following their election.

3. Special meetings of the society may be held at any time, at the call of the superintendent.

4. A collection shall be taken at the consecration meeting, and at the other meetings if desired, the money thus obtained to be held available for benevolent objects and to meet the expenses of the society.

5. All committees should meet at least once a month for consultation with the superintendent in regard to their work.

6. All expenditures shall be made under the direction of the superintendents.

7. Other committees may be added, whose duties shall be defined as follows:—

The *music committee* shall distribute and collect the singing books, and co-operate with the leader of the meeting in trying in every way to make the singing a success.

The *missionary committee* shall arrange for an occasional missionary meeting, and seek to interest the members in home and foreign work.

The *temperance committee* shall arrange for an occasional temperance meeting, and circulate a temperance pledge among the members.

The *Sunday-school committee* shall secure the names of children who do not attend Sunday school, and invite them to become members of the Sunday school.

The *flower committee* shall provide flowers for the Sunday school room, and distribute fruit and flowers to the sick and needy.

The *scrap-book committee* shall collect pictures and clippings, and make scrap-books for sick and disabled members, and for distribution in the hospitals.

The *relief committee* shall collect clothing for the destitute children found in the Sunday school and society, and bring it to the superintendent for distribution.

The *birthday committee* shall report all birthdays as they occur among the members, so that special prayer may be offered for each member on his or her birthday.

8. This constitution and by-laws may be altered or amended whenever the superintendents and pastor find it necessary.

No Unnecessary Differences. —It is very advantageous to make the constitution and work of the Junior society as near like those of the Young People's society as is possible. The reason for this is that then, when the Juniors come to graduate into the older society, the transition will be less difficult, and they will he better prepared to take up advanced work.

The First Meeting. — After all this preliminary work is done, call your first meeting of the children. Let it be on a Saturday afternoon, when all can attend. Advertise it as widely as possible, in church, Sunday school, and newspaper. Avoid disappointment by stating plainly the age limit, usually from six to fourteen. You will get a good attendance, especially of the boys whom you are most anxious to reach, if you announce that there will be some refreshments after the meeting. Get the best speaker from your Junior committee to prepare a little talk to the children. They will listen to those nearer their own age more readily at first than they will listen to you.

After the proposed methods of the new society are fully explained, being put in as attractive a form as possible, ask the children present who would like to join such a society to rise. With these, go over the constitution carefully, article by article. Explain each point, and let each division of the constitution and by-laws be adopted by those who intend to join the new society. Appoint a nominating committee to meet with the superintendent during the week and nominate the officers; then bring forward the refreshments, and at the close have an orderly adjournment to meet on the next Sunday afternoon.

The Call. — At this meeting the superintendent will preside. Have some lively singing and a few short prayers. Then let the superintendent talk earnestly about the conditions of joining the new society, briefly explaining the pledge and its importance, and what a solemn thing it is to sign such a pledge. Then ask the children to tell you whether they wish to join as active or associate (trial) members, and make a note of each on your list. Announce a topic and leader for next Sunday's meeting, and close with singing, " God be with you till we meet again," and with the Christian Endeavor benediction.

Go Slowly. — You will notice that up to this point you have not received a single member, nor has a single pledge been signed. During the following week visit each child separately. Talk over the pledge. See that they understand it perfectly, and accept their signatures to it only after you are thoroughly assured of their sincerity, and that they are not merely attracted by the novelty of the affair. Admit them as associate (trial) members unless you are certain that they are deeply in earnest as active members.

Receive no signature without the signature of the parent to the pledge, and do not accept the latter until you have talked with the parents yourself, and shown them just what the pledge means both for their child and for themselves.

Now you have your body of Juniors, and can go to work to form your committees and choose your officers. The meetings from this time on should be conducted by the Juniors, and along regular lines.

This is a slow way to begin, and it may seem to some that it is too cautious, but the most experienced workers know that a little caution at the beginning will save much discouragement and vain effort farther on. A society thus founded will be founded on the rock.

Outside Help. — It is always well, in organizing a new Junior society, to get the assistance of some experienced Junior worker, having her upon the ground, having her talk with the children, and consult with the new superintendent and her assistants at every point. In addition to this, it is helpful to have present Juniors from other societies, especially at the first meeting, when the Juniors come together to decide for or against membership in this society.   Let two or three of these speak to the young folks, and tell them what their society is doing, and how much they enjoy it.

A Recognition Service. — It will be pleasant for the older society to hold a recognition service as soon as their younger brothers are organized.   Both societies will be present.   The president of the older society will congratulate the Juniors on their organization, and the Junior president will respond briefly. The older Endeavorers will discuss plans for aiding the Juniors in their work.   The pastor will give some hints as to the tasks all his Endeavorers might undertake.   There will be much prayer.   Be sure to assign to the Juniors themselves some decided part in the meeting, having them recite, give responsive readings, sing, and take part, it may be, in sentence prayers.

Don't Wait. — In your church there may be (it is still possible !) some opposition to the Young People's Society of Christian Endeavor.   Do not wait for this opposition to die down before you organize a Junior society, provided the opposition would not extend also to that.   It has happened in many instances that the organization of a Junior society taught the older church members what Christian Endeavor really means, and prepared them to accept with readiness an older society of Christian Endeavor.

Do not wait either, before you organize your Junior society, to make too elaborate preparations and consult with too many workers.   If you delay too long, the children's enthusiasm, that you are so eager to utilize, will have vanished.

Do not wait too long, either, seeking for a single Christian with grit and grace enough to undertake the superintendency. If, after diligent search, no ideal or half-ideal superintendent appears, appoint a Junior committee from the older society.   It is a good plan to have a committee of six, two of whom are to carry on the society each month, all six serving in the course of the quarter.   Of course they will all be in constant consultation with one another.

An Impressive Beginning. — The plan of an Iowa superintendent in starting her Junior society will be suggestive to others.   She had carefully watched her trial members for some time before permitting any to sign the pledge.   After some weeks she found three boys and three girls who were, she decided, true Christians. After talking with them beforehand, she asked them at one of the meetings to take the front seat.

With her watch and a needle she showed how so small a thing as a needle can stop the entire machinery of the watch, and applied this to the principle of pledge-keeping, failure to hold to any of the things promised being the little needle that would stop the right action of their lives. Earnestly and solemnly the superintendent went on to speak of the seriousness of taking such a pledge.

She then gave each of the six a pledge card, and they all knelt, the other Juniors bowing their heads. On their knees the six Juniors read the pledge slowly together. Each little head then went down on the seat, and, taking turns, they repeated this sentence: " Dear Jesus, help me to keep this pledge." After an earnest prayer from the leader, each Junior went forward to the desk and signed the pledge, and thus the active membership of that society was started.

Junior Companies. — If you are compelled to start your society with few members, try the plan adopted by a Kansas Junior society at whose initial meeting only twelve young people were present. These twelve were made leaders of twelve companies, on condition that each promised to get three more members. Other young people later undertook the same task, volunteering to raise companies. This organization into companies was continued, and the work of each leader was recorded by a chart. If all four members were present, a blue star was placed on the chart. Five cents in the collection from that company placed a silver star there, and a new member added to their number glittered as a gilt star.

Committee Outlines. — At the outset of your society work, however familiar the plans may be to you, remember that they are all strange to the children. One of the best ways of setting the wheels smoothly to running is to give to each officer and to each member of the committees simple outlines of the main features of the work they are about to undertake. Such outlines are given for the committees in the chapter on committee work.

It is essential that each member of the society be set as soon as possible to doing something. Let each committee hold a meeting at the earliest possible date.   You cannot attend them all ; but you can see that some older Endeavorer, familiar with the work of that committee in his society, is present to superintend the planning of the Juniors.

Country Societies. — In country districts the children may be so scattered and the parents so busy that it will seem quite difficult to get them together at any one season for the purpose of carrying on a Junior society.   In some localities this difficulty has been met by holding the Junior society in immediate connection with the Sunday school, letting it occupy the last half of the Sunday-school hour.   Another good plan is to adopt a single centre convenient for the greatest number, holding the Junior meetings there, and permitting the other children who belong to the church to join this society as members of what might be called the home department.   They will be given committee work to do in their own neighborhoods.   They will sign the pledge and keep its provisions as far as possible under the circumstances, engaging in daily prayer and Bible-reading. They will make monthly reports to the central society to be read at the consecration meetings, and will attend whenever attendance is possible.

CHAPTER III.

PASTORS, CHURCHES, AND JUNIORS.

The Juniors at Church. — A pastor has truly said that the Junior Endeavor society is, next to the home, the best instrumentality in existence for insuring the presence of the children at church. The superintendent should keep the church meeting in mind in all Junior work. If the congregation is in the habit of repeating the Apostles' Creed, singing the Gloria or the Doxology, let these be taught the children, and frequently practised.

The training for responsive reading given in the Junior society will make the Juniors more ready than many of their elders in the responsive readings of the church services.

Above all things, teach the Juniors the church hymns, not to the exclusion of their own bright children's songs, but in addition to them. The pastor will be glad to tell the superintendent what hymns are to be sung in church the next Sunday, and these the Juniors may sing at the Junior meeting. Such methods in some churches have made the Juniors a strong factor in congregational singing. In fact, nobody else knows the hymns quite so well as they.

Sermons for Juniors. — If the pastor does not preach five-minute sermons to the children, it would be a good thing for the Junior superintendent to suggest that he take up this most helpful line of work. An Australian pastor has obtained the attendance of all his Juniors, — and he has a large number, — at the regular church services. He uses this excellent programme: The first Scripture reading is read by the congregation and the Juniors alternately. This Scripture lesson contains the text of the five-minute children's sermon, which the pastor then preaches. A child's hymn is next sung by the whole congregation, and the pastor then turns to the mature portion of his audience.

The Pastor in the Junior Meeting. — One Sunday a sturdy little fellow entered a Junior society. After looking around, he asked, " Where is the preacher? I thought he was here." The preacher was immediately sent for.

The children themselves will soon prove to the pastor that he is welcome to the meetings ; but it is well occasionally to give the pastor a special invitation to be present at the Junior meeting, and to set apart four or five minutes for his use, telling him beforehand just how much time he will have, telling the children also beforehand that the pastor is to speak to them, and awakening their curiosity and expectation.

It is needless to say, however, that the pastor should be present at the Junior meeting as often as he can, consistently with his other duties. Every true pastor will feel this to be a joy and privilege. He will take part with the children simply and briefly ; he will make them feel that he is one of them ; he will urge them to pray for him and for the work of the church. One of the best ways in which he can show his interest in the Juniors and draw them close to him, will be to give them an occasional social afternoon at his home.

Attendance Cards. — There are a great many methods of spurring the Juniors to better attendance on church services, but one of the simplest is this. Each Junior is given a card at the weekly meeting ; and on the following Sunday these cards, appropriately filled out, are dropped in a basket or box in the lobby of the church as the Junior enters. The card is like this : —

Christ's Church,
CATSKILL, N. Y.

For Regular Church Attendance.

SUNDAY..........................*1895.*

NAME..

Texts. — Ask the Juniors at every meeting how many of them have attended the morning service, and follow this question by the request that all who have so attended repeat the text that the minister used. At first you will not get a very good response; but very soon the Juniors will learn to listen to this part, at least, of the sermon.

Sermon Talks. — A sermon talk is effective in spurring the Juniors to better attendance on the church services, and better attention when there. All the Juniors who are at church are asked to stand, and are then questioned as to the name of the preacher, if he was a stranger, and as to his subject and text. Sometimes the superintendent asks questions on the main points of the sermon, but more often tries to get one fact or illustration from each Junior. This work can very profitably be placed in charge of one of the assistant superintendents.

A Roll of Honor. — A roll of honor is an excellent thing for promoting church attendance. Have a large list of the names of the Juniors pasted in some conspicuous place, and paste opposite the name of each Junior a silver star for each time he is present at church. Another plan is to make a wall roll divided into twelve sections, and at the close of the month write in the appropriate section the names of all the Juniors who have been present at church during the month.

For Church Attendance. — In order to promote attendance at church, some superintendents give a little prize every half-year to the Juniors who respond to the roll-call, " Present at church," the largest number of times.

Church Committees. — Some societies have church committees. The duty of this committee is to keep a record of all Juniors who do not attend church services, and to try in every way to bring them in. It also keeps a record of those who are regularly at the services, and makes an honor roll of all Juniors whose church attendance for the month is perfect.

It is a shrewd plan to place upon this committee at least two or three of the Juniors who are not in the habit of regular church attendance. Such work as this has been the means, in cases not a few, of inducing the parents of Juniors to attend church more regularly.

Thought Blanks. — One Baptist pastor of whom I have heard gives a prize every six months to the Junior who brings to the Junior meeting, during the half-year, the largest number of blanks like the following, filled out in the best shape with the best thoughts from the sermon. This is found very effective in securing not merely attendance, but attention.

Junior Christian Endeavor.

MORNING SERVICE.

Date..189

PREACHER..

SCRIPTURE LESSON..

TEXT..

....

THOUGHTS.

....

....

....

....

....

NAME..

A Junior Corner. — Of course most of the Juniors will wish to sit with their parents in the church services; but there will be enough of them who, for various reasons, cannot do this, to warrant in most churches the establishment of a Junior corner, which will usually be well filled at the morning church service. The secretary of the Junior society should notice what Juniors are present at church, and make a report of the number at the next meeting of the society.

Junior Pews. — Some Wisconsin Endeavorers have the habit of renting two pews near the pulpit for the use of those Juniors whose parents do not regularly attend church. These pews are filled with children, and the overflow crowds the neighboring pews also. The Junior treasurer, who pays the pew-rent in the name of the society, acts as children's usher. Almost the entire Junior society of this church are present at the church service, and the pastor always preaches to them a five-minute sermon, which is enjoyed by the elders as much as by the Juniors.

After Sunday school. — It is an excellent idea, when the church services come after the Sunday school, to invite the Juniors, if they are not accompanied by their parents, to gather after Sunday-school and attend church in a body. In this case a special seat, or several seats, should be assigned them, and a " Junior corner " might be established.

In the Church Service. — Five or ten minutes of some regular church service may, without harm, be set apart for the Juniors. They may be given some position in the front of the congregation, and requested to repeat some of the portions of the Bible they know, giving them in concert, to sing some of their songs, and in other ways to show what the society is accomplishing. This will serve to interest the parents, give fresh enthusiasm to the Juniors, and win new members to the society.

A Church Meeting. — The Junior society can do much to get the children interested in the church to which they belong, and in the wider work of their denomination, by holding occasional meetings that may be called denominational days, or church meetings. Such meetings are suggested in the uniform topics for each year. It should be the aim of the superintendent at these meetings to give the Juniors an idea of the most important points in their church history, some knowledge of the great men of the denomination and the striking events in their lives, of the fundamental principles for which the denomination stands, of the main facts in the organization of their churches, and the like. As bearing more directly upon their own relation to the church, they should be taught at such meetings the meaning of the Lord's Supper, and the reasons why church membership is both a duty and a privilege.

Work with the Pastor. — The superintendent can scarcely consult the pastor too frequently. She should remember that the Junior society is one part of the church, and that for the general conduct of the church in all its parts the pastor is responsible. He will not feel at liberty to advice her in her work unless she shows him unmistakably that such advice is desired. The pastor's aid is almost indispensable, too, if the superintendent would interest the parents in the Junior society. Words from the pulpit, or hints dropped by the pastor in his calls, will do wonders towards maintaining among the parents a lively interest in the work of the society.

How the Pastor May Help. — The pastor may do much for the success of the Junior society by a little thoughtfulness in giving the Juniors a place in the various exercises of the church. The small people will be eager to have something to do, and will be very thorough in the performance of whatever is within their power.

What One Minister Does. —It is wonderful how much can be done toward the success of the Junior society by even a little show of interest on the part of the pastor. I have heard of one minister who prepares for his Juniors every week the lesson for the following Sunday, making an outline of it on the mimeograph, and presenting a copy of it to each Junior. This results in a constant increase of interest.

Gifts of Testaments. — One pastor of whom I know has been especially successful in winning the children to the church, and he makes it his custom to present inexpensive Testaments each year to the Juniors who have attended church not less than forty-eight Sundays. One of the pleasantest exercises of Children's Day is the presentation of these Testaments, accompanied by a word or two showing what the church might be to the Juniors, and what the Juniors might be to the church.

Pastoral Letters to the Juniors. — It sometimes happens that the pastor cannot very frequently attend the Junior society, or take part in its meetings. There is no pastor in the land, however, who cannot occasionally follow the example of one good children's pastor I know, who frequently sends letters to his Juniors. These he manifolds, so that each can take a copy home and show to his parents. Through these letters the pastor is able to exercise a very real control over the society, to check any tendencies toward frivolity and disorderliness or carelessness, and to praise them, and inspire them in every good work.

For Helping the Pastor. — Every Junior society should have a "pastor's aid committee," which shall be set, either by the pastor or the superintendent, to doing things that are helpful in the pastor's work.

The Pastor's Boys. — The boys will like to be enrolled in a little sub-society of their own, which may be called the "pastor's boys," and set to doing work like the following: They must always be ready to serve the pastor at any time. They must make it their aim to invite to the church services at least one boy a Sunday who is not in the habit of attending church. They must sit in a body as near as possible to the pulpit, and must keep good order. They must agree to pray that the sermon may be effective in winning men to the better life.

Once a month the head of the committee must make a special report to the society. Of course this work cannot be carried on without the hearty assistance of the pastor, who should occasionally invite these boys, with their superintendent, to his home, spending a pleasant evening with them.

A Present for the Pastor. — It is a good thing, both for pastor and society, to have the Juniors occasionally give a little present to their pastor. Invite him to your next social, giving him a place of honor, and decorating his chair, and have the president of the Junior society present the gift with appropriate words.

A good present for your pastor, or your pastor's wife, may easily be made in this way. Give each member of the society a small sheet of nice paper, asking the Juniors each to write a greeting. They may be urged to decorate the sheets in ways of their own devising. When the sheets are returned, the superintendent will bind them into two pretty books, which the pastor and his wife will greatly treasure.

Another Present. — Give to each Junior a square card, the colors being different. Ask each Junior to write upon his card the Bible verse he likes best. At the following meeting, when these cards are brought back, each Junior will recite his Bible verse, at the same time handing the superintendent the card. These she will tie together with a ribbon of the Junior color, and will give the whole to the pastor, who will like to make these verses the opportunity for a little talk to the Juniors at the next meeting.

Close Connection. — The Juniors may be as closely bound to the church as the church itself desires. Some churches may prefer the very close connection between the Junior society and the church organization adopted by a certain Presbyterian church I have heard of. The executive committee of this Junior society is composed of the pastor, one elder, and three other persons appointed by the session of the church. This executive committee appoints the officers of the society, or, if it thinks best, permits the Juniors to select them. The pastor is himself chairman of the executive committee, and superintendent of the society.

Juniors in the Church Prayer Meeting. — I do not think it best to urge the Juniors to take any conspicuous part in the church prayer meeting. Such urging should come from the parents themselves, if they think it best for their children. If, however, the Juniors of their own accord raise their voices in the meetings of their elders, this pleasant addition to the hour should be gladly welcomed. The Juniors should be made to feel that they are wanted at the church prayer meeting, that their verses are helpful, that their voices are needed in the singing, and that, whatever part they may take now, they are expected at no distant date to take a very decided part, and in due time to conduct those meetings themselves.

A Visit of Investigation. — The officers of the church, and especially those that have to do with the reception of members, should be urged to pay an occasional visit to the Junior society. At these visits they should keep their eyes open, and especially notice signs of thoughtfulness and earnestness among the Juniors, and see if, in their opinion, some of these little folks are not ready for church membership. In no better way can the church officers and the pastor come to know the young Christians of the congregation, and they will find no better opportunity for the winning of new members for the church.

CHAPTER IV.

WORKING WITH THE PARENTS.

Parents Through Children. — For the sake of the parents, as well as for the sake of the children, the superintendent should insist strenuously on the signing of the parents' pledge that accompanies every Junior pledge. Many a parent has been brought to Christ by this means. A suggestive incident is given by Mr. William S. Ferguson.

At one of his Junior meetings a card was handed in, signed by the parents, with these words : " We are not professing Christian people. We want our children to be better than we are, and we will try to help them keep this pledge." The new Juniors took a great deal of interest in the meetings, and became very active ; and one day the little girl, taking part in the consecration meeting, said that she wanted her comrades to pray for her parents, that they might " soon become members of our Junior society." This was said with an expression of deep earnestness that showed her profound longing.

The prayers of the Juniors were answered. To-day the parents are both members of the church, and active members of the older Christian Endeavor society. They say that the signing of the Junior pledge first set them to thinking ; that, keeping it, they looked after their children to see that they read the Bible and prayed every day, and soon they began to pray with them. The following steps were easy.

To the Parents. — The following is an admirable and business-like letter, which is sent with a copy of the pledge to the parents of the boy or girl who intends to join the Junior society. It will be observed that the letter calls especial attention to the promises made in the pledge, and to the promise of the parent to help the child keep the pledge. A little carefulness of this sort at the beginning of the children's connection with the society will add greatly to the society's efficiency.

My dear Friend, — Your child has expressed the wish to join the Junior Christian Endeavor Society of this church. Will you please read the enclosed pledge carefully?

You will see that your child is to make certain promises. These promises are made to the Lord Jesus Christ, in dependence upon him. They are not meant to be assumed lightly. They are not temporary. They are meant to be life-long. These promises assume that your child may be converted, and live a Christian life.

Should you consent to your child's signing this pledge, please notice that you will promise to help that child to keep the pledge faithfully. Each week we shall issue a lesson paper, with verses to be marked and learned daily. Upon you must rest largely the responsibility for the way in which that promise shall be kept.

On our part, we shall try to train your child for Christ. And as soon as possible, we shall hope and labor to bring your child into church membership. You are cordially invited to come to all our services, unless you are a member of some other church or congregation.

Cordially and faithfully yours,

CORDA E. GARRISON, *Superintendent.*

A Pointed Letter. — Here is another practical letter, which one Junior worker is in the habit of sending to the parents of children who are thinking of joining the society: —

MR. AND MRS. ....

Dear Friends : — Enclosed you will find the pledge which............. is expected to take in order to become a member of our Junior Christian Endeavor Society. Will you kindly examine it, and only permit ....to sign it with your approval, and with your signatures attached? Please fill out all the blanks. This request is made in order to secure your support and co-operation; for I feel that without your constant sympathy, prayers, and help it will be useless for me to undertake the work.

Superintendent of the Junior Christian Endeavor Society.

A Plea for the Juniors. — The superintendent of a Friends' Junior society in Indiana makes use of the following admirable card, which he sends to the parents of his Juniors: —

A PLEA FOR THE JUNIORS.

That the Junior Society of Christian Endeavor may be effective to the greatest possible extent, the superintendent begs leave by this card to present a few suggestions to the parents of the members. While we believe the society has your sympathy and prayers, we desire your hearty support in the ways here spoken of.

1. Notice early in the week the topic for the next lesson, and call the attention of the children to it, that they may not forget it.

2. If the children should be negligent or forgetful of daily Bible-reading, remind them of the importance of forming the habit in childhood, using the daily readings, which will prove a helpful attendant to the study of the lesson.

3. Encourage daily prayer.

4. Help the children to draw some point from the lesson text or readings out of which they can give a testimony.

5. Encourage regular attendance.

6. Encourage benevolence by giving them money to contribute.

Prayer meeting every Sabbath at 3 o'clock P.M.

ALLEN C. DICKS, *Junior Superintendent.*

Let Her Test It. — The Junior superintendent, before she admits the Junior to the society, should always call upon the mother, and get her to attend a Junior meeting. In this way her support, which is essential, will be assured from the outset.

Put Them at Work. — Nothing interests like active work. If you want the cordial co-operation of the parents, you can gain it in no better way than by setting them at work for the Juniors and the society. Occasionally call on the parents for little talks before the children, giving them a plenty of time for preparation. On other occasions, invite them to be present at the society meeting, and to take just such part as they see the children take, speaking on the regular topic.

If any of the parents are gifted in this line, ask them to give object lessons to the children, or chalk talks. Some of them may be fine singers, and will be glad to sing beautiful songs at the society meetings. Others may play a noble piece of sacred music upon the organ or the piano. Others may have the gift of entertaining, and will prove invaluable assistants in the Junior socials. In all these ways the parents may be interested and kept interested in the work of the society.

A Mothers' Reception. — The Juniors will enjoy giving a reception to their mothers, and will preside at such an affair with surprising dignity and grace. They should present a pretty entertainment of some kind, and light refreshments. For such an affair be sure to appoint committees, one on reception, one on refreshments, and one on programme. Interest other members by appointing them waiters.

Monthly Reports. — It does much to interest the parents in the progress of the Juniors if the superintendent takes the trouble to send to the mothers a monthly report. The following form is in use for this purpose : —

Junior Y. P. S. C. E.

MONTHLY REPORT.

Dear Friend :

Your child, ...has been in.......................standing in the society during the month of.........................., having been.........................in attendance and.........................in behavior. ....has taken part ....Sundays in the month.

The consecration meeting is held the last Sunday in each month. Will you kindly see that............................... has a verse for response at roll call ?

Superintendents' signatures,

....

....

With the Mothers. — A quarterly mothers' meeting is not too often for any Junior society. Let this be made a joint meeting of the Juniors and the mothers, long thought of and carefully planned for by both. If there is a Mothers' Society of Christian Endeavor or a maternal association, the regular meeting of this organization should be merged in this joint meeting.

Work with the Parents. — Whatever the Junior superintendent does or does not do, he should call upon the parents of his Juniors, and in the course of the call should suggest to them ways in which they can help the Juniors in their work. Often the parents are greatly blessed through the work of their children, and in not a few instances have been led to Christ through the conversion of their boys and girls.

This visiting must be systematic, or it will fall hopelessly in arrears in a short time.

The Parents Leading. — Take every opportunity to get the parents of the Juniors to attend the meetings, and never fail, when they come, to urge them to be one with the Juniors, and to take part in the meeting like the rest. A bit of example from the parents will do much to spur the Juniors to greater faithfulness.

Juniors and Parents. — After you have talked to the Juniors about the topic of the meeting, urge them to go home and talk to their parents about the same matter. In private conversation, urge the parents also to question the Juniors about the subject of the meeting. In this way both will be interested, and each will interest the other.

From the Start. — It is an important point in establishing a Junior society to accustom the little folks to the attendance of older people. Unless older people come from the start, they will be likely to embarrass the children with their occasional visits. While this presence of older Endeavorers and parents at the meetings of the Juniors may at first render them more timid, yet it is an assurance that they will take seriously what part they do take, and they will soon develop confidence.

An Open Meeting. — It is good for the Junior society to give, once in a while, an open meeting. Let the Juniors have the church hour, if no other time can be found for them. They will delight to show their parents what they have learned and what they can do, and many friends will be won for the society, both among the Endeavorers and among the older people.

Willing Helpers. — Use the help of the Juniors in connection with your church entertainments, fairs, socials, etc., whenever you can. Set them in charge of a five-cent booth or a ten-cent table, and you will be astonished to see how eagerly they will take up the work.

Honorary Members. — I have heard about the advantage which honorary members have proved to be to a certain Junior society of Washington, D.C. At first these older people were made honorary members as a graceful recognition of their kindness to the society. Soon this honor came to be asked for, and now the society has twenty of such members.

There is a honorary membership committee, which writes letters, inviting the older Christians to become honorary members. They read to the society the letters received in reply, keeping the letters on file, and keeping a record also of what is done for the society by the honorary members. These honorary members are never asked for money, but yet they have given liberally to help the society, and have assisted it in other ways as well.

It is certainly worth while to have honorary members; and we believe that, much as these members may do for the Juniors, the Junior society, especially if the honorary members will work with it, will be of an immensely greater benefit to them.

Mothers' Societies. — Mothers' Societies of Christian Endeavor are of the greatest assistance to the Junior societies, and one of the most hopeful advance steps in the progress of the Junior movement is the springing up of these societies all over the country. If a mothers' society already exists, it is the easiest possible change to transform it into a Mothers' Society of Christian Endeavor, and associate it closely with the workings of the Junior society.

If you have no mothers' society, and wish to organize a Mothers' Society of Christian Endeavor, first do some preliminary talking, striving to interest as many as possible in the new plan. Issue to those interested a call for a meeting, and get the pastor or the Junior superintendent, or better, both, to present to this meeting the methods and purposes of this new organization.

The following simple constitution may be adopted, with any changes that may be necessary to fit it to the local needs:

CONSTITUTION OF THE MOTHERS' SOCIETY OF CHRISTIAN ENDEAVOR.

ARTICLE I. NAME.

This society shall be called the Mothers' Society of Christian Endeavor of the .... Church of [city] ....

ARTICLE II. PURPOSES.

The object of this society shall be to stimulate mothers to raise the standard of the Christian home, and to pray for aid to help the children in their Christian life, especially those that belong to the Junior Society of Christian Endeavor.

ARTICLE III. MEMBERSHIP.

SECTION I. Any woman interested in the welfare of children may become a member of this society by signing the following pledge: —

Trusting in the Lord Jesus Christ for strength, I promise him that I will strive to do whatever he would have me do; especially that I will endeavor to bring the children to Christ and to train them for him. To this end I will co-operate with the Junior Christian Endeavor superintendents in any way I can. I promise to seek daily the Master's blessing on the children. I will attend each meeting of the Mothers' Society of Christian Endeavor, unless prevented by a reason that I can conscientiously give to my Saviour, and will come prepared to add to the interest of the meeting. When obliged to be absent from the consecration meeting, I will, if possible, send a message to be read in response to my name.

Name..

Address..

Date..

SEC. 2. The relation of the Mothers' Society to the Junior Society of Christian Endeavor should be close and intimate, and it is expected that the members will in every way possible seek to promote the spiritual growth of the boys and girls of their church and Sunday school, as well as of the Junior society.

ARTICLE IV. OFFICERS.

SECTION I. The officers of the society shall be a president, vice-president, secretary, and such other officers as may be necessary.

SEC. 2. The president shall keep especial watch over the interests of the society, and it shall be her care to see that the committees perform the duties devolving upon them.

SEC. 3. The vice-president shall assist the president in her duties, and perform them in her absence.

SEC. 4. The secretary shall keep a record of the names and addresses of the members, and the minutes of all prayer and business meetings, and perform the other usual duties of a secretary.

SEC. 5. The officers and committees shall be elected by the society, and shall be chosen once a year, at the first meeting in [month]..........

The meetings should be held monthly. The United Society of Christian Endeavor issues topic cards with suggested themes for these meetings. The meetings should be devotional, as well as instructive. Into them should enter the Christian Endeavor principle that requires every one to take part who has no reason for not doing so that he could submit to the Master.

The essential thing is the Mothers' pledge, promising daily prayer for the children, regular attendance on the Mothers' meeting and participation therein, and co-operation with the Junior Christian Endeavor superintendent.

This co-operation will lead the members to attend the Junior society meetings as often as possible. to help the Juniors in their Christian Endeavor work, to assist in the Junior socials, to open their homes to the Juniors for committee meetings and the like, and in every way to show their interest in the Christian work their children are endeavoring to accomplish.

In some places this Mothers' society is a Parents' society, the fathers uniting with the mothers in this monthly meeting for prayer and consultation. It does not need to be said that this is infinitely better than the old one-sided arrangement. It requires only a change of name in the constitution given above.

A Mothers' Committee. — Where the mothers of a congregation are not willing to form a Mothers' Christian Endeavor society, a mothers' committee is the next best thing. The pastor should appoint this committee from among the mothers of the Juniors who are willing to serve. This committee stands ready to call, with the Junior superintendent, upon mothers who do not attend any church, to help out Junior socials, leaving the superintendent free to entertain, and to advise and assist in many other ways.

Your Assistant. — Where a mothers' society exists in the church, whether it is a Mothers' Christian Endeavor society or not, it is an excellent plan, if possible, to have the president of the mothers' society hold also the office of assistant superintendent of the Junior society.

The Parents' Pledge. — Many Junior workers do not think

it advisable to set on foot still one more society and one more set of meetings. They advocate simply the Parents' Christian Endeavor pledge, which is as follows : —

Trusting in the Lord Jesus Christ for strength, I promise him that I will strive to do whatever he would have me do, especially to show my interest in the Junior society of Christian Endeavor, by co-operating with the superintendents in any way that will prove beneficial to the welfare and spiritual growth of the boys and girls; that I will pray and read the Bible every day; and that, just so far as I know how, I will try to lead a Christian life. I promise to seek the Master's daily blessing on the Junior work. I will make a great effort to attend each Parents' meeting, and will come prepared to add to the interest of the meeting, with at least a verse or thought.

The Parents' meeting referred to in the pledge is simply one of the regular sessions of the church prayer meeting, one evening a month being given up to the needs of the parents ; or, rather, not an entire evening, but simply the last half of the regular meeting. This parents' half-hour is presided over by the pastor, and the regular subjects prescribed for the Mothers' Christian Endeavor society may appropriately be discussed. The co-ope-ration with the Junior society, the daily prayer for the Juniors, the pledge, participation in the parents' meeting — all of these points are held in common by the two methods, and great good will be gained by the adoption of either plan that local circum-stances may seem to favor

CHAPTER V.

OLDER ENDEAVORERS AND THE JUNIORS.

The Coming Workers. — The feeling should be inculcated in the two societies that the Junior society is really a branch of the older society. It will not be many years before the entire membership of the older society will practically have come from the Juniors. As the older workers care for the perpetuity of their work, they should seek in all ways to promote and strengthen the work of the Juniors.

Pray For It. — One of the best tests of the interest the older Endeavorers feel in their Junior society is the number of prayers offered for it and for its superintendent in the course of the society meetings.

Committee Superintendents. — It is sometimes well in a Junior society to have a superintendent for each committee, in addition to the chairman of the committee, the latter being one of the little people. The superintendents should be elected from the older society, and each committee is thus given in charge of some worker who is especially well qualified to super-intend the work of that committee.

It is a good idea for each superintendent to sit with her committee at the meetings of the Junior society, and they, as well as the Juniors, should take part in each meeting. In one society I know of, each of these committee superintendents asks one member of her committee to lead in prayer at the coming meeting, and, if necessary, assists that Junior to prepare for this important duty.

" Guardians " is an excellent name adopted by some superin-tendents for these members of the older Endeavor society that take charge of the work of the Junior committees. Others call them, just as fittingly, " advisers."

It is an excellent idea to place in charge of this work Juniors that have recently been graduated into the Young People's

society.   They are more familiar with the needs of the Juniors,
and, if they can accomplish the work at all, are more likely to
do it better than one that has not passed through the Junior
society.

The Officers Also. — Whenever this helpful plan is tried, it
should be extended to take in the officers, appointing, as part of
the work of the older president, secretary, treasurer, etc., the
assistance of corresponding officers in the younger society.
The executive committee of the Junior society may occasionally be invited to meet with the executive committee of the older
society, for the purpose of observing their methods.

Real Friends. — These helpers of the superintendent that
come from the older society should not confine their efforts to
the prayer meeting of the Juniors.   They can do wonders in
influencing the life of the Juniors at home and at school.   Each
of them should try, working upon the division of the Juniors
assigned to her, to make those children her friends, so that they
will confide in her, bring her their troubles, and get her help in
all their perplexities.   Each helper should report to the superintendent any conversation or incident that comes up in this outside work that will throw any needed light on the character of
the Juniors under her charge.

Each with His Wards. — Whether your society has adopted
the plan of a Junior committee, or of " committee advisers," or
not, at any rate it is an admirable scheme to divide the members of the Junior society among the older Endeavorers, a certain number to each, so that the older members may feel an
especial responsibility for the training of these Juniors; may
pray for them, help them in their society work, and be their
guides, through their Junior years, into the older society.   An
occasional invitation to their homes from these older Endeavorers would be greatly appreciated by the Juniors.

In the Executive Committee. — By every imaginable means
seek to tie together the Junior society and the older Endeavorers.   One of the best ways of doing this is to make the superintendent of the Junior society a member of the executive
committee of the Young People's society.   In this way she is
able to suggest ways in which the older Endeavorers can co-
operate with the Juniors, superintend their committee work,

assist their leaders and officers, and smooth the path of graduation from one society into the other.

Furthermore, if your Junior society is helped by a "Junior
committee" from the Young People's society, the superintendent of the Junior society should by all means be the chairman
of this committee.

A Superintendent in Sections. — In many a town, Junior
work is never taken up because the Endeavorers have a very
high ideal of a Junior superintendent, and because every one
shrinks from undertaking this great responsibility. It is forgotten that the qualities that cannot be found combined in any
one person may easily be found separately in four or five
Endeavorers, and that a Junior society can often be better managed by a Junior committee than by a Junior superintendent.

This committee should be appointed with exceeding care, and
always on consultation with the pastor. It should be composed
of both young men and young women, and various talents
should be represented upon it. There should be one who can
lead singing well; there should be one who is especially popular
among the children, one who is skilled in Bible work, one who
is able to inspire devotional zeal. As one Junior superintendent suggests, these Junior committees should be "put up
assorted."

Sharing the Work. — When this Junior committee of the
Young People's society constitutes the only leaders of the Junior society, it is customary for the members of the Junior committee to take turns, month about, in acting as superintendent,
the rest acting as assistants. In this way each member of the
committee keeps in touch with the work.

If the superintendent for the month is for any reason obliged
to be absent, there is always a properly qualified person to be
called upon. As the members of the Junior committee change
from time to time, there soon comes to be quite a body of
Endeavorers actively interested in the work of the Junior
society.

The difficulty with this plan is that it lacks continuity, and
leads to haphazard methods with the Juniors. In some communities, however, where long search fails to find any one who
is willing to undertake the work of a permanent superintendent,

this method may be adopted as far better than having no Junior society at all.

Meeting Together — Joint meetings of the Junior and Young People's societies should be held at least as often as once a year, and such meetings are provided for in the uniform topics of the United Society. These meetings should always be led by the superintendent of the Junior society, or by some one who is equally familiar with the work and the powers of the Juniors, and with whom the Juniors are equally familiar.

On either side of the leader should sit the president of the two societies. There should be a common topic, so simple that it can be grasped by the youngest of the Juniors, and yet thought-provoking enough for the oldest of the Endeavorers. Remember that the Juniors especially will find it difficult to take part in such a meeting, and plan the evening largely with them in mind.

The opening reading of scripture should be by the two presidents, alternating verses. Following that should come a short talk by the Junior superintendent. Following that might be responsive readings, first between the president of the Junior society and his Juniors, and then between the president of the older society and his Endeavorers. Next might come a set of questions and answers, led by the president of each society in turn, the president reading the questions for the day in THE GOLDEN RULE, and the Endeavorers responding by Bible verses, or with thoughts of their own, as they have made preparation.

Interspersed throughout might be songs from the Juniors. If you have a Junior choir, let the choir sing a stanza, and the Juniors take up the chorus. In the sentence prayers, all should take part, both the Juniors and their elders. When opportunity is given for the repetition of Bible verses, here again the societies should be united.

There should be an opportunity for brief testimony, and it would be well at this time for some of the Endeavorers to speak directly to the Juniors, telling them of the interest the older society feels in them, and how glad they will be to welcome them into their midst when the time comes for graduation. These remarks should, of course, be very brief, the object of the whole meeting being largely to make the Juniors feel that they will be at home in the older society. At the close, three or four minutes should be given up to the pastor for whatever he may have to say, and the society songs and the Mizpah benediction will make a fitting close.

Closing Together. — I have heard of a church whose Junior and Young People's societies, though they meet separately in adjoining rooms for the first half of the hour, yet come together in one room for the remaining half, and hold a joint meeting. This is a pleasant and very helpful combination; and though I am sure it would be hurtful as a permanent arrangement, yet I am sure it would be a charming variation from the ordinary separate meetings, helping both the Juniors and their elders by contact with each other. It might be best to begin together, the Juniors retiring to their own room at the close of the first half of the hour.

A Leader from the Juniors. — Occasionally ask the older society to request some of the better workers among the Juniors to lead their meetings. They will be astonished to see what excellent work the Juniors are able to do in this difficult line; and the Juniors, as well as the older society, will be spurred to more zealous efforts.

A Help from Outside. — Occasionally invite a member of the Young People's society to conduct a Bible drill among the Juniors. He will come provided with references, all relating to some particular topic, and will give out these references in the usual way, permitting the Junior who first finds each to read it aloud. A few words from him will connect the references together and enforce the lesson.

An Invitation. — The superintendent should occasionally invite some member of the older society to come in and give the Juniors a brief talk, being careful to emphasize the word *brief*, so that its meaning is unmistakable. If this invitation can come from the Juniors themselves, and be presented by one of their number to the fortunate senior, so much the better.

Missionary Meeting Leaders. — In one Junior society the missionary meetings held each month are led in turn by the members of the missionary committee of the older society. This plan works well. The programmes are greatly varied, as they are prepared by different persons, and the children enjoy the variety. The plan serves also to keep up an interest in the Juniors among the members of the older society.

An Auxiliary. — The president of the older society is not the president of the Junior society, and has no control over it. None the less he may be glad to consider the Juniors a sort of outside parish. He will be present at the Junior meetings occasionally, and will adopt the Junior president as a sort of younger brother, consulting with him regarding his work, and remembering that the older Juniors are soon to become members of the Young People's society.

Junior Visitors. — It should be so arranged that every member of the older society shall visit the Junior society at least once in the course of the year. In no way can this better be accomplished than by the regular appointment of visitors; and these should be one or more, according to the size of the older society. The president is the best officer to appoint them, and they need not be appointed more than a week in advance. These visitors should take some slight part in the Junior society, but no more than the Juniors themselves take, except by special invitation from the superintendent. They will help the Junior work greatly if, after the meeting, they say a word of encouragement to the Juniors who have taken part, to the leader, and to the society officers.

A Spur. — When you appoint visitors to the Junior society from the older society, be sure occasionally to appoint some of the more backward Endeavorers. In cases not a few these Endeavorers have been moved by the heartiness with which the Juniors enter into their work, have been ashamed of their foolish timidity, and have been spurred to more zealous service in their own society.

Delegates. — One of the best ways of knitting together the Juniors and the older society, is to appoint a Junior delegate to each meeting of the Young People's society. This delegate should be appointed by the prayer-meeting committee the week before. It should be the duty of the delegate to take some little part in the older society, and to bring back to the Junior society a report of what is done. This report should speak of the attendance and the way in which the older Endeavorers take part, of any helpful thought, or of any striking incident.

Not only are the Juniors thus led to take an interest in the older society, this interest making graduation from the Junior society seem easy, but the older society also is greatly benefited; and the presence of the Junior delegate, and the knowledge that he is watching their conduct with a view to reporting their success or failure, act as decided spurs to more vigorous efforts.

A Visit. — Occasionally have the Juniors visit the older society in a body, and take part by reciting the Twenty-third Psalm, by singing a song, or in some other special way. This will greatly help both societies.

Junior Reports. — Have the Junior president or secretary, or, if this is not possible, the chairman of some important Junior committee, present at the business meeting of the older society. They are to give the report of the Juniors, this report being previously prepared or corrected by the superintendent. Through attendance on the business meeting of the older society the Juniors will learn business methods, and will feel an added dignity because of this representation of their society.

Knit them Together. — The superintendent will do much to knit together the two societies if, when the Juniors come to her for advice, occasionally, instead of giving it herself, she send them to older Endeavorers. Especially she should seek to unite in their work corresponding officers of the two societies, and the members of corresponding committees.

The Graduates Consulted. — When a class of Juniors is ready to graduate into the older society, some especial attention should be paid them before the graduation day. It is suggested that the executive committee might step in here and ask the Juniors to meet with them for a social hour. Here they will talk over fully the plans for graduation, fixing the time, place, and programme, and showing these Juniors in a very practical way that they are to be welcome in the older society.

In Summer. — Union work between the two societies will be most useful in the summer, when the membership of both is small. Sometimes it will be well to hold union consecration meetings under these circumstances.

Pass them On. — Notices of union meetings come to the corresponding secretary of the older society, but they should not stop there. This secretary should pass them on to the secretary of the Junior society, so that the Juniors also may know what is going on in the wider Christian Endeavor world. All Juniors that wish to attend the union meetings should be given a cordial invitation, and every wide-awake union will give some part in this union meeting to the Juniors.

Learn the Older Song. — If the older Christian Endeavor society has adopted any song for its own, the Juniors should learn this in addition to their own song, so that when they come to graduate into the older society they may have at least this point of familiarity.

A Present from the Juniors. — I have heard of a Junior society that made a present to the members of the Young People's society of their church, the present being a Bible-mark. This Bible-mark was a long strip of paper, containing a list of all the missionaries of the denomination, grouped under the names of the different countries. The chairman of the Junior missionary committee, at the time the gift was made, asked each of the older Endeavorers to pray for these missionaries every day.

This incident is suggestive of some things the older society also might well do occasionally for the Juniors.

A Social for the Juniors. — One of the best things the older society can do for the Juniors is to give, once a year, a Junior social, to which the Juniors are especially invited. This is best held in the summer and in the afternoon, so that out-door games can be played. If the time is suitable, the anniversary of the formation of the Junior society may be chosen, and it may be called a Junior birthday party. Refreshments should be served; and the Junior boys may escort the young women of the older society, and the Junior girls be escorted by the older boys.

After refreshments might come a little programme, in which the Juniors should be especially prominent; though a bright little speech should be made by one of the older Endeavorers, welcoming the Juniors, and expressing the interest of the older society in them and their work. After this programme should come a little singing, a chain prayer, the Mizpah benediction, and then the older Endeavorers should see the Juniors safe home. If the Juniors should desire to return the compliment and give a social to the older society, let the older Endeavorers enter heartily into their plan.

CHAPTER VI.

THE SUPERINTENDENT'S WORK.

How Appointed. — No rule can be laid down as to how the superintendent of the Junior society is to be selected. Sometimes she will be chosen by the Young People's society, on consultation with the pastor. Sometimes the pastor, in conjunction with the officers of the church, will be the person to do the appointing. Sometimes, as explained elsewhere, no single person can be found who combines all the qualities requisite for a superintendent; and a Junior committee from the Young People's society may undertake the task, or there may be several superintendents acting jointly.

He — She ! — Let us not always refer to the Junior superintendent with the feminine pronoun. To be sure, the large majority of Junior superintendents are women, but a very respectable minority, to say the least, are wide-awake young men; and some of the most successful of Junior workers are pastors and laymen. In this book I have, on purpose, used masculine and feminine pronouns quite recklessly in referring to Junior superintendents, though the feminine predominate, as is only just.

Your Best for the Juniors. — It is part of the Junior superintendent's duty not to permit herself to be loaded down with so much work outside the society that she cannot bring full health of body and vigor of mind to this most important work of all. A great deal of the success of the society will depend upon her cheerfulness and the buoyancy of her spirit. Let her save her strength on Sunday, and on Saturday as well. Let her go to the meeting fully prepared by long meditation and careful study, not that she may make a long harangue before the Juniors — that is abominable; but that she may know how, by a few words here and there, by a shrewd direction, and by the uplift of an inspiring presence, to lead her young charges into the Christian life.

A Caution. — I wish I could write upon the hearts and consciences of every Junior superintendent in the world this stirring exhortation from a Junior worker: " Never go to the meeting feeling the least bit cross. Juniors can tell better than older people whether you feel all right. I went to the meeting just once feeling that I did not care what kind of meeting we had, and we came just as near having no meeting as could be. The little ones seemed afraid to read, and the older ones barely took part. Have a pleasant word and a smile for every one. Be bright and cheerful, and those around you will be the same."

"One Thing I Do." — In a letter from an active Junior superintendent I find another suggestion along this line, which, on account of its personal force, I give in the words of my correspondent: " If a Junior superintendent is doing good with the Juniors, he should never give up his Junior work to do some other church work. I, for instance, sing in the choir, and once attended a funeral to help with the singing, leaving the Juniors with a good leader ; but the carelessness formed in that meeting it took me quite a while to overcome."

The Four P's. — And again, here is a good specimen of common sense and alliteration sent me by a Junior worker: "A superintendent needs, most of all, prayer, patience, perseverance, and pleasantness." Nor is the last by any means the least important.

Be Prompt. — To these may well be added a fifth " P." A great help in keeping the children bright and alert is promptness, both in opening and closing the meeting. If in this particular the meeting drags, it is likely to drag in all other particulars.

Set Your Assistant to Working. — Take care to train your assistant superintendent, giving her abundant practice not merely in helping the children but in leading the meetings. It is a good plan to have her make the opening talk every other Sunday. Give her such chances for development that you may be able at any time to leave the society in her charge.

Junior Assistant Superintendents. — Sometimes, in a young society, the Junior superintendent is confronted with the necessity of putting new Juniors in office, and at the same time feels the need of retaining the services of the experienced workers trained during the preceding months. A happy solution of this difficulty was conceived by a certain Junior superintendent, who made the retiring president, secretary, and treasurer her assistants in superintending the society.

She talked with them earnestly, showing them the greater responsibility they were undertaking, and they entered heartily into her plans. It was her custom occasionally to have the three lead the meeting together, one giving out the hymns, another leading in prayer, and the third speaking on the topic. This plan was a great blessing, both to the society and to the superintendent.

Visit. — Probably in no work connected with the Christian Endeavor movement is visitation of other societies so necessary and helpful as in the work of the Junior superintendent. As just said, you should have an assistant, fully capable of taking your place; but if opportunity for visiting can be obtained in no other way, call in the pastor, or some older Endeavorer, to lead the meeting; or take your Juniors with you to visit.

"The Best." — It is a great misfortune for a Junior superintendent to have too high an opinion of her own society. This opinion is usually based on imperfect knowledge of what other societies and superintendents are doing. The following sentence I find in the correspondence printed by a State Christian Endeavor paper: " The Junior Christian Endeavor society of —— church is, I think, the best Junior society in the State, but, *as I have never visited another society myself*, probably I am not a competent judge." Most certainly she was not a competent judge, and most certainly a society whose superintendent never visits another society to get fresh inspiration and new plans is not, however good it may be, the best society in the State.

Let Them Do It. — "Oh!" said a disgusted Junior once, talking about his superintendent, " she does all the work, and all we have to do is to say Amen to it." Which means that that superintendent was not doing her work at all.

All through the work of the children the superintendent must remember that it is a great mistake to do anything for the children that they can be brought to do for themselves. Mrs. Scudder's illustration is a forcible one: " A leader is to be merely a trellis to support the young vine while it grows." This is the rule observed by all practical Junior workers: " A superintendent should never do anything a Junior can do instead." Though of course the rule is not to be followed with unvarying literalness, yet in the majority of cases it is certainly sound. It is as bad for the Junior superintendent to help the children too much as for him to help them too little.

On the other side, however, it should be urged that in all work the superintendent should herself set an example. Whatever you wish the Juniors to do, do yourself first before the society, asking them to follow. Said one pastor, for instance, to his Juniors, " If I tell you the way in which I found the Lord Jesus to be my Saviour; will you tell me how you found him? "

Let the Juniors Plan. — Ask the Juniors for their ideas regarding the work of the society. They will astonish you by the wisdom with which they propose new plans, and the eagerness with which they carry out the plans they themselves have suggested. They will hear from their comrades the methods in use in other societies, and they will pick up many a bright idea from *The Junior Golden Rule.*

Something New. — A wise teacher once said, " Remember that the best soon becomes second-best by constant use." This wise maxim is worth remembering by all our Junior workers. Remember that the best plan in the world becomes the second-best, if you stick to it too long.

Manage, if possible, to give the children something new each Sunday to think about. Do not exhaust all your plans upon a few Sundays. If, for instance, you have them select society colors at one meeting, do not have them at the same meeting select their motto, but postpone that to another meeting.

A model Junior superintendent will take care that the first interest the Juniors feel in their society shall not flag through lack of novelty, but will aim always to have on hand something fresh, some plan for a sociable, some new scheme for their prayer meetings or their committee work. Above all, a wise superintendent will seek to keep the Juniors at work along new and helpful lines for the good of others.

A Change of Face. — Most Junior societies begin with small numbers; and the superintendent, as the society grows, must constantly bear in mind that her plans must grow with it. The methods that are most helpful for a small society are quite certain not to be the most helpful for a large one.

Surprises. — The little folks will greatly appreciate anything in the line of surprises, and can be made to do a great deal of excellent service if they think it will surprise their friends. Such things as coming to church in a body to surprise the pastor, giving the pastor a surprise party on his birthday, and celebrating Thanksgiving or Christmas by giving a surprise dinner for poor children, will especially take their fancy.

Know Them. — Junior superintendents should use great pains to become familiar with the daily life of the little folks under their care. Truth uttered at random has little effect compared with truths carefully chosen to fit the needs of the children. Talks with parents will do much to give you this knowledge, talks with the Juniors' friends will do more, but frequent visits at the Juniors' houses will do most of all.

Christless Homes. — The Junior superintendent should, it is needless to say, have an especially tender and deep interest in all the members of her society whose parents are not Christians — this not merely for the children's sake but for the sake of the parents, for many a Junior has led his parents to the Master.

Praise Them. — Often, during the week, the superintendent will hear of some good deed which has been done by the Juniors. It is an admirable plan to speak of this at the next meeting with a word of commendation. Of course no name should be mentioned, and the story should not be told in such a way as to give a clew to the name of the Junior.

Superintendent's Letters. — A busy superintendent who has not much time to call upon the Juniors will find it very helpful to write occasional letters, especially to the leaders, giving them plans for managing the meeting; to the timid members, giving them suggestions for taking part in the prayer meeting; to those whose home influences are discouraging to the Christian life; and sometimes also to the very best members, showing that you appreciate their work, and stimulating them to increased efforts.

Indeed, one of the very best ways of rewarding faithful service in the Junior society, a method far superior to any giving of prizes, is a little note of appreciation sent quietly to the Junior whom you wish to commend. A slight gift may sometimes accompany it, such as a beautiful flower or a helpful book; but the note itself, and the consciousness that the superintendent is pleased, will be by far the best reward.

Believe in Them. — Children, who are quick to catch emotions, will speedily feel the contagion of distrust if their superintendent lacks confidence in their ability. On the contrary, if their superintendent is courageous both for herself and for them, they will soon gain the same confidence.

Explain. — If the superintendent finds that any of his boys or girls are growing careless in Christian Endeavor work, his first step should be to go to them personally and talk over the work with them. Many times he will find that their carelessness arises from the failure to understand what is required of them, and that when this understanding is given them they will do their work eagerly and faithfully.

Better than a Yardstick. — It is a great mistake for the superintendent to feel that the society is accomplishing nothing unless the members are engaged in some definite and easily measured work, such as the learning of Bible verses. Let it never be forgotten that the society exists primarily for spiritual purposes, to train the Juniors to habits of prayer and devotion, and to the expression of Christian testimony, as well as to the outward manifestation of the Christian spirit in acts of kindliness and charity. The results of the Junior prayer meetings cannot be measured as definitely as those of a Sunday-school class, but they are far reaching and deep, none the less.

Just for Drill. — The superintendent will make a mistake if she estimates the value of a method of work solely by its direct importance, or the need of it that would be manifest in an older society. A certain measure of "red tape" and detail in the Junior society is of value in setting the children to work; and they will enjoy it, though it may be plain to the superintendent that much of it is unnecessary and might be avoided by the adoption of simpler plans. At the same time the Juniors may be taught, by this seemingly unnecessary detail to be careful and painstaking, and may learn many valuable lessons.

A Reminder. — Whenever the topic card or programme calls upon all the Juniors to take part in some definite way at the next meeting, do not fail, as you see the Juniors during the week, and especially as you see the careless and indifferent ones, to remind each of them that he or she has some part in the next meeting. If they ask you what part it is, tell them to go home and look at their programmes or topic cards.

Passing Time. — The Junior superintendent of Wisconsin strikes at the secret of many a failure in Junior work, with this sentence in a private letter : " Still, in both Wisconsin and Minnesota, the tendency to *pass away* the hour, instead of to *fill in* the hour and make the most of the time, seems to predominate."

Name the Meetings. — Individualize the meetings by giving them distinct and attractive names, which should be announced several weeks beforehand, or possibly printed on the Junior topic cards. Such names as the following may be used : " Good Deed Meeting," " Sunshine Meeting," " Bible Bees," " Bible Search Meeting," " Cheerful Givers," " Willing Workers," " Star Meeting."

Variety Spice. — Frequently change the arrangement of chairs in your Junior meeting-room. Some superintendents make it a point to have different arrangements of chairs for every meeting. Here is one set, for example, sent me by a

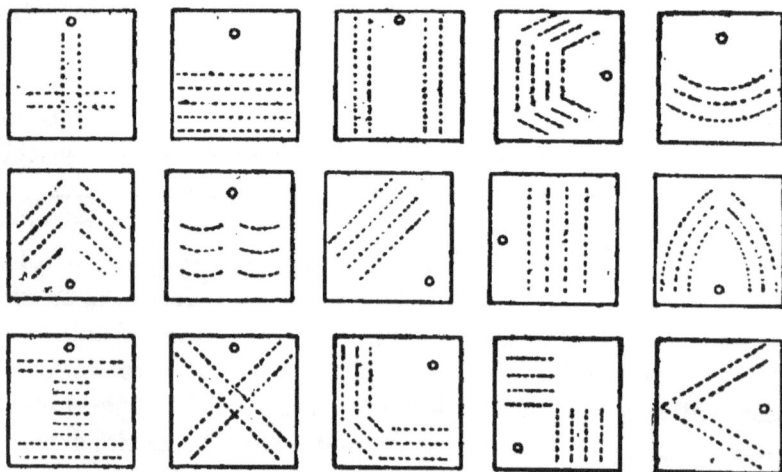

wide-awake superintendent. Thus the Juniors are seated facing in turn all points of the compass. A little surprise awaits them as they enter the room, and the novelty of the situation adds novelty to the exercises.

Draw Them Out First. — Many Junior superintendents make the mistake of putting their talk on the topic first in the meeting. A better plan is to get first from the Juniors them-selves all the suggestions you can. You will be astonished to see how fully the topic will be treated, and how much of your own talk will be rendered unnecessary.

Utilize Everything. — Start from what the children know and tell you. Do not permit yourself to be abashed by queer answers, but organize victory out of defeat. Mr. Thomas Wain-wright gives two illustrations of what I mean.

" If you ask: ' How many disciples were there?' a little girl may answer, ' Eleven.' ' Yes, but how many more?' A boy answers, ' Thirteen.' ' Not quite so many.' The next answer will be correct, and no one's feelings hurt.

"A superintendent once noticed a boy brimful of some idea. He was very restless, and she knew that he must relieve his mind; so she said, —

" ' Johnny, you've got something to say; what is it?'

" ' Baby's got a new tooth.'

"She took this piece of news, so wonderful to the boy, talked about it a little, wound her lesson about that tooth, and held the attention not only of Johnny, but the whole society. Pick up ideas that interest the children, and use the simplest language to express what you have to teach."

Numbers. — Whenever you give out to the Juniors sets of verses or other matter to be read, take pains to number them. In this way confusion will be avoided, since you can call for them by numbers.

Letters, not Epistles. — It is a small matter, but one that is suggestive of a large matter: the superintendent should never refer to Paul's letters as " epistles," but always as " letters," having the Juniors know to whom each letter was written, the place from which it was sent, and the place where his correspond-ents lived. In fine, the superintendent should always use the language of the present day, and make the Scriptures seem as vivid and familiar to the children as possible.

Some Model Programmes. — Few plans will add more to the interest of your Juniors than the preparation of regular programmes, copies of which, made by a manifolder, are distributed to the Juniors one week before the meeting. Excellent sample programmes are the following, which Junior workers will find very suggestive : —

PROGRAMME

OF THE

SLATE RIDGE JUNIOR CHRISTIAN ENDEAVOR SOCIETY MEETING,

Saturday Afternoon, Feb. 18, 1893, *at* 2.30 *o'clock.*

Opening exercises, conducted by the president.
Reading of the minutes of the last meeting.
Reports of committees and enrolment of new members

Subject for consideration : " Never use intoxicating liquors as a beverage."

Topic : " Reasons why we should never use intoxicating liquors as a beverage." To be discussed by Archie Wallace, Harry Baer, Samuel Jones, Willie Mobley, George Geiger, Joshua Green, Jr.

Temperance Readings, by Lula Stewart and Agnes Daughton.

SINGING.

Temperance Recitation, Willie Maffet.

" Should we drink wine or cider ? " To be answered by James Webster, Howard Sellers, Robert Stewart.

" Why should boys not stay around places where intoxicating liquors are sold ? " To be answered by Clarence Lloyd, Harry Street, Harry Cantler.

" What does the Bible say about drunkards ? " To be answered by Eva Heaps and Annie Torbert.

Essay, " Evils of Intemperance." — Bessie Dinsmore.

SINGING AND PRAYER.

General discussion and question-box.
Remarks by elder and pastor.   Roll-call and closing exercises.

PROGRAMME.

SLATE RIDGE JUNIOR CHRISTIAN ENDEAVOR SOCIETY.

Meeting Saturday Afternoon, July 8, 1893.

Opening exercises, conducted by the president.
Reading of minutes of the last meeting.
Reports of committees.   Enrolment of new members.

Address by the new president.
Subject : " How we can do more good."

Essay, " How we can help the Sabbath school."   By Lula Stewart.

Discussion : " The benefits of the Sabbath school."   By David Fulton, Robert Stewart, Hugh Jones.

SINGING.

Discussion : " How to get boys and girls who do not attend Sabbath school to come."   By Johnny Roberts, Howard Sellers, Bennie Baer, Willie Mobley, James Fulton, Harry Street.

" What is the best way to study the Sabbath-school lessons ? "   Mary Fulton, Annie Heaps.

General talk on the Sabbath school.

SINGING AND PRAYER.

Remarks by elder and pastor.

Question-box.   Roll-call.   Closing exercises.

PROGRAMME.

SLATE RIDGE JUNIOR CHRISTIAN ENDEAVOR SOCIETY.

Meeting Saturday Afternoon, Oct. 6, 1894, at 2.30 o'clock.

Topic for discussion : " Gambling."   Leader, Willie Maffet.

SINGING, HYMN NO. 328.

Reading Luke 2 : 40–52, by Mary Fulton.
The Lord's Prayer in concert.

SINGING, HYMN NO. 68.

Discussion : " What is gambling ? "   The question to be answered by each member.

" Why is it sinful and dishonorable to gamble ? " To be answered by Willie Mobley, Joshua Green, Ina Dooley.

" How do men gamble at horse races ? " To be answered by Harry Street, Ben Baer.

SINGING, HYMN NO. 451.

" What kind of gambling is there at county fairs ? " To be answered by Robert Bay, Plodwin Roberts.

" How do boys sometimes gamble in their play ? " To be answered by Johnny Roberts, Walter Stewart, Annie Torbert.

SINGING, HYMN NO. 27.

Remarks by pastor and elder.
Question-box.
Roll-call.
Reading of minutes.   Report of committees.
Closing exercises.

A Portfolio of Programmes. — Do not trust to a programme for a meeting that is kept in your head. Always write it down; and if you will write these programmes in a blank-book, each under the topic of the meeting, you will find that blank-book rapidly becoming invaluable for reference. Ideas that you have used a few months ago will be just as valuable for future use, but without this careful record you are likely to forget all about them.

A Glance Ahead. — The superintendent should be familiar with the topics of coming meetings as far ahead as possible. Plans for next week's meeting will often be greatly varied by a knowledge of the meetings that are to come. Often the superintendent is on the point of selecting a method for the next meeting, but finds that method more suitable for a meeting several weeks in advance, and reserves it for that occasion. Often, too, it is helpful to direct the thoughts of the children to the coming meetings.

If the superintendent can plan for five or six meetings ahead, she will find herself able to use methods that call for much preliminary work on the part of the children. If, however, she lives from hand to mouth in her Junior work, she can never call upon the children for any preparation that would occupy more than a few days.

The chief reason of all, however, is that Junior work should be a great whole, and all the lessons should be as far as possible interwoven. This cannot be accomplished if the topics are not thoroughly studied a good way in advance.

Take Them by Themselves. — It would be well for a Junior superintendent to accustom herself to giving an opportunity, at the close of every meeting, for private conversation with any Junior whose thought or conscience may have been stirred by something that has taken place in the meeting. Often this conversation may be invited, and the superintendent should always invite it by manner and readiness, if not in words. The few minutes after the Junior meeting may be made the time of genuine ingathering, and may often accomplish more good than the whole of the meeting preceding.

Put Opposites Together. — In selecting members for the different committees, it is a great mistake always to look at the likings and apparent aptitudes of the children. Committee work is often valuable because of developing unsuspected abilities, and because it rounds out character by compelling people to do what they do not like, and to keep on doing it until they like it. Children who do not care much for flowers may, if placed on the flower committee with flower-lovers, develop an excellent taste and a sincere appreciation of the beautiful. Children who are shy and reserved, placed on the social committee with those who are bright and sociable, will lose their shyness in due time. Children who find it difficult to pray in public may overcome their timidity if placed on the prayer-meeting committee with braver workers. Urge the Juniors to undertake hard things for the Lord's sake.

The Junior in Print. — It is to be hoped that you have a Christian Endeavor department in one or more of your town papers. The Juniors will be especially appreciative of items regarding their work that appear in its columns. They will like to see their names in print, and they will glory in the prominence thus given to their society.

Varicolored. — An invaluable possession to any Junior superintendent is a hectograph or a mimeograph, and very pretty effects can be produced by using different-colored inks. A card or an announcement can thus be printed in several different colors, to the great delight of the Juniors.

A Rally Day. — Rally Sundays are found useful in Sunday-school work; why not rally days also for the Junior society, to gather together in the fall the members scattered during the summer vacation, and set the society work promptly on its feet again? Make a special effort to bring out to this meeting the members of the society who have become sluggish and have lost their interest. Seek also to obtain the presence of the young people who may be expected to join the society. Do not leave out the parents, and plan the meeting largely with a view to increasing their interest in the work of the society.

Consult with the Juniors beforehand, and permit them to have a large share in planning for the rally. Let the society president preside, and have a society choir. Hold the meeting, if possible, in the large audience-room of the church.

Let the pastor have a few words to say to the Juniors, giving them inspiration and instruction for the work of the coming year. The president of the Young People's society will be glad to greet his younger brothers and sisters in Christian Endeavor, and of course the Junior superintendent herself will have a word for the parents, and for the children who do not yet belong to the society.

Quite a large part of the meeting, however, should be carried on by the Juniors themselves. The Junior secretary might give a little report of the past year's work of the society, including some figures of membership. The chairmen of the different committees should tell a little about their committee work, all of these papers being carefully written beforehand. Throughout the whole should be bright songs, with an occasional recitation.

The evening may fittingly be closed by a short consecration meeting, for which the Juniors have prepared testimonies and verses beforehand.

Opening Questions. — One of the first orders of business at the opening of the Junior meeting may well be the asking of questions by the superintendent, to which all the members respond by raising their hands. One superintendent uses the following set: "How many have read their Bibles every day? How many have prayed every day? How many have invited some one to attend this meeting? How many have made preparation for this meeting? How many took part in sentence prayers at the last meeting? How many took part in other ways? How many have done something for missions during the past week? How many have done some temperance work? How many remembered, when they came in, that this is God's house?"

In some societies such questions are presented to the Juniors occasionally on little slips of paper as they enter the room, and they write answers to them as the first exercise of the hour.

Searching Questions. — It is a good plan occasionally to set before the Juniors some heart-searching questions, with the view of disclosing to them their true spiritual condition. This of course should not be done frequently, nor with an air of solemnity, but it may be made very helpful. A set used by one well-known superintendent is the following: —

1. Do you desire always to do as Jesus Christ would do if he were in your place?

2. Do you pray every day that you may live unselfishly, and may show to your friends that you are one of Christ's children?

3. Do you strive to remember every day to read at least one verse in your Bible?

4. Are you willing that your father and mother, your schoolmates, and your friends in the Sunday school and Junior society, should know that you are a Christian?

These papers are given out, one to each Junior, with a pencil; and after the superintendent has explained quietly and earnestly what each question signifies, there is a very quiet time in the room while each Junior prayerfully examines himself as to whether he shall write Yes or No opposite the questions.

Ten Questions. — Doctrinal instruction may be given the Juniors by a memory exercise called "Ten Questions." These exercises may be prepared by the superintendent herself. For example, ten questions on repentance may be written, each being numbered. The Bible verses that answer these questions, also numbered, should be placed each in a separate envelope which has the same number, and these envelopes should be given out just before the meeting opens. The leader asks the questions by number, calling for the answers, and at the close of the meeting collects the envelopes again. After a while these references are learned, and the responses may be made in concert. When one set of Bible verses is thoroughly mastered, a new set, on a different doctrine, may be taken up.

Junior Questioners. — Occasionally, instead of asking the questions yourself, get the children to ask them. Give each child a topic, and ask him to think out at home one or two questions on the topic to propose to the society. These questions should be written out, collected at the next meeting, and again distributed, each Junior who draws a question doing his best to answer it.

The Catechism. — The catechism will afford to many Juniors both a strong basis of correct thinking, and an admirable drill in Bible principles. They will also greatly enjoy the task of committing it to memory, and repeating it at the meetings.

Blank Books. — If you are giving your Juniors any systematic Bible study, or if, in the course of each meeting, you are in the habit of presenting regularly anything for them to remember, you will find it a great aid to provide them with little blank books and pencils whereby they may write out these facts for study and reference during the week. These blank-books, always at hand, you will be able also to use in a great variety of ways.

Examine Them. — Both in missionary work and in Bible study written examinations are profitable. Indeed, if all the Juniors have learned nothing that they can put on paper, they have probably made no solid acquisitions at all. These examinations should, of course, be exceedingly simple; but neither the superintendent nor the Juniors should shrink from such a test.

Bible Exercises. — Many Junior superintendents do something in the way of arranging little responsive Bible readings and simple Bible exercises for the Juniors. Let the Bible texts that are made the basis of these exercises be carefully committed to memory. An exercise that is committed to memory is many times more valuable than one that is simply read from the blackboard or from printed slips of paper.

For such exercises you may begin with the Beatitudes, or with the shorter psalms, the children repeating one verse and you the second, or the boys repeating one and the girls the second, alternating. Interesting responsive exercises may be made of a series of questions repeated by the superintendent, the Juniors answering with Bible texts recited in concert.

Responsive Readings. — The back part of the popular Junior song-book, "Junior Endeavor Hymns," contains some admirable responsive readings, which superintendents will find especially useful in their society meetings.

Special Exercises. — Too few superintendents exhibit ingenuity in preparing their own exercises for special occasions. As a sample, one superintendent tells us about an exercise she herself prepared to teach the children kindness to animals, as she had noticed the boys killing a great many birds in her neighborhood.

She sent to Mr. George T. Angell, 19 Milk Street, Boston, Mass., for twenty cents' worth of his bird leaflets. She got eighty of them, and with some copies of *Our Dumb Animals*, she made up a fine programme. There were four pieces to speak, there was a song on the birds, there were Bible references, and there was a great deal of information regarding the use of birds, the numbers killed, the results of bird-slaughter, the abominable custom of using birds on the hats, and the opinions of famous writers on the subject.

A similar exercise for boys, on smoking, could be easily arranged ; and so with many other live themes.

A Flexible Blackboard. — The ordinary hard blackboard is a very poor surface on which to draw effectively. Superintendents who have not tried it will be astonished to find how pleasing their pictures are when they use large sheets of manilla paper.

But the most efficient blackboard consists of a large sheet of canvas stretched tightly on a frame, which may be so constructed that it can be taken apart and folded. This canvas must be painted black, and there are preparations which give it the finish of a regular blackboard.

Shading on such a surface may be done perfectly, and lines of varying widths are easily obtained. The figures stand out with wonderful distinctness when drawn on this yielding material.

A Paper Blackboard. — You may have no blackboard, and you may not see your way to get one soon ; but do not, for that reason, neglect the great aid given by pictures. Try how well crayon can be made to work upon coarse brown paper, and remember that the Juniors are not severe art critics.

A Folding Blackboard. — It is best that the Junior blackboard should not be a fixture upon the wall, as, for many purposes, the superintendent will wish to reverse it. If, however, a blackboard fixed on the wall cannot be avoided, the best way is to make it so that it will fold like two slates hinged together. In this way, whatever the superintendent does not wish the Juniors to see until the proper time comes can be written upon the inside of the board, which will then be closed and fastened with a catch.

A Trick with Chalk. — It is possible to draw or write upon the board with damp crayon, and then to add to what has already been placed there additional lines, figures, or letters with dry chalk — all this before the society comes together. Then with a sweep of the cloth the dry chalk may be removed, leaving upon the board what has been drawn or written with the damp chalk, thus producing a striking transformation.

Junior Artists. — Let the Juniors go to the blackboard as frequently as possible, occasionally asking them to draw objects connected with the lesson. At this work they will soon become surprisingly skilful. At the same time that one is drawing, another may be printing or writing on the board some name connected with the theme.

Picture Interpretations. — If the society is small, it is sometimes well, occasionally at least, to draw the illustration of the topic upon a piece of cardboard instead of upon the blackboard. Pass the picture around among the Juniors, and when all have seen it, call upon one or two to talk a little about it, telling what they think the illustration means.

Once for All. — Some Junior superintendents are too lavish of their labor in writing upon the blackboard. If it is matter that you are likely to refer to again, such as a copy of the words of a new song, a list of books of the Bible, a set of texts, etc., do not use the blackboard, but a sheet of manilla paper, writing with a coarse pen, or a large graphite pencil, and hanging the chart you have thus made upon the wall.

Tell Stories. — Junior superintendents should cultivate skill in story-telling. In no better way can the interest of the Juniors be aroused at the outset of the meeting than by telling some bright story, in which boys and girls figure, and which illustrates the topic of the meeting. Furthermore, every superintendent should be prepared with a large fund of interesting, soul-winning, brief stories, that she can use on an emergency when the Juniors get restless.

Read Children's Stories. — An experienced Junior worker testifies that she has obtained a good deal of insight into child character from the reading of many children's stories. The perusal of these, moreover, assists her to tell stories to the children in a plain and simple way. The narrative style of too many talkers to children is formed after the model of novels intended for adults, rather than after the simple and direct style that alone appeals to the minds of the children.

Telling Bible Stories. — Junior superintendents have great need of consecrated imaginations, especially in telling Bible stories. To tell these vividly you must think yourself back into the scenes you are describing, and remember how men and women must have talked and acted in such circumstances. A good illustration of what I mean is furnished by this outline of a description of Christ's walking on the waves. It is the way Rev. C. H. Tyndall tells it : —

" You and I know," he says, " how the disciples must have felt in that storm. One of them looked up, perhaps Peter, and saw something that looked like an apparition on the water; and he nudged John, and said to him, ' John, do you see that?' ' What is that?' John says: ' I do not see anything.' And pretty soon Peter says, ' There it is again!' And soon all the disciples see the figure of a man in the distance. Then, as a wave rolled on, it hid the figure from their view. Soon they saw the figure again, and nearer the boat; and then John said, ' It is the Lord.' And Peter stood up without a moment's hesitation, and cried, ' Master, if it is you, bid me come to you on the water.' And they all hear the word, ' Come.' Peter gets up from his seat, puts one foot over the side of the boat into the water, and tries it to see if it will hold, and all the disciples watch. It does hold; and he takes the first step, and then another, and step after step he goes, and seems to say, 'Look at me.' Then a great wave comes, and he takes his eyes from the Master to look at the wave. He becomes fearful, and down he goes, but is caught by the Master. Soon Jesus and Peter are in the boat, and then there is a calm. One of the disciples, perhaps Thomas, leans over to Peter, and says, 'Peter, how did it feel while you were on the water? What made you go down in that way? Did you get scared?' Peter says, 'You just go out there and see how it feels with nothing under you but water.'

"Now, we know there were some such experiences as these, because the disciples were men like the rest of us. And any one would have acted in about this way, and have asked about such questions. After relating an event like this in a picturesque way, how much interest the reading of this Scripture narrative would have to boys and girls! Boys and girls like stories; and you can take the most inattentive and mischievous boys and girls and say, 'Now I have a story to tell you,' and you will have their attention at once, and you will keep up their interest, and they will attend your meetings, if you do not tell them silly stories.''

A Junior Serial. — Not all Junior superintendents have the necessary gifts; but one consecrated worker makes skilled use of a Junior serial story, one chapter being read each Sunday just before the close of the meeting. The chapter was written in every case after a study of the Sunday's subject had been made, and after she had determined the particular lesson she wished to impress. The chapter was practically a review of the topic, and showed vividly by example how the lesson might be practised by the boys and girls themselves. This chapter of the serial, coming at the close of the prayer meeting, gained the attention of the more restless ones, and gave her a second opportunity to present the truth.

Golden Rule Illustrations. — Every week in *The Golden Rule* is given, on the Junior page, a brief, condensed story especially illustrating the topic for the week. Many Junior superintendents have already found the usefulness of these stories. Some have the Juniors read them. Others have the Juniors tell the story in their own words, and others tell the story themselves to the Juniors. Some, alas! read the story themselves; but this practice is surely not to be commended.

Many Junior superintendents make incidental use of these stories in their talks. Some of them make little sketches, and use the stories as chalk-talks. For this purpose most of them are well adapted.

Bottles and Traps and Things. — A little ingenuity in the use of objects pays a thousandfold. One superintendent uses a bottle to illustrate all her missionary meetings. She dresses it in the costume of the people about whom they are talking, and at the close of the meeting the children drop their pennies into the neck of the bottle! For temperance meetings, a trap makes an excellent illustration; or, better still, a set of traps of different kinds.

Sample Object Lessons. — The following bright illustrations, which I take from various Junior workers, are given as suggestions of ways of using common objects : —

Roll up a sheet of tissue paper into a little ball. Draw it out before the Juniors, and explain that that is how the influence of a single act is unfolded and extended.

Put a drop of ink into a glass of milk or of water, then another drop, then another, to show the cumulative effects of little sins.

Clean a tarnished piece of silver, to show how Christ cleans the heart, until his image is reflected there.

Extinguish a beautiful lamp, to show how worthless is a beautiful face without the light of Christ shining through it.

To illustrate the evils of bad company, rub a white stick with several charred and blackened ones. The latter grow no whiter, but the first becomes black.

Put an ugly picture into a thin glass tumbler. It shows through, just as the bad stories we put in our minds will show through our faces and actions.

Draw twelve cigarettes on the board, writing on each a reason why it should not be smoked. This reason is written on every cigarette that is bought, if one had eyes to see it.

Look Out ! — One of the most experienced of our Junior superintendents, Miss Jerome of Massachusetts, who is herself a mistress of apt illustrations, gives this wise warning: "Do not have your illustration like a glass of soda I bought one day, about nine-tenths foam. Do not let the means overcome the end. Be sure that the lesson is made very clear. Better no objects used than that the children should remember the objects only, and get a false idea of the lesson taught." An illustration of this error is given by *The Sunday School Times:* —

"Do you see this apple?" said a teacher. "How does it look on this side — good or bad?" "Good!" cried the children. "Yes, good — as if you would all like a piece! But on this side, is this good?" "No!" "It's rotten!" "It's soft!" came in varying tones. "Yes; this side is all bad and decayed, good for nothing! Now, your hearts are like this apple, unless you try to serve God. On one side it may be fair and apparently beautiful, but the other — how dreadful! Who wants a heart partly bad, like this?" Nobody wanted it. "Of course not" (producing a fine and sound apple). "But who wants a heart like this beautiful sound apple?" Evidently every child wanted a heart precisely like an apple, and an earnest exhortation from a conscientious teacher followed. But at least five of the small auditors went home and told their parents that children's hearts turned soft and got rotten if they were naughty, and one inquired anxiously if, when it became rotten on both sides, the child would die.

Flower Talks. — The Juniors will take great pleasure in flower talks, which the superintendent can carry on in this way. At the preceding meeting the Juniors select the flower which is to be the subject of the flower talk on the following Sunday. A flower with a short name should be chosen.

The superintendent will draw the flower on the blackboard, or have an actual specimen of it in a vase on the table. As to the drawing, no one need hesitate because he cannot use the crayon with the skill of a Frank Beard. The Juniors have strong imaginations, and will see a beautiful flower where eyes less kind would see only a few crude strokes.

The Juniors themselves may be permitted to suggest the words which shall be the basis of the flower talk, or these words may be given by the superintendent. In any case, the initials of the words must spell the name of the flower. If rose is the flower, it might mean to the Juniors, "Repentance, Obedience, Sincerity, Earnestness."

Silhouettes. — Junior superintendents will find a pair of shears of great assistance. They can cut out before the Juniors significant objects from white paper, and many a superintendent who cannot draw can make these silhouettes, and pin them to the blackboard. The Juniors will be interested in watching the process, and their attention will be firmly held.

Pricked Cards. — Imitate the kindergarten workers by giving the Juniors little designs illustrative of the topic, neatly printed on cardboard with some manifolding machine. Have the Juniors prick these designs, and work them with silk or worsted ; and while they work these cards let them be learning some Bible verses referring to the lesson.

Impromptus. — An ingenious superintendent will seldom be at a loss what to do if the Juniors become restless in the course of the meeting. Picking up the nearest object, she will begin to talk about it, and in some way or other make it contribute to impress the truth the Juniors are studying.

Taking up the bell, for instance, she will ask what bells are for, what they are made of, whence the material comes, and who created the material. Seizing a book, she will, by a series of questions, lead the Juniors to thinking about the Book of books. Taking up a soiled bit of paper, and asking how it can be cleaned, she will induce the Juniors to think about soiled hearts, and how God can cleanse them from sin.

The Temple. — Junior superintendents will get much help from a paper model of Solomon's temple, made up from the views given in any Bible dictionary.

Pasteboard Men. — A set of home-made pasteboard men and women, dressed as nearly as possible to represent the costumes of Bible times, will be found of the greatest assistance in Junior work. Pasteboard animals are also useful. Sand maps are to be made and used in connection with these figures.

For example, a man in a bit of a real tree will represent Zaccheus. To illustrate obedience, such a scene might be presented as the great draught of fishes in response to Christ's command. A large dishpan of water will represent the sea. There will be a child's wooden boat with sails, pasteboard men, and a torn net tacked to the sides of the boat.

A Sermon in Checkers. — A Junior worker sends us the following as a sample of how almost any common game can be utilized in teaching the Juniors. They all know something about checkers; and this is the way he talks to them, drawing moral lessons from that sprightly game: —

You all know how to play checkers. Now to-day I will play a game of checkers with you.

In playing checkers, you move your men in one direction. In what direction do you move them?

Yes; you have to move them towards the king-row.

But what is the opposite side doing?

O yes; they are trying to jump your men off, and prevent you from getting your men into the king-row.

Just so your superintendent is playing checkers. Her Juniors are the checkers she is trying to push into the king-row of Christ, step by step, watching to prevent the other side from jumping her men off. That king-row is the church.

Satan, with his many forms of temptation, is on the other side, playing against your teacher, and watching you all the time to find some weak spot where he can lead you into some temptation, and so jump you off the board, and prevent your getting into this king-row.

But after hard work some of the checkers are pushed into the king-row. What do we do then?

Yes, we crown them, to show that they are kings.

Just so, when we get you into the king-row, we put a crown on you. That crown is Christ's name. We call you a "Christian," showing that you are a king, but not one of this world.

But do we leave our king in the king-row?

No; we move him out, to make him help get our other men into the king-row.

So, as soon as we crown you by having you join the church, we want you to move out and help us get your companions of the society into this king-row.

We use our king in checkers to shield our men while we are pushing them into the king-row. So you can help shield your companions from their temptations, and in many ways help us push them into the king-row. Then they will accept Christ, and Christ will give them a power that no one knows, or can appreciate, until he has received it.

Candle Talks. — Candles may be made to illustrate many important truths in Junior work. Here is one. This exercise, by the way, has been honored by the winning of some souls to open confession. Taking for your theme Matt. 5:16, "Let your light so shine," prepare for its illustration a " C. E." made out of candles.

Procure a nice board about twenty inches by twelve, and three-quarters of an inch thick, painted black. Let a number of small holes be bored in this board so as to form the monogram, and place little wax candles in each hole. Question the Juniors, and bring out these truths : —

That the pretty little candles were made to give light, but cannot do so until they are first lighted. After this happens, one can light another. Many of them, lighted, give more light than one. Some can be extinguished after they are lighted, but then they seem more useless than those that have never been lighted. There cannot be a perfect " C. E." of light unless all the candles are shining at once.

God wants the Juniors to shine for him, but they cannot unless he illuminates their hearts by his forgiveness and his love. After this happens, they can light others by their beautiful lives and words. The unlighted candles are the associate members that have not become Christians. The extinguished candles are the members that have ceased to shine.

Sand Maps. — Sand maps are being used more and more to teach the children in the public schools and kindergartens. Why may they not be equally useful in rendering clear to the Juniors the geography of Bible lands and mission countries?

Get a large, shallow tray, and fill it with bright, clean sand. Teach the Juniors to hollow out the seas, and trace the outlines of the continents and islands. Have little paper pyramids for mountains, and toy houses for the cities and mission stations. Have toy ships for the mission vessels, like the Morning Star.

If you have time, you may make houses of different shapes, and miniature temples, to illustrate the differences in the buildings in the various countries. You will find that the children will learn a great deal from these; and it will be strange if the superintendent does not, in the process, learn a great deal herself also.

Home-made Symbols. — Junior superintendents can add a great deal to the interest of the Juniors by a little bit of work with the scissors and the paint brush. One Junior superintendent gave interest to a temperance meeting whose theme was

" The cup of cold water," by cutting out a piece of paper in the shape of a cup, and giving it to the Juniors, that it might be a reminder during the week.

At another time, when the theme was " The cures of the Bible," each Junior was given a little paper bottle inscribed with the sentence, " Who healeth all thy diseases."

On another occasion the superintendent's patient scissors cut out for each Junior, from yellow cardboard, a Christian Endeavor monogram, the E inside the C, and all of one piece.

To emphasize a lesson of benevolence and kindness, each Junior was presented with a white paper hand, on which had been printed the words, " Lend a."

For a Thanksgiving symbol, circles of white cardboard were used, each having a gilt heart in the centre of one side. Around the heart, in letters of liquid bronze, was the word " Thanksgiving," while on the other side, in a circle corresponding to the word " Thanksgiving," were the initials of the months of the year — twelve in all, one for each letter of " Thanksgiving," the year, 1894, being placed in the centre.

These paper symbols make excellent pegs on which to hang brief talks to the children. They cost very little, and the children are greatly pleased with them. If the Juniors are of sufficient age, they may themselves be set to cutting them out.

An Object Table. — The superintendent should have, in the meeting room of his society, a little table solely occupied with illustrative material, so that he may have a variety of articles at hand to use in the course of his talk on the topic, or to pick up and talk about when the meeting flags. An acorn, a grain of corn, a bottle of seeds, a bit of rock, a bell, a book, a globe, are samples of what will be likely to be useful.

CHAPTER VII.

THE GENERAL MANAGEMENT OF THE SOCIETY.

Go Slowly. — Beginners in the interesting work of managing a Junior society are often too lavish in the use of good ideas. Plans for work that could with profit be stretched over an entire year, or even a series of years, they use up in the meetings of a few months. Then they have nothing new to present to the Juniors, whose interest flags with their own. More than that, they have confused the young folks with the multiplicity of plans. It is better to take up the plans one by one, and make sure that the possibilities inherent in any scheme are exhausted before passing on to another.

Trust Them. — Let the superintendent trust her Juniors as much as possible Take the executive committee of the society into your confidence whenever you can. Present to them your new plans, and discuss them with them. If possible, get the Juniors to originate plans, and carry them out if they are at all practicable, though you may have to change them sometimes in some particulars. Few things will do more to spur your members to better work than this method of throwing responsibility upon them.

" Mr." — **" Miss."** — The Juniors will appreciate it if the superintendent, instead of calling them " John A." and " Bessie B.," calls them " Mr. A." and " Miss B." Everywhere outside the Junior society they are called John and Bessie, and an added dignity will be given them if this attention is shown them in the Junior meeting.

Society Names. — It will interest your Juniors if you permit them to choose for themselves special names for their society. The Presbyterian Juniors of Yellow Springs, O., for instance, are called the " Pure Gold " Juniors, while those of the Christian church are called the " All the Year Around " Juniors.

Lest They Forget. — One ingenious Junior superintendent, when she sets a task for all her Juniors for a coming meeting, such as giving verses beginning with a certain letter, telling something they are thankful for, or the like, is in the habit of seeing all her Juniors in Sunday school, and tying a small slip of paper by a thread to a button of their coats or to their Junior badges, telling them to write whatever she desires for the meeting on that paper, and bring it back to the meeting in the afternoon.   She has seen almost a whole class of boys march into Sunday school with these slips of white paper flying in the breeze. Usually, too, they wear them in that way when they come to the meeting in the afternoon.

Prizes. — Sometimes the Junior superintendent may wish to offer prizes for superior excellence in any line of Junior work. Appropriate prizes are Junior badge pins of various degrees of value, Junior hymn books, Christian Endeavor book marks, and subscriptions to *The Junior Golden Rule*.

Not On Sunday. — Some Junior workers are especially urgent in their advocacy of week-day Junior meetings, as this means one hour more of religious training, to break into and sanctify the activities of the busy week.

The Second Card. — Some Junior societies require that the Junior pay for the second card, if he loses his first copy. To guard against this loss, it is well to urge the Juniors to keep their topic cards in their Bibles.

A Useful Slip of Paper. — The cheapest and one of the best ways of obtaining topic cards is to get the uniform topics published by the United Society, the little book containing the daily readings.   If the society wishes, they can have some local printer print little slips of paper of the same size as the United Society pamphlet and containing the lists of officers and committees. These can be pasted on the covers of the uniform topics, and others can be pasted over these when the officers are changed.

To Be Sure. — Speaking of the intermission of Junior meetings during the summer, Indiana's Junior superintendent says: " I have heard from some superintendents, not very many, this reason for disbanding, ' It is so very warm to go out to the meeting on Sunday afternoon.' Now I know it is warm work, I have tried it ; but, dear friends, is it any cooler on Thursday, Tuesday, or any other afternoon in the week, when we go down-street, or calling, or upon some personal errand?"

Summer Work. — On account of the possibilities of outdoor work, summer should be one of the best of seasons for Junior societies. Change your hour of meeting, if necessary, to bring it in a cool time of the day. One summer some Juniors met outdoors every afternoon under the shade of the trees, making clothing for an orphan child, while their superintendent read a story to them. Others in the same way dressed dolls, made hoods, mittens, aprons, etc., to be sent to missionaries or used as Christmas gifts, while at the same time the Junior boys made scrap-books.

Another set of Juniors set up an ice-cream industry during the hot months, and cleared forty dollars for missions. The raising of flowers and vegetables for missionary purposes is a summer industry in which the Juniors may be engaged.

The children will be easily interested in the fresh-air work. If they live near large cities, they will like to entertain the children as they come out from the cities during their country week; or, if they live in the city, they will be glad to help to give them a taste of the country air.

Summer Missionaries. — Many of the Juniors spend their vacations in towns other than home. Before they leave, the superintendent should show them how they may keep their eyes open for opportunities for aggressive work. Many Juniors have used their vacations to organize new societies. They should be invited to write letters during their absence to the Junior society, telling of their experience.

Junior Circles. — It is helpful in many ways to divide the society into Junior circles. These may be utilized in the meetings, and for the accomplishment of special work. A Maryland superintendent who tried it had sixty Juniors whom she divided into twelve circles, appointing an older Junior as leader for each. These leaders gave some reference or Bible verse to each member of the circle one week in advance, and at the following meeting, when the circle was called, all its members rose, the leader gave the number present, told where the verse selected was found, how it bore upon the lesson, and then all recited it together.

When the superintendent divided her Juniors into circles, she told them that no circle would be complete without ten members, and urged them to see which circle would be completed first. In less than a month they had one hundred and twenty-five members instead of sixty. The responsibility thus placed upon the leaders of the circles developed some excellent Christian workers.

A Joint Society. — In some communities there are not enough young people to support more than one society. In such a case, rather than leave the youngest children out in the cold, it is better to have them join the older Christian Endeavor society as Junior members, signing the Junior pledge. Let the first half of the meeting be given to the Juniors, while their elders occupy the closing half-hour. Possibly there might be different leaders for these two divisions. In this way the Juniors will feel that they have an important part, for the successful management of which they themselves are responsible.

Junior Work by Sections. — For a small society, where it is especially desirable to furnish regular work for all the members, the following plan has proved exceedingly useful. Divide the society into sections, containing, as nearly as may be, equal numbers of young people. Seat these sections one behind the other, and put in charge of each row one member of the lookout committee. A little rivalry among these members of the committee will result in admirable attendance. Each section may also have its vice-president, and some special recognition may be given them in the regular order of service by having them rise and repeat a verse together.

In the society whose superintendent sends me an account of this method, the committee work was based entirely on these sections. For example, Section No. 1 would be for one week the prayer-meeting committee. From that section the leader of the prayer meeting would be taken, and each of the other members would be expected to offer a sentence prayer.

The same week Section No. 2 would be the social committee, its members coming early, arranging the room, greeting the strangers, and staying afterwards to put things in order again.

Section 3 would be the music committee of the week, its members having entire charge of the hymns to be sung.

Section 4, the flower committee, would keep track of the sick members through the various lookout committeemen, and would send them flowers and books, also putting flowers in the church when possible.

Each member of Section 5, the testimony committee, was expected to bring some personal testimony, or some story to illustrate the lesson.

Section 6 for this week would be the missionary committee. They would meet one afternoon during the week to study about missions, and to work for the missionary box.

The next week all these committees would rotate. Section 2 would be the prayer-meeting committee, Section 1, the missionary committee, and so on. Each section contained a chairman for each committee, so that nearly all the Juniors had an office.

When the section was on duty, as a prayer-meeting committee, for instance, its prayer-meeting committee chairman would consult with the superintendent, and set his committee to work in accordance with the superintendent's directions. The result of this method was to give all the children a feeling of responsibility, while at the same time the constant changing of committees gave to each member an intelligent interest in all departments of the work.

Meeting them in Groups. — One of the best ways by means of which the superintendent can put himself into regular and close communication with the members of his society is to divide the society into groups, one of which is to meet him for fifteen minutes before the prayer meeting each Sunday.

With the usual complement of committees, two committees can be placed in each group. The lookout and prayer-meeting committees will go well together, the social and music committees, the temperance and Sunday-school, the literature and sunshine. If there is a fifth meeting in the month, the superintendent should hold a cabinet meeting, consulting with the chairmen of all the committees.

These group meetings should be introduced by brief written reports, which have been carefully prepared beforehand. Then should come a general conversation on the work of the society in relation to those committees, and at the close a few brief prayers, all the group kneeling. This makes an excellent preparation for the regular meetings of the society.

Little Sheep. — For the very smallest of the Juniors who cannot read, one superintendent forms a class which she calls "Little Sheep." While the older Juniors are finding references which she gives out, she calls these to the front, and gives each in order one word of a text, calling it their "name." This "name" is whispered so low that no one else can hear, and the Junior is required to repeat it over and over again until she is sure that each remembers it. Then they are disbanded until after the references are read by the older Juniors.

The small ones then take their places just as they were before, and repeat their "names" loud enough for all to hear, the other Juniors being required to listen attentively, and see who can first repeat the text given by the little ones.

A simpler method of interesting these very little ones, who are too small to read and yet are regular attendants, is to have them learn at home some verse to repeat at the Junior meeting. Then, when they are of the age to join the society, they will be quite sure to do so.

A and B. — Sometimes it is found advisable to organize a section of the Junior society, to be composed of children who are not yet ready to join the Junior society. This may be called the B section, the regular society being the A section. The B section should be placed in charge of the assistant superintendent. Division into regular committees being unadvisable, the following plan has been found practicable: Divide the B section into two parts. One part meets the superintendent this week for scrap-book work, say. Next week the second part meets her for the same work. The third week the first band meets her for sunshine or flower committee work, and so on, thus minimizing the time and thought required of the superintendent.

The Sunshine Department. — Where the Junior society is divided into these two parts, the very small Juniors should be separated, during part of the meeting at least, from the older Juniors, in order that more suitable work may be found for them. By the way, refrain from calling the younger division the primary department, or any such minimizing name. An excellent title for this division would be " the sunshine department," if you do not adopt " Section A " and " Section B," as suggested in the last paragraph.

Intervisitation. — The older societies have found intervisitation exceedingly helpful. Why not the Juniors also? For this purpose appoint two members of your society to visit some other society. speaking at the meeting if possible, giving the greetings of your society, and to return, bringing back a full report of the meeting they have attended, and any helpful ideas they may have gained regarding the methods used by the other society. The delegate who speaks should be very careful to tell what society they come from, as well as their own names, to tell when their own society meets, and to extend a cordial invitation to the Juniors whom he is addressing to return the call. The Junior who does not make this speech is the one who should make the report to the home society, and it is a good plan to appoint to this duty some Junior whose voice is seldom heard in his own words at the home meeting.

CHAPTER VIII.

THE PRAYER-MEETING COMMITTEE.

Their Duties. — " The prayer-meeting committee," says the Model Junior Constitution, " shall, in connection with the superintendent, select topics, assign leaders, and do what it can to secure faithfulness to the prayer-meeting pledge." Most societies, of course, will find the uniform topics the best for their use. These are sold by the United Society of Christian Endeavor for $1.00 a hundred, special designs costing more. I advise all superintendents, however, to use the little leaflet containing the daily verses as well as the topics. These are prettily printed, and cost only $1.50 a hundred.

The list of leaders should be prepared by this committee, always in close consultation with the superintendent ; and the committee should notify each leader, promptly reporting to the superintendent if any are unable to serve.

Form this committee of pledge enthusiasts, Juniors loyal to the pledge in every fibre, and not afraid to speak a word for it whenever necessary.

Fit to be Examples. — All the members of the prayer-meeting committee should be able to lead a meeting, to offer prayer, and to give testimony before the society. It need not be said, in addition, that they should be good Bible readers. Whatever method of participation is adopted by the other members of the Junior society, the superintendent should see to it that at least the prayer-meeting committee *repeat* their verses, and do not read them. It is better, if you must, to begin with a very small prayer-meeting committee, and confine it to those who are well fitted for the work, waiting to enlarge your committee until you have developed appropriate workers upon it.

A Volunteer Committee. — An English society of which I have heard adopted the daring plan of forming the prayer-

meeting committee entirely by volunteers. It was decreed that
each member of the coming committee should promise to take
part promptly in the meeting, and should try, during the week,
to get some one else to promise to take part. These conditions
being fully understood, the superintendent was delighted to find
that the volunteers were more than double the number of the
desired committee.

Their Meetings. — Teach the prayer-meeting committee to
feel that each meeting held during their term of office is theirs;
that they will be largely responsible for its failure, if it fails,
and largely to be credited with its success, if it succeeds.

Her Aids. — The prayer-meeting committee are the especial
aids of the superintendent in all things connected with the conduct of the meeting. Let them clean the blackboard for her
drawings; and, if this work is not provided for by other committees, let them distribute the hymn-books and the Bibles, and
collect them after the meeting. If the superintendent wishes to
introduce certain objects in her talk, let the committee be called
upon to bring these.

The superintendent should not even select the pledge cards or
the topic cards without consultation with the prayer-meeting
committee, in whose province these things lie. They will enjoy
making their own selection of colors and designs, and will take
an added interest in all things connected with the topic cards
and pledges that they have virtually chosen.

Use Their Wits. — Let the superintendent invite the prayer-
meeting committee to suggest new kinds of meetings. Their
bright eyes will often find in *The Golden Rule* or *The Junior
Golden Rule* some novel idea that they will wish to try in their
own society. Whatever new schemes the superintendent may
wish to adopt, she should communicate first to the prayer-meeting committee, and win their co-operation. With this nucleus
the schemes will be quite sure of success.

A Wall Hint. — Hang upon the wall of the room in which
the society meets a sheet of paper containing, in large letters,
the names of the prayer-meeting committee, with this remark
below: " If you have forgotten to bring a verse for to-day, please
obtain one from any of the above."

Surveying The Ground. — In order that the prayer-meeting committee may know what work they have to do among the Juniors, let them, during occasional months at least, keep an extra record of the method of participation each member adopts, dividing the society into groups, one of which is taken by each committeeman.   When a verse is recited, mark the name of the reciter with a V.   P will stand for prayer, T for testimony, S for a song that is called for.   Those who have not taken part in any way, and those who continually take some very easy mode of participation, it will be the duty of the committee to talk with and improve.

A Prayer-Box. — The prayer-meeting committee may be placed in charge of the prayer-box, in which the Juniors may be encouraged to drop, as they enter the room, little slips of paper containing requests for prayers for any one or anything they choose.   The members should be made to feel that these requests are in place if given orally at the meeting, but many will be too timid to make this public request.   The prayer-meeting committee will open this box after all have entered, and read these requests, when the prayers will be offered by the Juniors.

As Ushers. — The arrangement of the prayer-meeting room falls naturally to the charge of the prayer-meeting committee. They should see that the air is good, that the room is not too dark or too light, that the door is not left open during the meeting, that there are no extra chairs to produce a straggling effect, and that newcomers are welcomed, and given hymn-books.

Care For The Trial Members. — If the associate or trial members of the society are divided up among the prayer-meeting committee, a certain few for each to pray for, that they may be brought to know and love their Saviour, this method will be found to move the children to a very real and affectionate interest in each other's spiritual welfare and progress.

Pilots. — The superintendent should impress it upon her prayer-meeting committee that it is their duty to initiate new members into right ways of working in the society.   Some member of this committee should for several weeks sit by each new member, making himself his friend, and urging upon him the best ways of participation of which he is capable, asking him to offer a sentence prayer as he sees the member of the committee doing, or to repeat his Bible verse right after the member of the committee has repeated his, and in similar ways giving him confidence.

At Home. — The private prayers of the Juniors fall also within the province of this committee. Not much can be done, of course, in this direction. It has been found helpful in some societies for the committee to write out little prayers on cards. These prayers are taken home by the Juniors, placed where they can often see them, and read over prayerfully every day during the week. The card is to be returned at the next meeting with an account on the other side, written by the Junior, telling how the prayer has been answered. Such sentences as, " Jesus, help me to be more patient ; " " Dear Saviour, teach me to be more helpful ; " and the like, thus followed up during the week, will insensibly lead the Juniors into the very spirit of prayer.

His Natural Assistants. — The members of the prayer-meeting committee are the most appropriate aids for the leader. They should know his plan, and be ready to co-operate with him in all its more difficult features. Especially should they be ready to come to the support of Juniors who have never before led the meeting.

The Meeting Before the Meeting. — The meeting of prayer for five minutes before the regular meeting, that is so helpful in the prayer-meeting work of the older society, is just as helpful in the prayer-meeting work of the Juniors. Be sure the members arrive promptly ten minutes before the regular time, accompanied by the leader of the meeting, for whom one member of the committee has called. Each committeeman will offer a short prayer, praying especially for the blessing of the Master upon the meeting that is to follow, and its leader. It is especially helpful occasionally to invite to this meeting a Junior who is not yet a Christian.

Pauses and Prayer. — The prayer-meeting committee should, in the Junior as in the older society, be a pause committee as well. The Juniors should not be taught to fear pauses when pauses are appropriate, as in silent prayer; but this committee should promptly respond to all the requests of the leader, offering the first sentence prayers when these are called for, and giving testimonies in particular ways at the request of the leader or superintendent. When prayer is requested for any special person or object, if others do not quickly respond, the members of this committee should be ready to. Teach them, also, how valuable is their example in the matter of prayer, coming as they do from a little prayer meeting of their own. Ask them to scatter themselves as far as may be among the Juniors. The contagion of their prayerful spirit will affect the entire meeting.

CHAPTER IX.

PLANS FOR THE PRAYER MEETING.

The Right Model. — There are two types of Junior meetings, one of which follows the analogy of the Sunday-school primary department, and the other the analogy of the Young People's Christian Endeavor prayer meetings. It is needless to say that, while the first is very much easier than the second, a Junior society is simply a work of supererogation, if that is all it accomplishes. The Junior society differs from the primary department of the Sunday school in the fact that it teaches the Juniors to do religious work for themselves, while the study of the Bible is only a secondary matter ; in the Sunday school that is the primary object.

A Way of Opening. — A good way to begin a Junior meeting is to divide the children into bands, placing some older Endeavorer, or some of the most steady of the Juniors themselves, at the head of each band. Ten minutes before the time for the beginning of the meeting, these bands are to meet in different parts of the church, and are to hold little prayer meetings. The very smallest will be given prayers, which they are to repeat after their leader. These opening services having been completed, at the tap of a bell the Juniors will all strike up a marching song, and proceed in order to the full meeting. Here the training just given in the band meetings may be utilized, especially by the smaller children, who will repeat the prayers they have learned there.

Begin Earnestly. — Open the meeting with some regular, solemn service. Here is a suggested one : One verse of " Nearer, my God, to Thee," or some other suitable hymn. Silent prayer, with bowed heads, closed with concert repetition of the Lord's Prayer, led by the leader of the evening. Then let all rise and sing, " Praise God from whom all blessings flow." Then let the leader begin.

Let Them Do the Reading. — It is a good plan to have the Juniors read the Bible lesson for the day at the outset of the meeting, either in concert or responsively. Occasionally the girls may read one verse and the boys the next, or the superintendent may read a few verses and then call upon the Juniors, one after the other, to read portions. In this way the attention of the Juniors will be held, especially if the method is frequently varied.

One Thing Learned, Anyway. — Be dissatisfied with your plans for the meeting unless they include the teaching of at least one new thing. Make it a point that the Juniors shall all learn certainly one valuable truth or fact a Sunday. The rapid accumulations will surprise both you and them.

One Task a Week. — It is helpful to assign to the Juniors one definite spiritual task a week. For example, you may ask them to endeavor during the week not to speak one unkind word. At the meeting of the next week ask all the Juniors to tell their experiences in this endeavor.

Lesson Stories. — Ask, each week, one of the most intelligent of the Juniors to select from any religious paper some story bearing on the lesson of the day, or some little article which will help the children to see the truths of the lesson. After this story or article has been read, another Junior, not appointed beforehand, is to be asked to rehearse the story. Thus the attention of the Juniors will be secured, and the story will be fixed in their minds. If a girl gives the story, ask a boy to rehearse it, and *vice versâ*.

A variation of this method is to give selected members, the week beforehand, stories bearing on next week's topic, with the request that they read them and tell them in their own words at the next meeting. These stories, of course, should be short and simple, and yet they should have a well-marked point. Missionary and temperance meetings are admirably illustrated in this manner.

Blackboard Stories. — The blackboard illustration of the Junior topic given each week in *The Golden Rule* may be put to various uses. Some of these uses are spoken of elsewhere. One of the best is this. With a gelatine pad, or other duplicating device, make copies of the illustration, one for each Junior, using the illustration for the next Sunday. Ask the Juniors to take these home, and to write out, each one of them, a story about the picture. These stories will be read at the next meeting, and will serve as an excellent review.

Leading Up To It. — You cannot get your Juniors to take part by original testimony in the Junior meeting without some trouble. Here is a plan that requires a great deal of care, but is very effective, as those who have tried it testify.

During the week, write out little stories illustrating the subject; select Bible verses, adding to them a sentence or two that explains them; or write a question bearing upon the topic, and follow it with an answer. Distribute these three forms of help to the Juniors, and ask them to read their slips over until they can tell the contents in their own words at the next meeting.

The next step is to send the story, verse, or question, with a little note, asking the Juniors to repeat the story, verse, or question, and comment upon them in their own words.

The third and final step is to request them to be ready with thoughts of their own at the next meeting, and then at every meeting.

Such thorough work as this decidedly pays. "I should not feel that I was keeping my pledge if I just read a verse," declared one Junior who had been led in accordance with this method.

Little Commentators. — A helpful variation in a common Junior exercise is the following: Let the superintendent provide himself, before going to the meeting, with eight or ten references in different parts of the Bible. Let these selections contain good, practical thoughts, readily comprehended by children.

Near the opening of the meeting the superintendent will say, " Now, boys and girls, I am going to read a reference. The one who finds it first will please rise promptly and read it; and I want each one who reads to add to the reading one thing that is to be learned from the verse."

In this way, before they know it, the Juniors will be learning to make little speeches before the society. The superintendent should pronounce his words very distinctly, repeating them just once, in order to insure attention. It is better to say, " Proverbs 20: 11," than to say, " The eleventh verse of the twentieth

chapter of Proverbs." The superintendent should take care to
commend the little preachers for their sermons.

The Meaning. — Occasionally assign to the Juniors before
the meeting a verse apiece bearing on the topic, and ask them
to write out the meaning of this verse in their own words. At
the meeting each Junior will read first the Bible verse and then
his explanation of it. Much interest will be aroused by this
exercise.

Lessons in Chairs. — I have spoken elsewhere about the
advantage of making frequent changes in the arrangement of
the chairs of the place of meeting. This variety in arrangement
may also be made the basis of several attractive meetings. If
you are studying a country in a missionary lesson, arrange the
chairs in the outline of that country.

For example, if it is on India, your triangle will easily be
formed. The Juniors who have something to say about Calcutta will sit at one apex, about Ceylon at another, about the
Punjaub will sit at the third, while those who have been studying about Bombay will sit near by.

Rev. F. B. Everitt suggests several other shrewd arrangements. Arrange the chairs in the form of a C. E. monogram.
The C might stand for China and the E for England; those
occupying the first chairs to wear Chinese flags, carry Chinese
curios to exhibit, or give to the society some interesting facts
about the country. Those occupying the E chairs will state
what England is doing for China, will wear English flags, and
carry articles from England.

Or the "C. E." may stand for "Call Every one," the C
chairs giving Scripture invitations, and the E chairs responding
with Scripture verses that emphasize the universality of the gospel, verses that contain "every one" or "all."

Many Bible passages can well be illustrated by the arrangement of chairs; for example, Christ's command to begin at
Jerusalem and evangelize the world. Let the leader sit in the
centre chair, and the Juniors in three circles concentric with
her. The leader will represent Jerusalem, the first circle Judea,
the second Samaria, and the third "the uttermost parts of the
earth." The leader will tell what can be done for her own
street and neighborhood, those in the next circle what the so-

ciety can do for the town, those in the second for the country, and those in the third for the world.

Placing the Juniors in a square facing the different points of the compass, those on the appropriate sides may tell about missionary work in the north, south, east, and west of our land. Placing the chairs in the form of a cross, those who are in the head of the cross may talk about speaking for Jesus, those in the arms about giving for Jesus, those in the foot of the cross about working for him and going on his errands, and those in the centre of the cross, where Christ's heart lay, should speak about love in Christ's service.

Let the Juniors Answer. — The questions on the topic given each week in *The Golden Rule* under the heading, "Let the Juniors Answer," will be found of the greatest service, not merely in themselves, but also as suggesting other questions that the superintendent may propose. These questions should be copied on slips of paper, which should be distributed among the Juniors a week in advance of the meeting, each being asked to answer the question at the coming meeting in his own words.

For the superintendent also the questions will be useful, as suggesting a synopsis of the topic, and various helpful lines along which he may make his talk. The more advanced of the Juniors should not receive questions, but should be instructed to read over the questions themselves in the paper, and get stimulus from them for their own original thinking.

Occasionally it is helpful to make use of these questions, not in the form of questions, but as incomplete sentences. If, for example, the question was, "What is the one thing necessary to be a Christian?" the superintendent might write it on her slip of paper, "The one thing necessary to be a Christian is ....," giving these slips to the Juniors, for them to complete and read before the society.

Impromptu Answers. — A series of simple questions, prepared by the superintendent before the Junior meeting, may thus be utilized. At some pause in the meeting the questions may be distributed ; and those who receive them will stand, one after the other, read the question, and call upon some other Junior to answer it. Some very bright answers will be brought out in this way, and the meeting will be greatly enlivened.

The questions, of course, must be exceedingly simple, and should usually bear upon the topic of the day, though occasionally a set may be prepared for the sole purpose of stimulating the Juniors to better work for their society.

Junior Question-Boxes. — Among the most pleasing devices for maintaining interest in the older Endeavor societies are the question-box meetings. The Juniors also will delight in these. For success in such a meeting, announce the plan several weeks before, that the Juniors may be thinking about their perplexities, both regarding every-day conduct, and regarding religious truth. These questions should be written out before the meeting, and received in a basket at the door as the Juniors enter.

The pastor should be present, and some older Endeavorers, to answer the questions as the superintendent reads them. Some she will also answer herself, and some of the easier questions she will ask the Juniors themselves to answer, occasionally calling upon the entire society for a response.

It is not a bad plan to have a question-box as a regular feature of every Junior meeting, giving no more than five minutes to it at a time. The box will seldom be empty, and sometimes it will be crowded; and the abundance of its contents will be, in a large measure, a test of the success of the superintendent in teaching the Juniors to think for themselves.

An Open Parliament. — It is sometimes pleasant for the Juniors to have presented to them a general question regarding which they are to write very short paragraphs, a little prize being offered, possibly, for the best one. One superintendent, for instance, proposed the topic, " How to keep off the blues." The three answers considered the best were : —

" Do some kind deed to some one near you, and try to make other people happy."

" Casting all your care upon God."

" Always keep a clear conscience, and look on the bright side of life."

Work Slips. — The Juniors delight in doing definite work, if the definite work is set before them. One of the greatest helps toward a successful prayer meeting is to write on little slips of paper, before the meeting, requests such as, " Please offer a sentence prayer in the meeting to-day."

Brief — Brief — Brief! — If you ask visitors to speak to the Juniors, be sure to warn them beforehand, or when you invite them to speak, that they must be very brief. Five minutes is long enough to talk to any Junior society, I care not how skilled the speaker may be.

Good for Reciting. — Many of the poems published in *The Junior Golden Rule* will be found helpful for the Juniors to commit to memory and recite at the meeting.

What Others are Doing. — Occasionally brighten the meeting by cutting out from *The Golden Rule* and *The Junior Golden Rule* items telling about what other societies are doing all over the world. Number them, and pass them around to be read when called for in the regular meeting. This will inspire the Juniors, making them feel akin to all the ends of the earth.

A Month's Programme. — It is a poor plan to have all the Junior meetings alike, and yet there is no harm in having four consecutive meetings alike in most particulars. If you agree with me, then you will be able to form a programme, copies of which you can give to the leaders for a month, and the members will soon become measurably accustomed to this order of exercises.

Let Them Rise. — The Junior society is the place to begin teaching Endeavorers to rise to their feet when speaking in the prayer meeting. Especially when the Juniors are taking part in any particular way, as in reading something that they have written, be sure to insist upon their standing.

A List of Members. — It is very helpful to place upon the society topic card the list of members in alphabetical order. If this is not on the topic card, it would pay any society to have such a list struck off, either from type or from a hektograph. Aside from the pleasure the members will have in reading their names in print, such a list is frequently useful in conducting the meetings. It permits, for example, the dispensing with the roll-call occasionally at consecration meetings, the members taking part in the order of their names on the card.

Key Words for Junior Meetings. — All Junior superintendents will recognize the danger that the Junior meetings will not leave definite impressions. One way to remedy this is by the use of key words descriptive of the topic of each meeting. Call one meeting, for instance, "The Stumbling-Block Meeting;" another, "A Trouble Meeting;" others, "Money Meeting," "Heaven Meeting," "Thankful Meeting." Give the children something for each meeting to focus the thoughts of the meeting, and to serve as a monument for the meeting.

These single words may be given out the week before, and they will help the children greatly in their work of finding references in the concordance — a work, by the way, which every Junior should be taught to do.

At the meeting, effective use may be made of them by printing them upon the blackboard, or upon a banner, and putting them in some conspicuous position before the children.

At the opening of the meeting the superintendent might call for Bible verses containing the key word; at another time she might call for songs containing the key word; and she might even ask the children to use the key word in a series of sentence prayers.

Another way to emphasize these key words is to give out to some of the Juniors slips of paper on which is written a passage of Scripture containing the key word underscored. These passages they are to commit to memory, and recite at the next meeting. This is better than simply to tell them what the key word is, and ask them to hunt up a passage of Scripture containing it.

An instructive and pleasant exercise might be contrived by giving out at the previous meeting a series of Bible verses, the first letters of which should spell the word chosen as key word of the next meeting, and these verses might be recited at that meeting in their proper order. Ingenious superintendents will find many uses for the key words; but their chief use will be to give point to the meeting, and to make its chief lesson easily remembered.

A Card a Sunday. — Some Methodist Juniors use a separate topic card for each Sunday. These cards are little slips of paper, two inches by an inch and a half, and bear upon them the name of the society, the topic, and the name of the leader. Many societies that could not afford to have these separate cards printed may contain amateur printers who would be willing to give their services.

Entrance Cards. — Some Methodist Episcopal Juniors of whom I have heard are very systematically shepherded. For admission into the Junior room an entrance card is required at the door. On this card are printed the months and days of the meetings; and as each Junior enters, his card is punched in the appropriate place by the sentinel or doorkeeper. Even visitors have to obtain entrance cards, or they cannot get in. These cards, of course, can be obtained with the greatest readiness by application to the proper officer; but this slight bit of secrecy and formality pleases the Juniors, besides contributing to the regularity of their attendance.

Out=Door Prayer Meetings. — For the pleasant days of summer it is a good idea to hold at least one out-door prayer meeting. The unusual surroundings will move the Juniors to renewed interest in the services of the hour. The theme for the meeting may well be one connected with out-door life, such as Bible flowers, or the trees of the Bible, Bible waters, or Bible animals.

Junior Open-Air Meetings. — The custom is more common in England than in this country, but some superintendents have found it possible to hold open-air evangelistic services almost entirely conducted by Juniors. These, of course, are held during the warmer months, and the Juniors soon pray and testify in a very beautiful way, their childish voices influencing the hardened men and women that listen, as older people would scarcely be able to do.

A Home Prayer Meeting. — If you find your Juniors slow in taking up the devotional work of the society, try the effect of a prayer meeting held at your own home. The familiar and home-like surroundings will inspire the young people with courage, and many voices will be heard that before have been silent.

Summer Meetings. — During the summer the superintendent may well make the meetings shorter if the days are warm. The time may well be transferred to a cooler hour if the meeting has been held near the middle of the afternoon.

Definition Meetings. — Helpful Junior meetings may be based on definitions. For example, the Juniors may be asked to bring original definitions of the word, "Christian," each telling in his own simple way what sort of person he thinks a Christian should be. At another meeting the society may in the same manner define the word " Endeavor." Other topics for definition might be " the Bible," " Christ," " love," " unselfishness."

Midweek Meetings. — For the purpose of rousing in the Junior society a greater spiritual interest, a midweek meeting is an excellent aid. Invite all the Juniors to come together after school on Wednesday. You will get, of course, only those who are especially interested. Talk with them earnestly about their Christian duties, and about getting into close relations with Christ, and have earnest prayers and testimonies. These midweek meetings, of course, should not be continued indefinitely.

A New Idea Meeting. — A " new idea " service, originated by a Junior society in the Emerald Isle, is thus conducted. Upon the blackboard this diagram is printed : —

Let all

Christ's

Epistles

Say:

" Trusting in the Lord Jesus Christ,

I am   **H**EAR.
                      EED.
READY to   ELP."

The pastor gave a little talk upon this diagram, asking the Juniors to repeat it thoughtfully in concert three times. Before the meeting each Junior had been set to studying copies of *The Golden Rule* of various dates, as well as of *The Junior Golden Rule;* and after the pastor had finished his talk they read reports from societies in different parts of the world. The ideas that were new to that society were commented upon by the superintendent, and resolutions were adopted regarding the use of several of them.

A Testimony Meeting. — A testimony meeting was held by a society of Belfast, Ireland, managed upon the following plan. Folded sheets of paper bore plainly printed upon the outside the question, " How were you led to Christ?" and on the other, " What hinders your coming to Christ?" the first printed in blue, and the second in red ink. At the meeting of the previous week a basket containing these papers was presented to the Juniors, and each chose a paper as he passed from the room.

The superintendent had explained what was desired; and at the next meeting, in accordance with his invitation, the papers were brought in, each containing some bit of personal experience. As a result of the meeting, some of the Juniors were strengthened, and others, who found themselves in a difficulty about answering, were led to careful consideration of the question to which their attention had been called.

A New Year's Souvenir. — One pleasant feature of a New Year's meeting of a Junior society I know of was a folded piece of paper given to each member. Upon the front leaf were the words, " Turning over a new leaf, January 1, 1895." The next page was headed, " A lamp unto my feet;" the next, " A light unto my path;" while the last contained the name of the society and church. Upon the second page each member of the society wrote a verse of Scripture with his name, and returned the sheet to the superintendent. These sheets were then redistributed; and the last recipient wrote upon the third page a verse of Scripture, and kept the folder as a New Year's souvenir, these verses being adopted as each Junior's mottoes for the coming year.

A May Day Meeting. — As near May Day as possible hold a flower meeting. This should be the especial care of the flower committee. You will easily find suitable recitations and songs. The room should be nicely decorated, and the flowers at the close of the meeting sent to the sick. The superintendent's talk will have the beautiful theme of " Lessons from the Flowers," showing how the lily teaches purity, the pansy thoughtfulness, the violet modesty, and the like.

Scrap Meetings. — An occasional scrap meeting will be pleasing to the Juniors. To this meeting let them bring clippings that they have made from *The Golden Rule* and *The Junior Golden Rule*, — whatever each thinks will be most helpful to the society and its work, — and let the reading of these clippings be their participation in the meeting.

Lessons from the Immortal Tinker. — Cheap copies of

Bunyan's *Pilgrim's Progress* may be furnished the Juniors. They will delight in reading the matchless allegory, and in talking about it at their meetings. It would be a good plan to go through the entire book, taking one scene a week, the Juniors telling the story in their own words, turn about, and the superintendent applying the lessons to modern conditions and experiences.

Needs and Promises. — A need and promise meeting will furnish a pleasing variety. Let the superintendent prepare for it by making out a list of needs that are likely to be felt by every child, as, for example, " We need help in trouble ; " " We need strength ; " " We need sympathy ; " " We need courage ; " " We need salvation ; " " We need purity ; " " We need wisdom," etc. Give each of the Juniors a copy of this list, and ask each to find in the Bible as many promises as he can that fit the different needs. At the next meeting call out the needs one by one, and have the Juniors respond by repeating the promises that fit them. Let the Juniors vote as to which is the best promise to remember in connection with that particular need. Make a note of it, and drill the Juniors upon it afterward.

A Church Meeting. — You will do a wise thing if you set apart at least one meeting in the year to interest the Juniors in the different branches of the work of their own church. At this meeting they should especially consider the pastor and his different lines of work, praying for him, and bringing to the meeting poems and extracts that will be helpful, collected and sent to him. A special prayer should be offered for the success of his work. The Sunday school, the church prayer meeting, the missionary activities of the church, the older Christian Endeavor society, the mothers' meeting, the church officers — these and every other activity of the church should be remembered in this meeting, the object being to give the children as comprehensive an idea as is possible of the manifold labors of their church home.

See Other Chapters. — Though this chapter concerns one of the most important of all topics connected with this subject, it is a comparatively short chapter, for the reason that nearly every chapter of the book contains hints on the Junior prayer meetings. A large number of different forms of prayer meetings and ways of managing them will be found in the chapters on the consecration meeting, the Bible work, missionary work, temperance work, good-citizenship work, the Sunday-school committee, the music committee, prayer, the daily readings, the birthday committee, the flower committee — and, in fact, in almost all the chapters hints may be found on this topic of Junior prayer meetings.

CHAPTER X.

THE CONSECRATION MEETING.

What It Is. — " A consecration meeting," says the Model Junior Constitution, " shall be held once a month, at which the pledge shall be read and the roll called, and the responses of the members shall be considered a renewal of the pledge of the society. If any member is absent from three consecutive consecration meetings, without excuse, his name shall be dropped from the list of members." The by-laws fix the time for this meeting on the last of the month, subject, of course, to local circumstances.

No Junior should be dropped from the society until persistent, prayerful efforts have been made to retain him. The test of faithfulness given in the constitution is never to be enforced literally, except when the best interests of the society and of the delinquent seem to require it. Do not long keep unfaithful members on your lists, but exhaust all your resources before you let them go. No public announcement should be made when a member is dropped.

One a Month. — The superintendent, or the assistant superintendent, should lead at least one meeting a month, and this meeting should usually be the consecration meeting, in which should be made an especially urgent appeal to the Juniors, turning their thoughts toward personal consecration.

Begin in Time. — You cannot make as much of your consecration meeting as you should if you do not begin to plan for it and talk about it among the Juniors a month beforehand. Occasionally get them to promise to pray every day during the month for the next consecration meeting. At the opening of this meeting, let them all kneel down and pray for God's blessing upon it. Your prayers will be answered.

A Definition. — Consecration is a long word, and the Juniors may be pardoned if they fail to understand it. Let the superintendent explain its meaning carefully, not hesitating to repeat his explanation at every consecration meeting until he is sure that it is understood. An excellent plan is to ask each Endeavorer, one week beforehand, to bring to the consecration meeting some account of what consecration means, expressed in his own words.

Consecration Roll-Call. — The secretary should not be permitted to call the roll in the same way on two consecutive meetings. Now let her call the names in alphabetical order; now let the names be written on little cards, the cards shuffled, and called in the order of chance; now let the Juniors be called by rows as they sit in the room. Sometimes, instead of calling the names in alphabetical order by ones, call them by groups of three, the members responding in the order in which they are named. At another time place a list of the members upon the blackboard, asking each Junior to take part in that order, the secretary noting the responses.

If you have a printed list of the society, occasionally give each member a copy, asking them to take part in the order of that list. Sometimes take the society by sections, asking all in a certain part of the room to speak in any way they please, then turning to some other portion. Again, arrange for committee responses, asking the chairmen of the committees to call the roll of their committees, and when these have each taken part, the committee will rise and repeat some appropriate consecration verse previously determined upon.

The Roll of Associates. — It is not best, in my opinion, to call the roll of the associate or trial members at the consecration meeting. Such a roll-call implies that they are under a corresponding obligation to the society with the active members, and this is in no way implied in their pledge. It also, in a measure, places them on an equality of Christian confession with the other Juniors, and that is not best. If, however, this roll is called, these members should merely answer " Present."

Send a Message. — Though nothing is said about it in the Junior pledge, I believe it to be well to teach the Juniors that which will be a very important part of their duty when they join the older society, the sending of a message to the consecration meeting from which they are obliged to be absent.

This message should be an appropriate verse of Scripture, a bit of a poem, or some words of the Junior's own. The message may be read by the friend who brings it, or may be handed to the secretary or superintendent for him to read.

The Pledge in the Meeting. — No consecration meeting should pass without the concert repetition of the pledge, which may come either at the beginning or at the end of the meeting. It should be followed by the singing of the pledge song.

Consecration Responses. — Responses to the roll-call at consecration meetings should not be permitted to fall into a rut. One of the best methods, of course, is the giving of memorized verses of Scripture. At one consecration meeting these verses may all begin with the first letter of each Junior's name. At another meeting, each Junior may give a verse beginning with the last letter of his name. At still another, the verse chosen may mention the particular sin or fault of which each Endeavorer is conscious.

Hymns may be used, and the Juniors may come prepared to give each his favorite verse of his favorite hymn. Again, they may give three verses each of a hymn that commences with the first letter of their Christian names. Ask the Juniors on another occasion to give, at roll-call, some instance of God's especial kindness shown to themselves or to some one they know.

Seven Meetings. — Seek in every way to promote variety in the manner of conducting the consecration meeting. Here are some different plans : *A voluntary meeting*, in which no roll is called, though a record of participation is kept, the members taking part in any order they please. *A biography meeting*, in which the Juniors participate by giving, each one of them, a brief account of some beautiful consecrated life, taken from the Bible, history, or from personal knowledge. *A " next step " meeting*, in which the Junior is expected to take part in some way different from his usual method, and in some manner more difficult for him. *An after-election consecration meeting*, in which the newly chosen officers and committees speak of their plans for work, and pray for God's blessing upon it. *A " C. E." consecration meeting*, in which each Endeavorer repeats two Bible verses, one beginning with the letter C, and the other with the letter E, these verses to be appropriate to the significance of the initials. *A prayer consecration meeting*, in which prayers alone shall constitute the mode of participation. *A song consecration meeting*, each Junior responding, as his name is called, by singing or repeating one stanza of his favorite hymn.

Committee Responses. — One portion of the consecration meeting may well be devoted to committee responses, each committee having learned some appropriate verse which they repeat in unison. The temperance committee, for example, might say, " Look not upon the wine when it is red," etc.; the sunshine committee, " Do unto others as you would have them do to you; " the birthday committee, " So teach us to number our days," etc. At the close, let all the members, with the officers, recite in concert the society motto, or the motto of the United Society, " One is your master, even Christ, and all ye are brethren."

Definite Consecrations. — Give point to the consecration meetings by teaching the Juniors to make definite consecrations for the month to come. Call upon them during one month, for example, to consecrate their hands to doing kind deeds. During another month let them keep special watch over their tongues, that they refrain from everything that is harsh, and that they accustom them to speak bright and cheery words. Let the next consecration meeting look backward upon the month which has been passed. Call upon the children for their experiences, asking each to testify as to how he has been enabled to keep this definite consecration.

A Number Meeting. — An admirable plan for conducting the Junior consecration meeting has been used successfully in the First Congregational Church of San Diego, Cal. The secretary stands at the door, and as each Junior enters the room he is given a number which is placed opposite his name on a list. At the same time the secretary finds out whether the Junior has come prepared with a Bible verse to be used as his response to the roll-call. If not, the secretary furnishes the Junior with a Bible verse which has been supplied by the prayer-meeting committee.

After the opening of the meeting, the leader asks all to rise and take part who have numbers between one and eight. These rise and take part in the order of their numbers. Then comes a song, and another set. In this way the formal calling of the roll is avoided, and every member takes an active part in the meeting.

Confessions. — Sometimes confessions will make a good opening for the consecration meeting. Ask the Juniors to tell the ways in which they have failed to keep the pledge during the past month, the points in regard to which they have found pledge-keeping difficult. After this exercise the Juniors will be far more ready to repeat the pledge in concert, with the spirit and understanding.

" Sealed Orders." — A " sealed orders " consecration meeting will have the cordial co-operation of the Juniors. It is thus carried out. Just before the meeting begins, the chairman of the prayer-meeting committee will pass around a plate containing little slips, each of them bearing some direction as to how the Junior will take part. Some will be told to pray, some to repeat a verse, some to answer a question about the subject of the meeting, some to tell of their experience in certain matters during the past month. These slips may be addressed to the different Juniors, or they may be apportioned by chance. In either case, many advance steps will be taken during the meeting.

Consecration Questions. — Write upon the blackboard before the consecration meeting such questions as the following, asking each Junior to select one, and embody his reply in his response to the roll-call : —

How did being a Junior, with the Junior pledge, help you this past month —

1. To be more truthful?
2. To be kinder to others?
3. Not to swear?
4. Not to cheat in school?
5. To be pleasanter at home?
6. To read your Bible oftener and better?
7. To pray more earnestly?
8. To be more unselfish?
9. To listen better in Sunday school?
10. To do your home duties without grumbling?

No Meaningless Terms. — Take especial pains to nip in the bud any tendency among the Juniors to use stock phrases in the consecration meeting, such as that nuisance in the older society, " I want to reconsecrate myself." Teach the Juniors in all things to be sincere, and to speak out of their desires and experience. Any failure in this respect may mean for them a life of canting insincerity.

A Consecration Exercise. — This little exercise for the consecration service was originated by Miss Laura Wade Rice of Baltimore, the well-known Lutheran mission worker. All our Junior superintendents will be glad to see it.

Leader. — We are met in the name of the Lord Jesus Christ, who loved us, and gave himself for us.

All. — " For the love of Christ constraineth us ; because we thus judge, that if one died for all, then were all dead ; and that he died for all, that they which live should not henceforth live unto themselves, but unto him which died for them, and rose again." Therefore we make him this pledge : —

Trusting in the Lord Jesus Christ for strength, I promise him, etc. (Juniors repeat membership pledge.)

Leader. — " I beseech you therefore, brethren, by the mercies of God, that ye present your bodies a living sacrifice, holy, acceptable unto God, which is your reasonable service."

PRAYER HYMN.

Dear Jesus, take me as I am,
  And make me more like thee,
Till, when God looks into my heart,
  Thine image he may see.

Dear Jesus, take these lips of mine,
  And may the words they say
Be kind and gentle, pure and true,
  More Christ-like every day.

Dear Jesus, take my hands, my feet,
  Set them to work, I pray ;
Help me to make this earth more sweet,
  More like to heaven each day.

Leader. — " Whether therefore ye eat or drink, or whatsoever ye do, do all to the glory of God. For none of us liveth to himself, and no man dieth to himself."

All. — " For whether we live, we live unto the Lord ; and whether

we die, we die unto the Lord ; whether we live, therefore, or die, we
are the Lord's."

> " I will go where you want me to go, Lord,
> Over river or mountain or sea,
> I will say what you want me to say, Lord,
> I will be what you want me to be.
> Whenever you speak I will listen,
> I will read your sweet words every day,
> And belong to you only and always,
> At my home, in my work, in my play."

SUNSHINE MOTTO.

" I expect to pass through this world but once. Any good thing,
therefore, that I can do, or any kindness that I can show to any human
being, or any word I can speak for Jesus, let me do it now. Let me
not defer it, or neglect it, for I shall not pass this way again."

New Members and Graduates. — The consecration meeting, as it is the most serious meeting of the month, the meeting
at which the pledge is uppermost and the thought of personal
loyalty to Christ at its height, may well be made the meeting
for the reception of new members and the graduation of old
ones. For the proper performance of these two things, see the
chapter devoted to them.

Avoid Monotony. — Be careful that the calling of the roll is
well broken up by singing. Instruct the leader beforehand to
interrupt the secretary at suitable intervals by announcing a
hymn. It is best to have only one verse sung at a time, the
Juniors being asked to keep their books open at the place until
all have been sung.

A Consecration Hymn. — Let your Juniors choose for themselves some consecration hymn, to be sung only in consecration
meetings, and to signify consecration always to them. With
this the meeting may well be closed.

Arise ! — It will serve to emphasize the consecration meeting
and the importance of the part each member takes in it, if, at
this meeting, all the Juniors rise as they speak or read, though
at other meetings they remain seated.

Prayer in the Meeting. — Each consecration meeting should
be largely devoted to prayer. Silent prayer will come fittingly
at the close. If any of the members are sick, prayer should be
offered for them when their names occur in the roll-call. Dur-

ing seasons of sentence prayers the Juniors should be taught to kneel, in the consecration meeting especially. It will be found wise to devote occasional consecration meetings entirely to prayers, no roll being called, though the secretary keeps an account of the participation. You will find, if the plan is announced a week or two beforehand with an earnest little talk, that you will have slight difficulty in getting all the Juniors to pray.

Consecration Gifts. — One of the most beautiful teachings of the consecration meeting will be the teaching of practical charity. A consecration basket may well be placed at the door of every consecration meeting ; and in this the Juniors will drop, as they enter, gifts for the poor, their monthly missionary offerings, papers and magazines for sailors, flowers and fruit for the sick in the hospital, and similar things. If this is not thought best, certainly a missionary collection should be received, and the Juniors should feel that they are actually consecrating part of their possessions to the Lord's service. The superintendent should offer a prayer after this collection has been taken, or the Juniors should sing some appropriate song.

How They Earned It. — Occasionally, at least, have your Juniors during the month earn the money that they bring for their consecration meeting offering, and then spend some time at that meeting hearing from the Juniors the ways in which the money has been earned.

How to Close. — It is always best to close a consecration meeting with some concert features, something that will fuse the thought and purpose of the entire society in one. This may be the Lord's prayer repeated in concert, a consecration hymn sung with bowed heads, the concert repetition of the pledge or of some appropriate psalm, silent prayer, the singing of the Gloria or the doxology, the repeating of the child's creed, or the like.

A Little Prompting. — If you find the Juniors becoming careless of the consecration meeting, and forgetful of its sacred import, it would prove helpful to write out little notices something like the following, and send them around by willing Juniors from house to house the day before this meeting : " As you know, tomorrow's meeting will be a consecration service. Please come to the meeting with some verse of a hymn, or some Bible verse, which expresses your need or your prayer. Please pray for the meeting, that it may be a blessed and a helpful one for all of us. If you cannot be present, be sure to send some message."

CHAPTER XI.

PRAYER IN THE MEETINGS.

Teaching to Pray. — The superintendent should select from the Bible short prayer passages and teach the Juniors to use these as their own. The psalms especially abound in fitting quotations. One Methodist pastor taught his Juniors to pray by having them kneel down and repeat, one after another, any prayer he might know, even " Now I lay me down to sleep." In this way they became accustomed to their own voices, and since all were praying, no one was willing to refuse.

Another admirable method is for the superintendent, at the opening of the meeting, to ask the Juniors some question, such as, " What do you wish to ask God for to-day? " and then, after a good many answers have been given, call for sentence prayers embodying these answers.

Leading in Prayer. — One of the best ways of instructing the Juniors how to pray is for the superintendent to offer a prayer with short and simple sentences, pausing at the end of each sentence, or portion of a sentence, for the Juniors reverently to repeat in concert after him what he has just said. Here is an example, the prayer offered by Mr. Sewall and the Juniors who were present at the Junior rally of the Montreal Convention : —

" Our dear heavenly Father, we thank thee for this day — for the Bible — for Jesus Christ our Saviour — and that each of us may be a Christian now. We pray for thy blessing upon our meeting. Help all those who shall speak to us. Help us to remember and understand what they say. May some of us become Christians before we go from this room. Wilt thou bless this city, and all the boys and girls in it, — and wilt thou bless all the boys and girls in all the world. For Jesus' sake. Amen."

And here is another example, a prayer offered by Mr. Ralph Wells and the children at a Sunday-school convention : —

" Dear Saviour, — we do thank thee — for coming so far — to save us. — We remember — how thou wast a little boy — in Bethlehem's manger; — how thou didst go about — doing good; — without **any** home; — men ill-treating thee; — until at last, after thirty-three years, — thou didst die for me — on Calvary. — O Saviour ! — help me to call thee — my Saviour, — and to love thee, — like thy little child. — May I show my love for thee — by trying to keep — all thy command-ments ; — by being very kind to everybody ; by keeping the Sabbath day — by not saying bad words — by helping my father and mother. — Bless all that I love, — make them all thy children, — and in a lit-tle while — may we meet thee in heaven, — for Jesus' sake.   Amen."

Written Prayers. — Some superintendents have found it helpful to inspire confidence in public prayer by this method, to which many Junior workers will object.   I give it because it has been found useful.   The superintendent writes a simple prayer, and gives it to one of the Juniors to read. " Now let us all bow our heads," says the superintendent, " while Lucy reads a prayer."   After several repetitions of this method, the superin-tendent advances to the step of asking the Juniors to form their own simple prayers.

Instead of this method, little slips of paper, each bearing a sentence prayer, may be given out, and many set to praying during the meeting.

Transformed into Prayers. — Teach your Juniors to pray by showing them how any of their Bible verses may be trans-formed into prayers.   For example, the beatitude, " Blessed are the pure in heart, for they shall see God," may become the prayer, " Make me pure in heart, dear Father, that I may come to see thee."   And in the same way they may be taught quite indefinitely to pray in the language of Scripture.

Praise and Petition. — In teaching the Juniors to pray, it is a good plan to ask at one meeting solely for sentences of thanks, beginning, " I thank thee, Jesus, for—— ."   At the next meeting teach them to pray prayers of supplication, beginning, " I pray thee, Jesus, that thou wilt —— ."   At the third meeting they will be asked to unite the two forms of prayer, praying little prayers containing two sentences, one of thanksgiving, and one of sup-plication.

Talk It Over First. — A little conversation between the superintendent and the Juniors may be made the basis of follow-ing prayers.   Ask the Juniors to tell, each one, what he or she needs that the topic of the day suggests to them. After all have done this, ask the Juniors to kneel down and simply ask God for the things about which they have been talking to their superintendent.

The Parts of Prayer. — Do not permit your Juniors to make the mistake of thinking that all prayers must be prayers of petition. Familiarize your young charges with the different portions of a model prayer, namely, adoration, thanksgiving, supplication, and confession. Do not use these long words, or, if you use them, explain their meaning to the Juniors. Occasionally the Juniors may be asked to pray prayers containing something under each of these heads.

The Model Prayer. — When the Juniors are slow in forming their own prayers, let not the superintendent forget the Lord's Prayer. Train the children to pray that in public, and be sure to ask different Juniors at each meeting. It will soon become easy for them to offer their own petitions.

In Turn. — An admirable way to get the children to take part in sentence prayers is the following: Ask all to rise and repeat the pledge in concert, and request them, on the conclusion of the pledge, beginning with the leader of the meeting, to offer sentence prayers in turn, the sentences passing from each to each in order. Any Junior that, for any reason, may not wish to take part in this exercise, is to take his seat instead, at the moment when his turn comes. Each Junior is to stand until his turn, so that in case of refusal it is an active rather than a passive one. This plan will secure a very full participation in sentence prayers.

Beginnings and Endings. — The Juniors will find it much easier to engage in prayer, if they are taught some appropriate beginnings and endings of prayers. A short time may well be spent some day in a drill on this subject. The superintendent may write appropriate forms on the blackboard, and may get the Juniors themselves to suggest others.

Begin with Few. — Much may be done in committee meetings toward the promotion of sentence prayers in the prayer meetings. Many will begin to pray in the smaller committee meetings that will be too bashful to make the attempt before more of their companions.

Their Thanksgivings. — An impressive way of opening the Junior meeting with prayer is the following: Let the superintendent ask the Juniors each to think of just one thing that he is thankful for, without mentioning it to the superintendent or any one. Then the society is to stand up, and the Juniors, taking part in order, are to offer sentence prayers, thanking God for the one thing of which each has thought.

No Mumbling. — In teaching the Juniors to pray, remember that it is very essential that they learn to pray very distinctly, not mumbling their prayers. Teach them that it is manly and womanly to speak in meeting with sufficient loudness and clearness that all may hear.

Prayer Circles. — The Juniors will like to form prayer circles, rising and standing with hands joined, circling the room, bowing their heads and praying in turn.

For Understanding. — A season of prayer should never be entered upon with the Juniors without at least a word from the superintendent, explaining to the children the sacredness and the meaning of what they are about to do. The spirituality of the season will be increased if the Juniors are taught to kneel. At any rate, they should be required to bow their heads.

Prayer Lists. — See that the members of the prayer-meeting committee are each furnished with a printed list of the members of the society. Such lists are useful also for the lookout, social, and other committees, as well as the officers. One prayer-meeting committee of which I have heard has the helpful habit of dividing the Juniors among the members in such a way that each committeeman shall have one Junior to pray for each day. In this way all the members of the society are remembered in prayer by some one of the committee in the course of the week, with the result of deepening very greatly the spiritual life of the entire little band.

Don't Do Too Much. — The Junior superintendent will make a mistake if he permits the Juniors to call upon him very frequently to lead in prayer. They will soon come to depend upon him, and will cease to take this responsibility upon themselves.

Calling by Name. — In some societies the members are so ready and have so conquered their timidity that the leaders dare to call upon the members by name, as they desire to have them speak, pray, or repeat Bible verses. If your Juniors have sufficient confidence, this method may occasionally be adopted in your society, though with exceeding tact.

In general, the leader or the superintendent should never make this request in public until in private he has learned whether the Junior is willing thus to be called upon. If a Junior is asked to pray and refuses, the meeting is hurt, and all future efforts in that line are discouraged.

Prayer Themes. — In order to give definiteness to the prayers of the Juniors (and the Juniors delight in such definiteness), propose for each meeting some special theme of prayer. Often it should be in harmony with the topic; but sometimes there may be suggested special persons or objects, such as missionaries in whom the society is interested, or persons in the church who are sick.

Prayer Slips. — Sometimes the superintendent will do well to distribute prayer slips before the opening of the meeting. Each Junior will read upon his paper the name of some object for which he is to pray. One will be told to pray for the superintendent. Another will be asked to pray for " our officers." A third will be asked to offer a short prayer for increase in the numbers of the society. Thus the Juniors will be led to widen their themes, and to find them for themselves in the future.

Silent Prayer. — Silent prayer should often be used, though not more than once in the course of a meeting, and the time for it should vary. It should come after some impressive thought or experience. Always it is well to tell the Juniors for what to pray during this time of silent prayer; and occasionally it is best to announce a series of themes of prayer during this silent moment, one after the other. Show the Juniors that this is the way in which they are to follow one who is praying audibly.

Subjects for Prayers. — If the society is just beginning to make sentence prayers, it is a good plan to write upon the blackboard and keep in plain sight some fruitful themes for such prayers. The following list will be suggestive : —

1. Truth.	5. Our committees.
2. Sinning.	6. Our superintendent.
3. Bad company.	7. Our pastor.
4. Heathen lands.	8. Sad homes.

Stand or Kneel. — Occasionally call upon the Juniors to rise and repeat in concert the Lord's Prayer. At other times they may be asked to stand, and with bowed heads sing some prayer-song, like " Nearer, my God, to Thee." It is best for them to stand during such exercises, as this will be a relief for their restlessness. In general, however, prayers of any sort, and especially sentence prayers, will be more effective if the society kneels while praying.

A Prayer-Hymn Service. — A good prayer service for the Juniors groups itself around some fitting prayer-hymn, such as " Just as I am." The first verse is sung, and three or four of the boys are called upon to lead in prayer. After the second verse, three or four girls are called upon in a similar way; and so it alternates until, after the last verse, the superintendent herself offers prayer, at the close of which all join in the Lord's Prayer.

For Opening and Close. — Here is a fitting verse of prayer to be repeated in concert at the opening of a meeting : —

> " A prayer we lift to thee, dear Lord,
> Ere we shall listen to thy word.
> The truth thy Spirit brings from thee
> Help us to study patiently.
> For Jesus' sake. Amen."

The following verse is a good one for the Juniors to repeat in concert, with bowed heads, at the close of a meeting : —

> " Our Father, through each coming day,
> Watch o'er our every step, we pray :
> And may thy Spirit hide the word
> Deep in our willing hearts, O Lord.
> For Jesus' sake. Amen."

The Week of Prayer. — During the week of prayer, the Juniors should by no means be omitted. Though it may not be best for them to attend all the meetings, one meeting certainly should be theirs ; and they should be asked to join their prayers with those of their elders during all the course of the seven days. In some places, Junior work during the week of prayer has been crowned with abundant conversions.

CHAPTER XII.

JUNIOR MUSIC.

The Music Committee. — No part of the superintendent's work can be made so delightful as the direction of the singing and other music. Every society should have a music committee. The Model Junior Constitution lays down its most important duties: " The music committee shall distribute and collect the singing books, and co-operate with the leader of the meeting in trying in every way to make the singing a success." Other work is suggested in the following pages.

In addition, a large society, and many a smaller one, will find useful a Junior choir, whose leaders should, if possible, be the music committee. This choir should meet for occasional practice under a skilled leader, and will furnish the efficient nucleus for all the society singing.

Music Everywhere. — An Illinois Junior had a music-box, and played a tune every time she gave a cent for missions. After this fashion a shrewd superintendent will teach the Juniors to put music into everything they do. This will need guidance rather than urging; for children are filled with the spirit of song — a spirit that some, alas! repress, but all should delight to train.

The Best Instrument. — To lead the Junior singing, nothing is better thon a strong and well-trained voice. Of course a piano or an organ is a great assistance, or a violin, cornet, clarinet, and the like. Some of these instruments the Juniors themselves play; but all of these may be dispensed with, while the human voice is indispensable.

Some Technical Knowledge. — A Junior superintendent, who has the management of so many unformed voices, will find it well worth while to become familiar with the management of the vocal organs. It is nothing short of a sin so to train children as to strain their voices, and unfit them for future usefulness.

Give them songs within the range of a child's voice. **Never** permit screaming. Remember that the young throats need rest oftener than you yourself do. Show the Juniors that singing is a part of worship, and that to sing a prayer without feeling it is as bad as to repeat it without feeling it. Though you should not make the Junior meeting a singing-school, yet a word about singing from note, the different kinds of time, the pitch, and the like, will not be out of place, and will help you greatly.

Transpose. — As the voices of the Juniors range low, and as it is especially important to avoid in any way straining them, a knowledge of the principles of transposition is especially helpful to the Junior organist or pianist. These principles are easily learned; and a little practice will make the player proficient, so proficient that she can readily lower the key of any piece whose range is too high for the undeveloped voices of the Juniors. In this way she can be far more useful in Christ's service.

Expressive Singing. — Do not fall into the mistake so commonly made of estimating the excellence of Junior singing by its loudness, rather than its correctness and feeling. Teach the Juniors to sing with expression. Teach them to make marked variations in softness and time in accordance with the thought of the words, now sinking almost to a whisper, now louder with some joyous thought. If the children are made to feel what they are singing, you have gained the greatest possible triumph.

Learning without Book. — Do not hesitate to attempt to teach the Juniors new songs without books or music. Place the words before them written upon the blackboard. Sing a line or two, and ask them to repeat it. Keep this up until they are familiar with that portion, and then go on to another. They will soon pick up a tune, which will thus be added to the permanent possessions of the society. They will enjoy it if one new tune is learned at each meeting. Do not fail, however, to practise the tunes for several meetings before you conclude that the Juniors know them.

Good Humor. — "Good air and good humor," says Rev. W. W. Sleeper, "will be found of great assistance in Junior singing." Anything approaching scolding is an immediate destruction of spiritual harmony, and it is hard to see how the harmony of sound can be expected to result. Keep in good humor, and your Juniors will be a thousand times more likely to keep in good voice.

Suitable Songs. — Take care to set before the Juniors songs that are in harmony with their own experiences. Remember that the hymns that voice the sterner experiences of older people are not always most fitting for the Juniors. You cannot judge of this by the zeal with which they sing them, because the children will be caught by the pleasing tune, and will sing an unfitting hymn for the sake of the tune.

Start Right In. — You have no idea how much it will help your Junior meetings if your organist is able to do without her notes, at least in playing the pieces most commonly used in the society. Then she can strike up a tune as soon as it is called for by the Juniors. Their ready memories have possessed themselves of the words of their commonest songs, and usually they are waiting impatiently for the organist to find the hymn in the book and play the prelude. Life and vivacity will be added to the meeting if this fumbling can be dispensed with.

Without Books. — As soon as you have become quite sure that the Juniors know a song, then do not permit them to make any use of the book while they are singing that song. Accustom them to sing from memory. This training will be of the greatest advantage in their future Christian service.

Standard Music. — Devote much attention to teaching the Juniors some of the many beautiful songs by standard composers especially adapted to their work. These should be learned by heart, so that they will always abide with the young Christians. A Junior superintendent suggests as especially fitted for this purpose such hymns as Sir Arthur Sullivan's, "Hear us, Holy Jesus;" Luther's hymn that he wrote for his own children, "Away in the manger, no crib for his bed;" Dr. Holland's beautiful Christmas hymn, "There's a song in the air;" and Baring-Gould's exquisite evening song, "Now the day is over."

The grand hymns of the church, such as, "Lead, Kindly Light," "Nearer, my God, to Thee," "Rock of Ages," and the like, should, in a similar way, be made the lasting possession of their memories, rather than the property of their hymn-books. One of these hymns may well be selected each month, committed to memory, and sung at the opening of all the meetings, until it is thoroughly learned.   At the next meeting a new one may be chosen.

Teach the Juniors to sing the Lord's Prayer, the Gloria, the Doxology, and some of the easier chants.   You will find that they can be taught to chant beautifully.   Obtain some easy prayer response, and teach the Juniors to sing it at the close of the opening prayer or at the close of sentence prayers.

Junior Hymn-books. — In my opinion, the best book published for the use of Junior Christian Endeavor societies is "Junior Christian Endeavor Songs," edited by Mr. Ira D. Sankey, with the co-operation of Mr. William Shaw and Mr. John Willis Baer.   It is sold by the United Society of Christian Endeavor for twenty-five cents a copy (postage five cents), and you should at least examine it before you make any selection. For the use of Junior conventions and union meetings, the United Society has prepared a sixteen-page leaflet of selections from this song-book.   These are not for sale, and cannot be loaned to individual societies, but will be loaned for the occasions first mentioned, on condition that expressage both ways shall be paid, and payment be made for the missing leaflets.

Take Care of Them. — If it is worth while to have Junior singing-books at all, it is worth while to take good care of them. Have them gathered up before the society is dismissed.   One of the Juniors will take pride in being appointed to this office. Have a bookcase or a box in which they can be locked; and thus you will never lose any, nor need to use books that are ragged and soiled.

A Hymn-book Committee. — A hymn-book committee will be helpful for occasional endeavors.   These have charge not merely of the Junior song-books, but of the church hymn-books. In one Kansas society, such a committee went to the church an hour or more before the regular meeting.   They took with them erasers and mucilage, erasing all writing they found in the hymn-books, and pasting in the leaves that had been torn out.

In Church. — A Methodist Protestant Junior society, on buying a new hymn-book, was so proud of it that they gained permission to sing a song from it at each church service.   Why would not this be one pleasant way of interesting the Juniors in the church service, and the older Christians in the Juniors?

The History of Hymns. — Songs and hymns may be made much more vivid to the Juniors by a little knowledge of hymnology. The superintendent should make a collection of anecdotes illustrative of hymns, and of bits from the biographies of famous hymn-writers, occasionally giving one of these in the meetings. If such a method is used, the Juniors will always think of these stories when they come across those hymns.

A Hymn Service. — A service your Juniors will appreciate is a hymn service, wherein all the songs shall be taken from the work of some great hymn-writer, such as Watts, or Fanny Crosby, or Ray Palmer. Tell the Juniors about the beautiful lives of these sweet singers, inserting anecdotes between the hymns, occasionally questioning the Juniors so as to fix in their memory what you have already told them, using the map to show where these writers lived, showing the children pictures of their homes and of their faces. Aim to make each character vivid and real to the Juniors, so that whenever the name is seen in the hymn-book henceforward, it will carry with it helpful associations.

Initial Hymns. — It is a common custom for the Juniors to learn Bible verses whose initials coincide with the initials of their names. The same plan may be applied to the learning of hymns, each Junior committing to memory three hymns whose initials are the same as his own.

"Picking out Hymns." — Few older leaders know how to make judicious selection of hymns, and the Juniors can hardly be expected to have this knowledge. A little teaching along this line might well be given before the whole society, so that the spirit of the meeting may not be spoiled by some ill-considered selection of inappropriate hymns. Occasionally the Juniors may take an exercise in hymn selection. The superintendent may say, "Suppose we had a meeting about Christ's love, what hymns would you pick out?" and as the Juniors name hymns, turning over their hymn-books, the superintendent may commend each selection as fitting, or show in what ways it is inappropriate.

Introductory Praise Services. — A praise service of five minutes just before the regular meeting of the Juniors is an admirable plan. The younger members of the society who would not feel competent to lead the regular meetings may well be set to leading these brief introductory services, and they will make for them an excellent stepping-stone into the more difficult work.

Preparation for Singing. — It will add much to the interest and understanding with which the Juniors sing their Christian Endeavor songs if, before a hymn is sung, especially if it is an old hymn, the stanzas be recited by one of the Juniors. If it is a new hymn, it will be well to ask one of the Juniors to read it first.

Sometimes the entire society may be called upon to read the hymn in concert. It may be read through and then sung; or, on another occasion, it may be read a stanza at a time, each stanza being sung after it is read.

If the thought of the hymn is unusually difficult, the superintendent may give a little explanation of it, and then the singing will come with more than the customary zeal.

The Spice of Singing. — A very impressive way of using a song that is in especial harmony with the thought of the meeting is to get some Junior to read it or repeat it before it is sung. Other variations in the use of hymns should be made. Have occasional solos, asking one Junior to sing the stanzas, while the rest come in on the chorus. Vary these by appointing duets and quartettes; by having a girl sing one verse and a boy the next, while all sing the chorus; by having the girls sing the verses while the boys sing the chorus, or the reverse; by appointing different members of the society to sing different stanzas as solos; by dividing the society into two divisions, those on the left singing the first stanza, and those on the right the second, while all join in the third, and in many other ways.

When you make a separation between the boys and girls, having the girls sing one verse and the boys another, appoint a girl to lead the girls and a boy to lead the boys. It is a good plan to vary the singing by calling for the favorite songs, first letting a girl name a piece, and then a boy. When the Juniors become restless in the course of a meeting, sometimes it is advisable to drop everything else, even the most carefully prepared programme, and have them stand up and sing.

Alternate. — Utilize your Junior choir by setting them to sing one verse, while the rest of the Juniors sing the chorus of the song. Those Juniors who are not in the choir, by the way, should be called " the chorus."

Emphasize the Music Committee. — If possible have the music committee and the choir the same, in order to avoid confusion in authority and responsibility. This committee should sit in front, facing the society, at each meeting. Their office may be emphasized by requesting them occasionally to sing a song by themselves, and by occasionally choosing members from their number to sing solos or duets.

An Organized Choir. — It is not a bad plan to organize the Junior choir with its own president and secretary; its treasurer, to collect fines for absence from rehearsals, and the like; its lookout and membership committee, and so on. Membership in the Junior choir should be made a reward for progress in singing; and the Juniors should feel that it is possible for each one of them, by attending faithfully to the instructions of the superintendent, to gain this coveted position. In some societies the Junior choir for the day is appointed at the opening of the meeting, and thus all are given a chance.

A Hymn-leader. — Occasionally ask some Junior besides the leader to select the hymns for the meeting, placing the name of this Junior upon the programme as assigned to that duty.

Boys' Choirs. — A boys' choir is helpful to any Junior society, and the boys will enter into the work with great zest, and take pride in their success. A boys' choir and a girls' choir, singing alternately, would make a pretty feature. All Junior choirs should be changed as frequently as possible, in order to avoid all suspicion of favoritism, and to give all the members the needed practice.

Musical Boys. — I have heard of a Junior society in which the boys play the pieces on their mouth harps. Other boys may be found that are skilled with the violin, and all such ability should certainly be utilized.

A Daring Venture. — A bold and ingenius Junior superintendent of Iowa, finding that her boys could not sing very well, adopted the daring expedient of permitting them to whistle the songs. This kept them out of mischief and maintained their interest, but was a rather hazardous experiment.

One Junior worker in Connecticut, having ventured upon this

risky innovation, writes me: "It has been a great success with us. My boys enjoy the singing now even more than the girls."

Young Musicians. — If any among your Juniors plays the organ or the piano, have him or her preside at that instrument at the prayer meetings in preference to an older performer.

Motion Songs. — Junior superintendents have many lessons to learn from kindergarten teachers. One of the most important of these is the value of motion songs. I do not mean, of course, the same class of motion songs used in the kindergarten; but many familiar religious songs may be illustrated by simple motions which the children may be taught to execute together. For instance, in hymns of consecration, have the Juniors lift up their hands; in hymns of prayer, have them fold their hands; in hymns of work, let the hands be extended; in hymns of union and fellowship, let neighbors' hands be joined. A little thought will make out of more than half our hymns appropriate motion songs.

These motion songs, used at the beginning of a meeting, or in the middle of it when the children are becoming a little tired, will serve to remove their restlessness. Besides that, the songs will become more vivid through the use of motions, and the children will be greatly interested.

The Bible and Song. — Couple the hymns with Scripture in this way. Occasionally, as the children enter the room, give to each the number of a hymn in the book you use, asking him to find a Scripture verse for the next meeting suitable to the theme of the hymn. At that meeting each in turn will repeat his verse and announce his hymn, one or more stanzas of which will be sung.

Song and Prayer. — An entire service devoted to song and prayer will be helpful. Spend the whole time, first in singing, then with a prayer, and so on, alternating.

Antiphonal Hymns. — A little ingenuity will find in the hymn-books many hymns that can be divided into antiphonal songs, such as, "Watchman, tell us of the night," the girls singing the questions, and the boys the answers. Another hymn of this nature is, "Art thou weary, art thou lanquid?"

Various Services of Song. — In some societies the Juniors leave the room in a very orderly way, with no talking, jostling,

or laughing. After the Lord's Prayer, they all strike up a stirring song, like "Onward, Christian soldiers," and march out,
keeping time to it with happy feet.

Prayer songs should be used in connection with sentence
prayers, the children singing one stanza of such a hymn as
"Nearer, my God, to Thee," or "My faith looks up to Thee,"
then following it with sentence prayers. At any break in these
prayers another stanza may be sung, which may be followed by
more prayers.

Sometimes the meeting is preceded by a song service, at the
close of which, to wear off any restlessness, the Juniors may
march around the room while they are singing the last song,
after which the regular meeting will open.

Society Songs. — Each Junior society should have a song
of its own, calling upon some friend of poetical gifts for the
words, which should be adapted to some favorite tune of the
Juniors. One society of which I have heard goes so far as to
have a separate song for every meeting. The first verse and
the chorus are always the same, while the second stanza, new
for each meeting, bears directly upon the lesson that is studied.

This rallying song, whatever it is, should be frequently practised in the meetings, so that it can be used with good effect on
anniversary occasions, at union meetings, at socials, Christian
Endeavor picnics, and on innumerable other pleasant occasions.

A Musical Surprise. — Do not let the music of the Junior
society run into a rut, any more than you permit the same fate
to any other part of the society work. For each meeting think
out some little surprise, such as a solo, or a song from some
older Endeavorer, or an easy anthem by the choir, or an antiphonal song service, with which to incite the Juniors to fresh
interest in this branch of their work.

Collection Songs. — Many portions of the meeting may be
vivified by song. The following collection verses are in use,
sung or repeated in concert by the children while the missionary offering is being collected.

> "I am but a penny in a little hand.
> Can I bear glad tidings over all the land?
> Yes, if love goes with me, then shall I be blessed,
> For God's love is promised unto all the rest."

"Dropping! Dropping! Dropping! Hear us fall?
Crowding in the mite-chests, offerings great and small.
Surely God will bless as we gently fall,
Many prayers rise upward; for his help they call,
Till we form together such a mighty band,
As to bear salvation over all the land."

Their Favorites. — Occasionally ask the Juniors to select during the week each his favorite hymn for announcing at the next meeting. If there are too many Juniors for this, ask the boys to take charge in this way of the music for one meeting, while the girls do the same for the next.

A Free Parliament. — Has your society yet had a meeting a portion of which is taken up with answers to the question, "What song do you like best, and why?" This might occupy fifteen minutes after the regular topic for the day has been discussed; and the selections made by the Juniors will give the superintendent an insight into their characters, and an opportunity to say many a word in season.

His Favorite Verse. — Once in a while permit any Junior present to select hymns, and let the Juniors understand that when permission is given them to announce a hymn they may, if they wish, rise and read their favorite verse in that hymn.

CHAPTER XIII.

THE LEADERS OF JUNIOR MEETINGS.

Let All Lead that Can. — One of the most important duties of the prayer-meeting committee is to obtain the leaders. Every one in the society at all capable of the work should be invited to lead a meeting. The superintendent will be surprised to see how good work will be done by many of those whom he believes to be quite incompetent. This work of the selection of leaders should be done at least a month before each meeting is to occur, and the prayer-meeting committee should hold themselves ready to take the place of the leader in an emergency.

Plan Far Ahead. — Appoint your leaders far enough in advance so that they will have a plenty of time to talk their plans over with you and with the prayer-meeting committee. No leader should be appointed less than three weeks before his meeting; and, in my opinion, it is best to appoint at the beginning of the quarter all the leaders for the quarter. This schedule, however, should be flexible, so that new members may be asked to lead if it is thought best. By giving them some subordinate part in conjunction with the regular leader, this need will be met.

The Leader Announced. — In the older society, it is not the best plan, in my judgment, to have the name of the leader announced at a previous meeting. In the Junior society, however, the leader may without harm be made more conspicuous, and this will serve to enlarge his sense of his responsibility. If possible, the names of the leaders for the quarter should be printed upon the topic card. Children think a great deal of seeing their names in print. An alternative plan is to post in the society room a written list of the leaders for the quarter, giving dates. The prayer-meeting committee may well announce at the end of each meeting who is to be the leader for the next.

A Programme. — Young leaders especially are rendered much more confident if they have a regular programme to carry out. This programme should be carefully fixed by consultation with the superintendent, who should go over it with the Junior often enough to be sure that the young leader is familiar with it, and will not get confused. In order to make sure of the smooth running of the plan for the meeting, let the leader acquaint the prayer-meeting committee of any especial points in which he desires their co-operation. Unless the Scripture to be read at the opening of the meeting is exceedingly simple, be sure to have the leader read it over with you, that you may correct mispronounced words, and that he may gain a ready utterance.

Suggested Introductions. — When the superintendent aids the Junior leader to make out the programme for the prayer meeting, let her at the same time suggest neat little ways of introducing the various divisions of the programme. For example, instead of simply writing down, "The Lord's Prayer in concert," let her write, "Let us join in repeating the Lord's Prayer, and after that will as many as possibly can make a prayer of their own?" Instead of writing, "Bible verses," let her write, "And now will not the Juniors tell what the Bible itself says about our topic?"

Study the Leaders. — Be careful, in your plans for the leader, to introduce as much variety as possible into the general conduct of the meeting. Study the capacities of the young leaders. One is strong in Bible knowledge; another is a skilful story-teller; another has unusual confidence in prayer. Use all these different abilities, and form the plans of the meetings in such a way as to develop them.

Interest the Leader. — Strive in every way to make the leader feel that it is *his* meeting and take a pride in it. Whatever novelty you propose to introduce, let him feel that he is introducing it. Get him to consult with his parents regarding his plans, and thus you will interest them as well as him. Have the leader meet for prayer before the meeting with the prayer-meeting committee. Above all, make him feel that in order to insure a good meeting he must pray much over it at his own home, and then, after the meeting is over, do not fail to praise the young leader for the good work he has done.

Voluntary Leaders. — Try the plan, some quarter, of giving the Juniors an opportunity to volunteer to lead the meetings. Go before the society and name a date, asking for a girl to volunteer to lead on that date, the next date for a boy, and so on, alternating.

Two Leaders. — If the Juniors are any of them timid about leading the meeting, couple each timid member with another more confident, and divide the meeting between them, giving one, say, the Bible-reading and the announcement of hymns only. It is possible to use even more leaders; and, if the society is large, this is a good plan. One leader might open the meeting, calling for sentence prayers and singing. The second might read Bible verses responsively with the society. The third and fourth might treat different divisions of the topic. The fifth might put a little drawing upon the blackboard, or say a few words about a drawing that has previously been made; the sixth might tell a little story about the lesson, and the seventh might close the meeting. It is almost essential, if the Junior society is to be an effective training-school, that all of the Juniors shall be taught to lead meetings, and shall be appointed leaders as frequently as is possible.

Some Points for the Leader. — The following set of leader's hints I find on a leader's programme used in a certain Presbyterian Junior society : —

1. Begin on time and close on time.
2. Prepare by prayer and Bible study.
3. Write out your own thoughts.
4. Write out a prayer and learn it. Ask others to be ready to follow in sentence prayers.
5. Repeat distinctly the numbers of hymns.
6. Invite all visitors to take some part.
7. Be sure to make this *your* meeting.

An Effective Disposition. — Some Junior superintendents find it advisable to place the assistant superintendent by the side of the Junior leader, while they themselves sit in front of the leader and among the Juniors.

Committee Aids. — Occasionally give the leader of the meeting the support of an entire committee. If the meeting is on Prayer, for example, ask the prayer-meeting committee to consider itself an associate leader. The same use may be made of other committees when the theme is appropriate.

Hints to Leaders. — One very helpful division of the treatment of the prayer-meeting topic in *The Junior Golden Rule* is its hints to leaders. These the Juniors can carry out, and they will add variety to the meetings.

The Leader and Order. — Tell the Junior leader that he or she is partly responsible for the order of the meeting. Though the superintendent should always interfere to preserve order, if such interference is necessary, yet if the order can be kept by the leader, so much the better. Instruct the leader, when the Juniors become restless, to interject some bright song, calling upon them to rise as they sing. Let this be a motion song, if your society is happy enough to know such. Above all, teach the leader that, if he is reverent and thoughtful, all in the society will be likely to be the same.

CHAPTER XIV.

BIBLE WORK IN THE SOCIETY.

An Important Distinction. — One of the most cheering facts about the Junior society, and one of the strongest omens of its perpetuity and permanent usefulness, is the prominence given in its work to the Bible; and yet at this very point a note of warning must be sounded.

In some cases the Junior society is scarcely more than a second edition of the primary Sunday-school class. It should be kept constantly in mind that the Bible work of the Junior society is not to teach about the Bible, so much as to teach ways of using the Bible in Christian work and for inspiration and helpfulness. Bible texts are to be learned, to be sure; but the special reason for learning them must have reference to the conduct of life.

Any Bible work may be taken up that could not suitably be accomplished in the primary department of the Sunday school. The teacher of this department should be in closest league with the Junior superintendent, and they should not duplicate each other's work. In the Junior society the children should be taught how to handle the Bible speedily, find texts promptly, select texts bearing on certain subjects; how to study the different books of the Bible, and how to compare Scripture with Scripture. The Bible work of the Sunday school can seldom proceed along these large lines, but must be more minute and detailed. The Junior superintendent has this wider scope.

Bring Bibles. — Insist on the Juniors bringing their Bibles to the Junior meeting. For many of your exercises, the Bible will be needed. At the opening of the meeting, ask how many Bibles have been brought. Let the Juniors hold them up, and let the secretary note the number, so that she can state in her monthly report what progress has been made in this particular.

A Bible Roll of Honor. — For special inducement to the

Juniors to bring their Bibles regularly to the meeting, prepare a large roll of honor on which their names are to be placed when they bring their Bibles for six consecutive Sundays. Place a star at the end of each name when they bring them six more Sundays in succession, and ask the Juniors to see who will get the most stars.

Responsive Readings. — The most important use to be made of the Bibles in the Junior meetings will, of course, be in responsive readings. The Junior superintendent can so plan these that no two responsive readings in the course of many months shall be carried on in precisely the same way.

Concert Reading. — When you desire to have a long passage from the Bible read, it is well to have the Juniors read it in concert, instead of reading it yourself. An excellent plan is to ask the leader to read the first verse, the boys the second, the girls the third, and so on to the last verse, in which all are to join. This plan may, of course, be varied indefinitely.

Bibles of Their Own. — A Junior society in Chicago had an entertainment, and with the money they gained bought a Bible for each member of the society. It would be well for all Junior superintendents to find out how many of their Juniors are unable to purchase Bibles, and in this way, or some other, to see that each is so provided.

Large Type. — The careful superintendent, moreover, will find it well worth while to see that his Juniors have large-type copies of the Bible wherever possible ; and Bibles are so cheap now that there is usually no reason why the children should be compelled to destroy their eyesight and spoil their reading by Bibles that require a microscope to decipher.

Concordances. — If you can possibly manage it, see that your Juniors possess Bibles that contain concordances, and drill them in the use of this indispensable tool of the Bible student. An excellent plan is to announce the key-word of the meeting, and have the Juniors open their concordances and look out, each at his own pleasure, some Bible verse containing this key-word. These are to be read, one after the other, the Junior making brief comments.

Bible-Marking. — The Juniors will take great delight in marking their Bibles, and no superintendent should fail to instruct them in Bible-marking. A cheap outfit consists of five little glass bottles, five-eighths of an inch each in diameter, obtainable of any druggist, placed in five holes in a block of wood, and filled with different colored inks. They should also obtain a brass-edged rule.

One superintendent has them underline with red all verses about salvation, the atonement, and forgiveness of sin. Black is used to underline verses about sin and condemnation or punishment. Verses about love are underscored with purple; promises, with green; things Christians should do and lessons for Christian living, with blue. Other colors may be used, such as gilt for words about prayer.

A simpler way of marking the Bibles of the Juniors is to place after each verse containing a promise the letter P in red ink, after each command the letter C, after each lesson the letter L, after each warning the letter W, etc. Then the Juniors may underline with red ink the passages that seem to them most beautiful and helpful.

Daily Bible-reading is thus made attractive to the Juniors, and they are led to think about the meaning of the words they are reading, and to compare Scripture with Scripture. Besides, the work thus done speaks for itself; and the superintendent, by examining the Bibles of his charges, can make sure that the work has been done well and faithfully. The outfit above described may be given by the superintendent, or purchased by the parent.

A Bible Hand. — One of the most common tasks set before our Juniors — and rightly — is to learn the names and order of the books of the Bible. A Kansas superintendent teaches these to her Juniors by drawing on a large sheet of paper a hand. The five fingers stand for the five divisions of the books of the Bible, each finger bearing opposite the name of the division the initials of the books that belong to that division, as follows: —

In the thumb: Pentateuch, 5. — G. E. L. N. D.
In the first finger : Historical, 12. — J. J. R. 1 and 2 S. 1 and 2 K. 1 and 2 C. E. N. E.
In the middle finger : Poetical, 5. — J. P. P. E. S.-S.
In the fourth finger : Major Prophets, 5. — I. J. L. E. D.
In the last finger : Minor Prophets, 12. — H. J. A. O. J. M. N. H. Z. H. Z. M.

An Object Lesson. — Another admirable method of teaching
the names of the books of the Bible is reported by a well-known
State Junior superintendent.   A small bookcase is provided.
The shelves of it are divided into compartments, one for each
book of the Bible.   These compartments vary in width according to the size of the books.

In these are placed books made of wood covered with paper,
each book of a different color.   These colors should be chosen
with an eye to the appropriateness of the color to the subject
matter of the book.   John's Gospel, for example, might be scarlet, because he makes so much of love; the Psalms might be
gilt, as they are the gold of the Old Testament; Revelation
might be white, as through it shines the brilliancy of the great
white throne; Lamentations might be black, and so forth.

This bookcase is placed before the society, and is used in
this way: The wooden books are taken from the case, and
given to the Juniors.   On a given signal the Juniors come forward, one by one, and each tells the name of the book he holds,
the name of its author, and gives some fact about it.   Then he
places it, or tries to place it, in its proper place in the Bible
bookcase.

This is an admirable method, not only because of the facts
it teaches, but because it is lively enough to keep the Juniors
thoroughly interested.

To Teach the Books of the Bible. — From Mrs. Charles
A. Savage, of Orange, N.J., I have an account of a third plan,
which is most excellent.   She has set up two long boards in
which are fastened at certain intervals some hooks.   Strips of
card-board of equal length are prepared to hang from these
hooks, the strips each representing a book of the Bible.   They
vary in width with the size of the book.   Moreover, the strips
are colored so as to indicate the groupings of the books; the Pentateuch bearing one color, the minor prophets another, the poetical books another, the Gospels another, and so on.   The
names of the books are plainly printed upon the strips.   To
use this apparatus, these strips are distributed among the children, who are then required, one after the other, to place the
strip each holds upon the proper hook of the board, one board
representing the Old and the other the New Testament.   This
plan may be varied in many interesting ways.

Several at Once. — To drill the children to find quickly the books of the Bible, it is a common plan for the superintendent to call out a Bible reference, permitting the one who first finds it to read it. A good variation of this plan is to call out several references at once, asking the members to rise as soon as each has found all the references. A little of this practice will speedily make the Juniors very expert.

Book, Chapter, Verse. — An excellent way to vary this common Junior exercise is the following, which one live superintendent uses once every month. She prepares at home on a slip of paper a list of Bible references — short, easy verses that all the Juniors can read and understand; and after the lesson, which is made shorter than usual on that day, she tells them to get their Bibles ready, and reads first the book in the Bible that is wanted, which they all find quickly, the first one who gets it putting up his hand. Then she reads the chapter, which is found in a similar way, and finally the verse. The first hand up belongs to the Junior who is given permission to read the verse, though the Juniors are required to wait until all are ready before the reference is read.

Both Ways. — In setting the Juniors to learn the books of the Bible, remember that it is just as useful for them to have a knowledge of their order backwards as forwards. In finding a Bible reference we work in one direction as frequently as in the other.

Their Neighbors. — It is an admirable plan not merely to learn the order of the books backwards and forwards, but also, with respect to each book taken at random, what book follows and what precedes it. For example, when Hosea is called, the Juniors should be able to say, " Hosea is in the Old Testament, Daniel at the left, and Joel at the right."

To Spell Them. — While your Juniors are at this work, be sure that they also learn how to spell the names of the Bible books. A good practice for this is to send them in turn to the blackboard, and have them write the words, the other members correcting in case of misspelling.

It is the practice of some superintendents to instruct the Juniors at the same time in the number of chapters contained in each book. If this is not thought necessary, some plan at least should be devised to teach the Juniors the relative length of the books.

The Author Also. — And in connection with learning the books of the Bible, the Juniors should by all means be taught to name also the authors of these books, wherever the name of the author is not expressed in the title of the book, as in the Revelation and in Paul's letters. Besides, they should be instructed in the proper contractions, as " Isa., Dan., Ps.," and should know which ought not to be contracted, as " John, Luke, Ruth."

Bible History. — While you are teaching the Juniors the books of the Bible, why not add also a little information, that may easily be given in that context, regarding the order in which the books were written? You may also go on to tell them something about the time when the different books were put together to make the Bible, and something also about our own English Bible and the different translations.

Book Outline. — After a Junior society has committed to memory the names in order of the books of the Bible, often the question comes to the perplexed superintendent, " What next? " It is an excellent plan to have the Juniors read through a book at a time, making a simple outline of it as they go, each point of the outline to include several chapters. As an illustration, take this outline of the book of Genesis:

GENESIS.
THE BOOK OF THE BEGINNING.

CREATION. { Six days' work. / One day for rest.

SIN. { Adam and Eve. / Murder of Abel. / Great increase of sin.

THE FLOOD. { Noah and the ark. / Tower of Babel and the dispersion.

ABRAHAM. { Covenant with him. / Offering of Isaac on the altar.

JOSEPH. { Sold by his brethren. / A man of God in Egypt. / The Egyptian bondage.

These outlines should be printed distinctly on large sheets of paper, and kept for future reference. It will do no harm for the children to write them upon the margins of their Bibles.

Learning a Book. — A book of the Bible may be studied by chapters, after the fashion of the study of the Gospel of John by a certain Junior society of which I have heard. One chapter was taken for each week. Each Junior was requested to learn the verse he liked best in the entire chapter, and read it or recite it at the meeting.

The pastor prepared a design for a chart, representing the principal subject found in the chapter; and one of the Juniors enlarged the design on a sheet of paper. After the members had given all the verses, the pastor exhibited the chart, and talked a little about it. A name was then selected for the chapter, and the Juniors made choice of a verse which would stand to them for that particular chapter.

These names and verses were often reviewed in connection with the charts, and thus the Juniors soon got to know the entire book of John by the names and special verses of its chapters. They gave a special exercise in public, exhibiting the fruits of this study.

Bible Divisions. — There are certain facts about the Bible that the Juniors should be taught, if these are not already taught in the primary Sunday-school class; for example, the number of books in each Testament, and the division of these books into the five books of the law, the twelve historical books, the five poetical books, the seventeen prophecies of the Old Testament, and the five historical books, the twenty-one epistles, and the one prophecy of the New Testament.

Things to Do. — Here are some of the things that Juniors may be set to doing to spur them to Bible study: They may learn the Commandments, the first chapter of John, the names of the parables and of the miracles, the thirty-fourth psalm, the names of the apostles, ten verses containing promises, five verses containing commands, twenty-five names by which Christ is called.

Good Topics. — Interesting topics for Bible study, each of them sufficing for one meeting, are: mountains of the Bible, rivers of the Bible, precious stones, animals, birds, etc. Mrs. Hill gives a capital list of these in her "Meetings for Juniors," sold by the United Society for ten cents.

The Life of Christ. — The Juniors may, with great profit, be set to studying in a systematic way the life of Christ, taking as the basis of the superintendent's talks some such books as Dr. Stalker's *Life of Christ*, or Geikie's, or Farrar's.   One fact might be learned every Sunday, and a few minutes be spent in reviewing what has been learned already and in adding this new point.   Dates for the prominent events should be carefully fixed, as well as the places.

A few minutes spent this way every Sunday by the superintendent will speedily give the Juniors a definite idea of the life of Christ such as is possessed by comparatively few Christians. It is an excellent plan to teach the events by numbers; so that the Juniors can tell, when called upon, what was the first recorded event in Christ's life, the second, the third, etc.

If each event is associated carefully with the place in which it occurred, the Juniors should be able to go to the map, and, pointing with their finger, follow the footsteps of the Master up and down through the Holy Land, as the numbers of the events are called.   For another exercise it is well sometimes to ask the Juniors what events that they have studied occurred at Cana, at Nazareth, in Samaria, at Jerusalem, and so forth.

Incidents in Christ's Life. — A helpful Bible exercise is to call upon the Juniors to rise, as many as can think of an incident in the life of Christ, and are willing to tell about it.   Let those who have risen give their incidents in order, and encourage them to relate the story at some length.   If the incident chosen by one is the same as that repeated by some one who has preceded him, let him think of some other event in Christ's life, or, failing that, tell the same story in his own words.

A Whole Book. — Set the Juniors occasionally to reading through entire books of the Bible in the course of a week.   At the next meeting, ask them ten easy questions on the book they have read, and see if they can answer the questions.

Bible Campaigns. — When there is a Boys' Brigade connected with your Junior society, you will find a series of talks on Bible campaigns of the greatest interest to the boys.   For the sake of the boys, it would be well to prepare such a series of talks, even if you have no Boys' Brigade.

One pastor who tried this plan with great success made his talks a military history of the Israelites.   He began with the campaign of Chedorlaomer, in the Jordan country, and Abraham's finishing stroke. Then he told the story of the passage of the Red Sea by Moses, and went on to the fight with the Amorites, the defeat at Kadesh Barnea, and so on through the stirring history.

He pictured the scenes vividly, describing the country and the costumes of the times, the political and religious surroundings, the methods of military practice, and the character of the commanders. The value of this in giving the Juniors a knowledge of Bible history, at least in outline, is invaluable; and the best of it is that the boys will be fascinated by the story.

A Relief Map. — Your Juniors will enjoy building a relief map of Palestine. Here is the way a certain pastor set his Juniors to work. He had made a large light frame six feet by three feet, well stayed at the back, and backed all over with thin board. Upon this he laid a complete lining of heavy builders' paper, well sized with glue on both sides, gluing it to the boards at the back.

He instructed the children to draw upon this with charcoal a map of Palestine. He made this work easy by dividing the map they were to copy into squares corresponding to squares formed upon the larger surface by threads stretched across.

The drawing being completed, the threads were removed; and taking clay, the Juniors built up the mountain ranges. They took a little space each day, studying, as they went along, books, pictures, and maps. To make the clay hold fast, they put in slender brads at an angle with the back, and anchored the clay frequently to these.

After completing the larger features, they spread glue over the level country, and sprinkled sand over it lightly, painting the top of Hermon white to indicate its snow cap. They painted the rivers and the seas in water colors, with different shades of blue.

They then located the principal towns and cities named in the story of Jesus' life, printing the names on narrow slips of paper, and placing them, flag-like, on long pins stuck in the clay, marking the more important places by little white houses. The expense altogether for this useful map was not more than two dollars. The Juniors worked upon it for two months of weekly meetings.

Vacation Work. — A Massachusetts Junior worker suggests this plan to keep the Juniors at Bible work during vacation. Tell them that the Bible is God's garden, and that their own hearts are their garden. Name certain kinds of verses after certain plants, as, verses that speak of love, forget-me-nots; of purity or cleansing, lilies; of forgiveness, pansies; of prayer, morning-glories. At the beginning of the vacation ask the Juniors to see during the coming weeks how many flower verses each can transplant from God's garden to the garden of his own heart, bringing a list of the verses that he has learned when he comes back to the society in the fall. If the Junior is too young to select the verses himself, the superintendent may make the selection for him, drawing opposite each division a picture of the plant that symbolizes it.

A Bible Sunday. — Devote one Sunday in the month especially to Bible-study; that is, make the exercises of that particular Sunday bear more directly than usual on the Bible. It would not be at all out of the way to do nothing that day but teach the Juniors how to study the Word of God.

An Examination. — An occasional written examination is a great stimulus. Scatter the members over the room, and write upon the blackboard ten carefully selected Bible questions, which the Juniors are to answer upon paper provided for them. The results of this examination should be read at the next meeting, and an oral drill given on the same questions.

Bible Biographies. — Set the Juniors to writing little biographies of Bible characters. Give them Bible references, including the principal points in the lives of such men as Moses, Joshua, Joseph, David, Abraham, Lazarus, and ask them, after reading the Bible, to tell the stirring story in their own words. This they will greatly enjoy doing. The essays should be limited in length, say to three hundred words.

An Essay Alphabet. — If you have met with success in obtaining these short papers upon Bible characters, your Juniors will like to fill up an alphabet with such essays. Ask one Endeavorer to write a short life of some Bible character whose name begins with A, another to take one beginning with B, and so on.

A Bible Exercise. — An interesting Bible recreation that may be used to diversify the meetings of the Junior society is this : Let the superintendent repeat any good Bible verse that comes to his mind, for example, " Ye are the light of the world. A city that is set on a hill cannot be hid." The first Junior who can recall another Bible verse beginning with h, the first letter of the last word of the text quoted, now rises and repeats it.

Suppose he repeats, " Honor thy father and thy mother." Instantly the Juniors try to think of another text beginning with m. The first to think of this rises and repeats it, and so the quoting goes on until the superintendent thinks best to close the contest. This is done by asking all to repeat in concert the last text given. All Bibles are closed, of course, during this exercise.

Filling Out Texts. — A Bible drill in which the Juniors will delight consists of giving small portions of familiar texts, as, " God so loved," the Juniors to add as promptly as possible the missing words.

A Sword Drill. — The boys will be especially pleased with a Bible sword drill, which consists in a selection of Bible texts that may be called swords, such as the sword of preparation, " Seek ye first the kingdom of God," etc. ; the sword of warning, Gal. vi. 7 ; the sword of strength, 1 Thess. v. 17 ; Matt. vii. 7 ; the Damascus blade, John iii. 16, etc. The superintendent may call for these swords one after the other, and as she calls for them let the boys bring them forth out of their armory.

Word Hunts. — These Bible word hunts should be made to bear upon the topic to be studied at the Junior meeting. Suppose the prominent thought in this topic may be summed up in the word *forgiveness*. Ask the Juniors to hunt through their Bibles at home, and find all the passages they can that contain the word *forgive*, showing them how to use the concordance, and at the same time telling them not to include in their list passages that do not help to explain the topic. These Bible verses they are to copy in little blank-books, and at the next meeting are to report how many they have found. The one who has the largest number will then read his list; and the lists will then be compared, those that are deficient adding, so far as there is time, the texts that they lack.

Bible Stories. — One of the most interesting Bible exercises is the following, which may be prepared beforehand. Ask some bright Junior to learn at home the principal facts in the life of some Bible hero or heroine. At the next meeting the Junior will tell the story, omitting all the names. When the story is ended, the society must guess what character has been told about. The story should be so selected that it will bear upon the topic for the day.

Bible Objects. — An interesting way to tell Bible stories is by the use of objects. In one Junior society, for instance, one of the Juniors came forward with a leather bottle of water, a piece of bread, and a bow and arrow — objects involved in the story of Hagar. She asked if any of the Juniors could tell the Bible story that mentioned these things. None could; so she told of Hagar's journey, referring to the objects, but leaving them to guess all the names connected with the story.

A Verse Alphabet. — Every Junior society should form for itself an alphabet of Bible verses. This is the way to do it. At one meeting ask all the Juniors to bring Bible verses beginning with A. These should be committed to memory. When all have been spoken, ask the Juniors to vote which they will select as the society's A verse. In the same way at the following meetings select verses for all the letters of the alphabet. At each meeting review the verses previously chosen.

Bible Anatomy. — The Juniors will take great delight in learning passages of Scripture that are applicable to the various parts of the human body. Let the superintendent draw, upon manilla paper or muslin, a large outline of a man; and after the appropriate texts are learned, let her call for the recitation of them as she points to the parts of the figure. Mr. Thomas Wainwright has selected the following appropriate passages : —

Skin, flesh, bones, Job 10:11.	Lips, Ps. 141:3.
Head, Prov. 16:31.	Teeth, Job 4:10.
Hair, Matt. 10:30.	Tongue, Ps. 34:13.
Forehead, Rev. 22:4.	Neck, Rom. 16:4.
Mind, Isa. 26:3.	Shoulder, Isa. 9:6.
Eye, Ps. 33:18.	Breast, John 13:25.
Nose, Prov. 30:33.	Heart, Matt. 5:8.
Ear, Prov. 18:15.	Bowels, Col. 3:12.
Mouth, Ps. 141:3.	Liver, kidneys, Ex. 29:13.

Thigh, Gen. 32:25.	Arms, Deut. 33:27.
Loin, Isa. 11:5.	Hand, Eccl. 9:10.
Leg, Prov. 26:7.	Fingers, Ps. 8:3.
Knee, Rom. 14:11.	Joints, Col. 2:19.
Feet, Ps. 119:105.	Bodies, Rom. 12:1.

The Chautauqua Drill. — This exercise, originated by Rev. H. N. Kinney, is an admirable one to introduce into the middle of a meeting when the Juniors show symptoms of weariness : —

1. Right hand raised, with concert repetition. — "Lift up your hands in the sanctuary, and bless the Lord."
2. Clap hands once. — "O clap your hands, all ye people."
3. Fold arms. — "Thy word have I hid in mine heart."
4. Both hands raised, palms to front. — "Stand up and bless the Lord."
5. Join the tips of the fingers over the head. — "His banner over me is love."
6. Hands to sides. — "Happy is the man that findeth wisdom."
7. Right hand extended, palm up. — "Length of days is in her right hand."
8. Left hand extended, palm up. — "And in her left hand riches and honor."
9. Both hands extended. — "Her ways are ways of pleasantness."
10. Right face! — "And all her paths are peace."

Christ's Titles. — Have you tried teaching your Juniors the different titles of Christ, as "Good Shepherd," "Physician," "Door," "Vine," "Lamb," etc.? If not, ask the Juniors to bring each to the meeting a verse containing one of these titles. Be prepared to add verses containing titles that they may not select. Get one of the boys to write the titles on the blackboard as the verses are repeated. It would be well for all the Juniors to learn as many of these verses as possible, as they all contain rich truths for their future living.

A Good Exercise. — Junior superintendents will find the following table useful as an exercise for home work. Let it be copied on a hectograp , and handed out to the children, each being asked to fill out the blanks, and bring them in to the next meeting. At that meeting the superintendent will read in order the descriptions, the Juniors answering in concert with the appropriate names.

A—, the first man.

B—, the favorite son of Jacob.

C—, a man of Cæsarea who had a vision.

D—, one cast into the lions' den.

E—, a prophet fed by ravens.

F—, a governor of Cæsarea.

G—, a giant.

H—, son of Noah.

I—, son of Abraham.

J—, who was swallowed by a whale.

K—, the father of Saul.

L—, the poor man covered with sores.

M—, one careful and troubled about many things.

N—, an officer who was healed of the leprosy.

O—, one in whose house the ark of the Lord continued three months.

P—, an apostle who wrote thirteen of the epistles in the New Testament.

Q—, one whom Paul called a brother, when writing to the Romans.

R—, Isaac's wife.

S—, a wise man who built a temple

T—, one who knew the Scriptures from a child.

U—, one who put forth his hand to stay the ark of God, and God smote him.

V—, a beautiful queen.

Z—, one who climbed a sycomore-tree to see Jesus.

Bible Puzzles. — Some Junior workers make use of Bible puzzles, rebuses, etc., constructed after the following fashion : —

My 5, 6, 7 is one of the sons of Noah.

My 7, 6, 3, 4, 5 is the place where Moses made bitter water sweet.

My 1, 2, 2, 1 is a name by which Christ called God.

My 1, 2, 3, 4, 5, 6, 7 is the name of a great patriarch.

These Bible puzzles should always relate to the topic, and should bring out some particular application thereof. They are easily made, and will serve for home work.

Acrostics. — It is an excellent plan to string the Bible verses you wish your Juniors to learn upon some acrostic. Choose, for instance, such a word as "Christian," and select Bible verses, each of them descriptive of some Christian attribute, their initial letters forming the word "Christian." Print these initials on large shields of pasteboard, giving one to each of the Juniors who are to learn the verses. They will enjoy stepping in front of the society in order, holding up their shields, and repeating their verses until the members can spell the completed word ; and the verses thus learned will not readily be forgotten.

Their Own Questions. — Ask the children occasionally to bring in Bible questions to present to the society — any questions they please arising from their reading of the Bible. Devote a few moments of the next meeting to these questions, which the Juniors will propound, and which the superintendent may either answer herself or refer to the society.

Twenty Questions. — Mrs. Scudder suggests this plan of stirring up a lagging Junior meeting : Let the superintendent take some object mentioned in the Bible, and allow the children to ask twenty questions, and find out within that limit what it is.

Bible Queries. — The society as a society might well utilize the Bible questions given in *The Junior Golden Rule*. Some societies make a practice of studying these every month, and learning the answers so well that they are able to recite them in concert.

Bible Questions. — One Junior superintendent finds it an excellent plan to spend fifteen or twenty minutes of each prayer meeting in systematic Bible work. The Bible is read in course by the Juniors, a small portion at a time. For each portion of the Bible the superintendent makes out a set of easy questions that can be answered by any one who has read the portion selected. Mimeograph copies of these questions are distributed to the Juniors at the preceding meeting, and at the next meeting they are answered and discussed.

The last question of each set is always one bearing upon the central thought of the topic for the day, so that the superintendent is thus enabled to close the meeting with a discussion of the theme with which the meeting opened. At the end of each two months the superintendent selects ten out of the eighty or ninety questions the Juniors have answered, and holds a written examination. He may award prizes at the end of the year to the five examination papers that are found to be best.

A Question Meeting. — A Bible question meeting may be arranged in the following way: Place the boys on one side of the room and the girls on the other, in rows, and ask Bible questions back and forth after the fashion of a spelling-match. Allow only a limited time for the answers, and keep a record of each side, announcing at the close whether the boys or the girls have been victors.

A Bible School. — A contest in Bible verses arranged like a spelling-school, though simple, will excite great interest among the Juniors. Choosing sides and beginning at the head, let each repeat a Bible verse, and continue the exercise as long as possible, each side watching the other to see that no Bible verse is repeated incorrectly, or given more than once. Whoever gives a verse already given, errs in repeating it, or fails to think of one when his turn comes, is counted out and sits down; and so it continues until none are left.

A Reference Contest. — A reference contest will add spice to an occasional Junior meeting. The superintendent brings a certain number of references, which are written upon the blackboard. Those who find the most of these within a certain time will be accounted the victors. It should be required that the verse not only be found, but be read.

A Bible Contest. — Though some Junior workers may consider the method too close on the borders of a game, yet I find much that is suggestive in the following scheme for inciting the Juniors to learn Bible verses: Each member is asked to commit a verse for each day in the week, and to write this verse upon a sheet of paper.

When the time comes to recite these texts in the meeting, the members stand in a row, one end of the row being head and the other foot. The papers are then handed to the leader, who holds them in the order in which the members stand.

The Junior at the head of the row then recites his texts, and so it proceeds until some one fails to recite a text perfectly. When this happens he moves down, and is passed by the first one below him who can recite correctly all his texts.

Whoever is head at the close of the exercise receives a head mark, and starts in at the foot the next time. The children are eager to get these marks, and it is wonderful how much Scripture they learn.

Book-Marks. — Bible book-marks are very easily made, and will form a very acceptable gift from the superintendent to the Juniors. A little strip of bright ribbon with the name of the society printed upon it, the date, and " Happy New Year," or " Merry Christmas," or some other pleasant wish, — this is all that is necessary. It will give the society a feeling of solidity when the members see its name in print.

A Handy Method. — An excellent use to make of *The Junior Golden Rule* Bible references is the following, though the method is not to be commended for regular, but only for occasional use : Before the Junior superintendent hands to the Juniors their copies of the paper, let her mark for each the Bible reference that he is to copy and bring to the meeting prepared to read, or else to learn at home and repeat at the meeting. Different Bible references being marked in the different *Junior Golden Rules*, the prayer-meeting committee is saved the trouble of writing out the references for the members to use.

Parable Meetings. — A parable meeting will be greatly enjoyed by the Juniors. Assign a parable to each member, the Juniors to tell the beautiful stories in their own simple words. Arrange the parables in sets of four and five, and at the close of each set let the choir sing a hymn touching on the last parable ; such hymns, for instance, as " The Ninety and Nine."

The Twelve Disciples. — In learning the names of the twelve disciples, superintendents will find the following rhyme of use : —

" These are the twelve disciples' names :
Peter and Andrew, John and James,
 Two pairs of brothers, who lived by the sea
 When Jesus said to them, ' Follow me.'
Then James the Less and Jude were called too,
Philip, and also Bartholomew,
 Matthew, and Thomas who doubted the word,
 Simon, and Judas who sold his Lord."

Nazarites. — Papers on Bible Nazarites will furnish interest for a series of meetings, one paper being given at each meeting. On this cord may be strung little biographies of Samuel, Elijah, Moses, and John the Baptist.

Bible Cities. — Bible cities will furnish an interesting theme for the Bible portion of the Junior hour. Let one Junior name a city beginning with A, telling an interesting fact about it; another Junior will take B, and so on. Of course these letters will be assigned the Juniors a week beforehand.

Symbolic Cards. — If, as in some societies, it is your custom to write upon little slips of paper the Bible reference each Junior is to commit to memory, it will be advisable occasionally to cut the paper into shapes symbolic of the truth that is to be uppermost in the next meeting. For example, if it is to be a meeting about the Bible, cut your slips into the shape of a lamp; a temperance meeting, cut them into the shape of a bottle; a Christmas meeting, into stars; an Easter meeting, into lilies, etc.

Cards. — A certain Methodist pastor prepares his young Endeavorers to take regular part in their weekly prayer meetings by buying cheap picture cards with a Bible verse on each, and giving them to each child at every meeting. The verse is to be learned, and repeated at the meeting of the next week. The Sunday school and Christian Endeavor society pay for these cards, and are glad to do so.

A Book of Cards. — One Junior superintendent I have heard of presents to her Juniors every week a card with some Bible reference upon it. Whoever fills out this card with the Bible verse correctly copied, and recites it perfectly at the next meeting, receives the card back again with an embossed picture pasted on the back. When the Junior has eight of these cards, they are made into a little book with stiff covers and a picture on the front.

Calling the Roll. — The roll-call may be utilized in various ways; but probably no way is better than to ask each Junior, as his name is called, to respond with a verse of Scripture, not read, but committed to memory. In a certain Canadian society they take the verses alphabetically. One week they will all begin with A, the next with B, and so on.

Their Favorites. — Distribute cards at the prayer meeting, and ask the Juniors at their homes to write upon these cards their names and their favorite Bible verses, telling at the next meeting why they like them.

Precious Verses. — One of the nicest plans for Junior societies is to have the Juniors commit to memory lists of " precious verses," each being asked to select four or five of his favorites.

Two or three of the Juniors may be asked to repeat their entire list in the course of a single meeting.

Committee Verses. — A pleasant way to familiarize the Juniors with certain important texts is to set the committees to learning texts appropriate to their work. Each committee may choose a verse for its term of office. The temperance committee, for example, "Look not upon the wine," etc. ; the sunshine committee, the Golden Rule; the birthday committee, "So teach us to number our days," etc. The superintendent should frequently call upon the committees to recite their texts in concert ; and thus the other Juniors will become familiar with them, even though they are not on the committees. After each election these verses will be changed, and thus a considerable range of texts will be secured.

"Love" Verses. — Occasionally call upon all the Juniors to give, at the next meeting, a praise verse, or a love verse, or a sin verse, leaving them to discover for themselves what you mean.

Verse Names. — Each Junior in your society should be able to spell his name in Bible verses; selecting, that is, a set of Bible verses that he has made peculiarly his own, the initials of which spell his own name. The children will delight in finding these verses and committing them to memory, and will enjoy hearing each other repeat them.

In Promises and Commands. — A variation of this plan is to ask the Juniors first to spell their names in Bible promises and then in Bible commands. This method may be varied quite indefinitely.

Every=Day Verses. — Store the minds of your young charges with verses that you may call every-day verses — Bible gems, that is, that are especially applicable to the tasks and the worries, the little cares and the common joys, of every day. This will be more helpful to them than you can tell, in their future life.

Seven-Day Texts. — Occasionally give the entire society a text, such, for example, as "Bear ye one another's burdens." Request them to make this the text of their living for the coming week, and to report at the next meeting how they have succeeded in obeying its precepts, what difficulties they have found, and what rewards have come to them.

Concert Verses. — It is helpful to teach the Juniors Scripture verses to be recited uniformly at certain stages in the meeting. For example, before the opening hymn, Ps. 95 : 1, "O come, let us sing unto the Lord, let us make a joyful noise to the Rock of our salvation." Before the opening prayer, Hab. 2 : 20, "The Lord is in his holy temple, let all the earth keep silence before him." Before the Bible-reading, Ps. 119 : 18, "Open thou mine eyes, that I may behold wondrous things out of thy law."

"Name Texts." — Set the Juniors to learning Bible texts strung upon the name of some Bible character; five texts, for instance, suitable to the character of Moses, and beginning successively with the five letters of his name.

The Location. — As your Juniors learn Bible verses, be sure to have them learn also the chapter and verse number. You have no idea what a help this will be in all their later Bible work. Simply knowing the words, "God so loved the world," etc., is of course the main thing; but it is also a great help to know that these words are found in John 3 : 16.

Initial Words. — Many Junior superintendents have tried the plan of asking the Juniors each to bring to the next meeting a verse beginning with "be." Not so many, however, extend this useful exercise to other words, — "let," for instance, "come," "go," "send," "speak," "pray," and so on.

A Swarm of Bees. — The occupation of learning "Bible be's," so common among our Junior societies, may be pleasantly varied in the following way: Have a bush with a cushion among its branches. Give each member an imitation bee, made of tissue paper, larger than natural size, and with pins for legs. Each member, as he says his verse beginning with "be," will place the bee upon the cushion. The cushion will soon be filled, and the Junior superintendent will explain to the children then how it stands for a character fully equipped for the Master's use.

Bible Committees. — Bible committees of the Junior society can help the superintendent very greatly. In some societies they even select the passages of Scripture or the chapters of the Bible that the Juniors are to learn. Of course, when they do this, their work should be carefully gone over by the superintendent.

Learn the Psalms. — The Juniors should be set to learning the Psalms. No portion of Scripture is so well adapted to being committed to memory. Let the Juniors themselves select the psalm they will memorize during the coming month, and try to get them to learn twelve psalms in the course of the year. Extracts may be made from some of the longer psalms.

CHAPTER XV.

THE JUNIOR PLEDGE.

Hold To It. — The pledge of the Junior Christian Endeavor society is the following: "Trusting in the Lord Jesus Christ for strength, I promise him that I will strive to do whatever he would like to have me do; that I will pray and read the Bible every day; and that, just so far as I know how, I will try to lead a Christian life. I will be present at every meeting of the society when I can, and will take some part in every meeting."

Every word of the pledge is carefully thought out, and there is a reason for it. Experiment has proved the usefulness of it. Do not change the form except for the very best reasons, carefully considered and prayed over.

An Essential. — The pledge is an absolute necessity for the Junior Christian Endeavor society. Indeed, I have never heard of an attempt to organize one without it. For such an attempt nothing but failure could be predicted. Older people may object to the pledge, but no objections will come from the children. They are always ready for definite obligations.

How About Objectors? — In most communities will be found one or two who argue against the pledge, and refuse to let their children join the Junior society because they do not believe in it, thinking that the children are too young to take upon themselves so solemn an obligation. They forget that children's consciences are more sensitive even than those of their elders. It is far better to keep them sensitive, and train them in this delicacy by the pledge, than to permit them to grow hardened without this training.

It is difficult to say when little hands are too young to be set to work, and little tongues too feeble to be taught to talk. It would be equally hard to say when consciences are too young to be trained.

Mr. Gough was in the habit of telling the story of a boy six or seven years old, who wanted to sign the temperance pledge with the other members of his family. His father objected, thinking he was too young; but he insisted. Afterwards the father, on a journey, called for a drink of water at an inn. It was not obtainable; but cider was brought, and, being very thirsty, he drank it instead. He told about this when he reached home, and this little boy came up to him with his eyes full of tears. " Father," he asked, " how far were you from the James River when you drank that cider ? " " About fifteen miles," was the reply. " Well, I should have walked there and back again rather than break my pledge."

I have heard of a hot-tempered ten-year-old Junior, who was put in a trying position where the injustice of a comrade tempted him to a declaration of war and something worse. But he kept the peace, saying afterwards, " If it had not been for that pledge, I should have fixed him ! "

I have heard of a ten-year-old Junior who went to bed without reading her chapter in the Bible. Remembering it, she got up and lighted the gas, and read it, and did not read it in a hurry, either. This same Junior, who lives in a sceptical family, has conducted family prayers.

On the whole, the best answer to those who argue against the pledge, is simply to show them that it is in harmony with the Bible, and then to keep quiet. Do not try to argue in reply, because thus you only confirm them in opposition. Begin with the children whose parents heartily agree with the pledge principle. Aim to show forth the benefits of Christian Endeavor work; and in this way, if in any way, you will convert objectors.

An Examination. — As the Juniors enter the society they should be tested very carefully regarding their understanding of the requirements of the pledge. The lookout committee and the superintendent should talk this matter over with the applicant for membership, reading the pledge and carefully explaining it. Then a set of questions should be formally propounded. The shy young people may be permitted to write their answers to these questions. Those who are more confident may give their responses in open meeting. Such questions as these will furnish satisfactory tests : " What do you promise in your pledge as to the Junior meeting? About the Bible? About prayer?

About your conduct in life? To whom are your promises made? How will you get strength to keep your pledge? Why do you wish to take it? How long must it last?"

Go Carefully. — Junior superintendents should realize what a heavy responsibility they are taking upon themselves in asking the Juniors to sign a pledge so solemn and far-reaching in its influence as the Junior pledge. If the Juniors take this pledge carelessly, and do not live up to its requirements, the carelessness regarding promise-keeping thus inculcated will have an effect on their future life. On the contrary, faithfulness to their Junior pledge will probably mean for them a lifetime of fidelity and truth.

I know of one superintendent who worked with her new society for more than four months before she permitted any members to join. She preferred to have the boys and girls think over the step very seriously, especially before signing the active members' pledge, and took particular pains, before receiving a new member, to inquire into the home and school life of the boy or girl, to learn whether he was trying to do what Jesus would have him do.

Committed to Memory First. — It is not unwise for the superintendent to require the Juniors, as some superintendents do, to commit to memory the Junior pledge before they permit them to sign it. This is, of course, not because any special importance is attached to the committing to memory or to the mere form of words, but because in this way they can be assured that the Junior has thoroughly considered the contents of the pledge.

Two Pledges. — It is a good plan for the Junior to sign two pledges, one the original pledge, which the parent signs with the Junior. This is returned to the superintendent, and kept on file by her. Then the Junior should sign a second pledge and take it home with him, keeping it in the Bible or in some place where he can often see it. The fact that the superintendent holds a pledge signed by him will be a constant spur to fidelity.

Some societies have the pledge kept by the Junior printed on cards bearing the pansy, — the Christian Endeavor flower, — printed in colors. These are called " pansy cards," to distinguish them from the pledge that is kept on file. The United Society sells these for $1.25 a hundred. The plain card costs 50 cents a hundred; on heavy card-board with gilt edge, $2.00 a hundred; and embossed in purple and gold, 75 cents a hundred. An ingenious superintendent will find a use for all these varieties.

The Pledge Memorized. — Be sure that all your Juniors are able to repeat the pledge from memory. Its every word cannot be too firmly embedded in their minds. Insist on this memory repetition at the beginning of each consecration meeting, or, if you prefer it, at its close.

Occasionally call on some Junior to repeat the pledge by himself, asking the entire society to be ready, as soon as he is through, to sing a verse of some appropriate song, such as " Our Pledge " (No. 7, in " Junior Christian Endeavor Songs "), or " Strong in Thy Strength, O Jesus " (No. 33, in the same book), or " Keep Your Covenant with Jesus " (No. 10, in the same book).

The Substance. — Instead of requiring the Juniors always to repeat the pledge in the exact words of it, occasionally vary this proceeding by requesting them to tell *in their own words* what things they have promised to do. One minister condensed it thus : —

> " Trust and obey,
> Read and pray."

I shouldn't wonder if some of your Juniors would make paraphrases as bright.

You will make no mistake if, in some form or other, the pledge is brought into every meeting. Hammer it in.

A Pledge Song. — Occasionally, instead of repeating the prose form of the pledge, it is well to sing a versified form, and I have prepared the following for this purpose. It is to be sung to the tune Hursley, " Sun of my soul."

> I promise Jesus I will pray
> And read the Bible every day;
> Here at the meeting I will be,
> And do my duty faithfully.
>
> All of my life I'll try to do
> Just what the Lord would wish me to,
> Trusting to Christ whose power is given
> Freely to all in earth and heaven.

I have also written the following version, rather for concert repetition than for singing.

I.

We promise, dear Jesus, to try to be true,
And do what our Saviour would like us to do.
We promise to read in our Bibles each day.
We promise that daily to God we will pray.
Trusting in Christ,
Trusting in Christ,
Saviour, dear Saviour, we promise to pray.

II.

When our Juniors meet we will try to be there;
We'll say a few words, or we'll pray a short prayer.
And all our life through, just as far as we know,
We'll go where our Saviour would like us to go.
Trusting in Christ,
Trusting in Christ,
Saviour, dear Saviour, we promise to live.

III.

While all of these duties we promise to try,
We're trusting in Jesus his strength to supply;
His love will infold us, his wisdom will guide,
His power uphold us whatever betide.
Trusting in Christ,
Trusting in Christ,
Help us, dear Saviour, our pledges to keep.

The Good of It. — An occasional half-hour may be given to a pledge meeting in which the Juniors may be asked to answer by personal experiences how the pledge has helped each of them to live a better Christian life.

A Bible-Reading. — A Bible-reading on the pledge may easily be arranged. Miss Kate Haus has selected the following illustrative texts : '' Trusting in the Lord Jesus Christ (Prov. 3 : 5) for strength (Ps. 29 : 11), I promise (Rom. 9 : 9) him (Acts 5 : 31) that I will strive (Col. 1 : 29) to do whatever (John 15 : 14) he would like to have me do (Col. 3 : 17) ; that I will pray (Ps. 55 : 17) and read the Bible every day (Rev. 1 : 3 ; John 5 : 39 ; Acts 17 : 11) ; and that, just so far as I know how (Ps. 143 : 8), I will try to lead a Christian life (Ps. 25 : 5 ; Phil. 3 : 14). I will be present (2 Sam. 20 : 4) at every meeting of the society

(Mal. 3:16) when I can (Heb. 10:25), and take some part in every meeting (Isa. 43:10; Luke 12:8)."

In using this Bible-reading, divide the society into two parts, asking one part to repeat the pledge, pausing at the appropriate places for the recitation of the confirmatory passages of Scripture from the other half.

Pledge Acrostics. — A pleasant exercise for the Juniors is to set them to making an acrostic on the pledge. These acrostics should explain what each Junior thinks the pledge ought to mean in his life. The following sample comes from Ireland: —

> **P**raise God,
> **L**ove Jesus,
> **E**ver more
> **D**oing
> **G**od's work
> **E**verywhere.

A Pledge Record. — Many Junior superintendents find a personal record of pledge-keeping very valuable. A sample of these cards is the following, each blank to be filled with one word, such as " well " or " ill," or possibly with a figure, graded from one to ten, or from one to four, faithfulness in each of the four particulars counting one point. There are five spaces, because sometimes the month has five weeks.

I PROMISE

To do what Jesus would like to have me do.　To pray every day.

HOW KEPT:

First.	Second.	Third.	Fourth.	Fifth.

To read the Bible.　To attend all meetings of the society when possible.

Month................... *Name*.....................................

A Wall Pledge. — No Junior room is at all well equipped without a large, clear-type pledge. It should not be placed, however, in such a position that the Juniors will rely upon it for the concert repetition of the pledge; but they should be taught to commit the pledge to memory. If they have to turn their heads to see it when it is referred to, all the better. Such a pledge, 28 by 36 inches, ready for hanging on the wall, is sold by the United Society of Christian Endeavor for 75 cents.

A Novel Pledge. — The idea of the pledge must not be carried too far. A multiplicity of pledges has a tendency to confuse. Nevertheless, under certain circumstances, it may be very advantageous to introduce definite pledges for such matters as are not referred to in the Christian Endeavor pledge. The Juniors of a certain Cumberland Presbyterian society have taken the following pledge, which explains itself, and certainly is most desirable in its aim : " Trusting in Jesus for strength, I promise him that I will not repeat or tell any bad thing which I hear of any person, but will try to find all the good I can of every one, and tell *it*." This is a pledge that might with profit be taken by many of the older Endeavorers.

Sunday Observance Pledges. — Some Junior workers, especially those whose work lies in mission schools and churches, may find a Sunday observance pledge of service. The pledge used by one Chicago worker is a promise on the part of the Junior not to buy, sell, or trade on the Lord's day. and to teach others also not to do so.

CHAPTER XVI.

THE LOOKOUT COMMITTEE.

Their Duties. — The Model Junior Constitution thus defines the work of the lookout committee: "The lookout committee shall secure the names of any who may wish to join the society, and report the same to the superintendents for action. They shall also obtain excuses from members absent from the roll-call, and affectionately look after and reclaim any who seem indifferent to their pledge." The duties will be seen to be two-fold — partly toward outsiders, and partly toward those already members. The first set of duties especially requires enterprise; the second, tact.

A Firm Guide. — On no committee should the superintendent keep so firm a hand as on the lookout committee. Lack of tact in the members, and hasty action on their part, may do the society irreparable injury. Forbid the members of the committee to invite any children to join the society without first speaking to you about it, for fear they should get in those who are unprepared. Unless you can thoroughly trust them, do not permit them to speak to any who have been remiss in their duties until they have first talked the matter over with you.

Working for the Future. — In all your work with the lookout committee, remember that it is not the results this committee may accomplish that will be especially valuable, but the effect of this work upon the members of the committee themselves. You are training in these young people the pastors and evangelists, the Sunday-school teachers, and the earnest Christian lay workers of the coming years. As you make them earnest and consecrated, sincere and unselfish and frank, such will be the characteristics of the church of the next generation.

Modest Overseers. — Of course one of the dangers of lookout committee work, though it is a danger which those who do not know children are likely to exaggerate, is Phariseeism.

The superintendent should never permit the lookout committee to rebuke the Juniors, or in any way to set themselves above the delinquents. Remind the committee how often they themselves fail to do their duty. If, in the progress of the committee meetings, you see any trace of a harsh judgment, let all kneel while you offer up an earnest prayer for the right guidance of the committee and of the Juniors who are not doing their duty. Urge the committee themselves to pray earnestly before they speak to any who are remiss.

Hold, in the progress of the committee meetings, frequent drills of the following nature: "You, Mary, are to see Martha, who has been absent from two meetings. What are you going to say to her?" "You, Tom, are going to speak to Ned, who does not take part faithfully in the prayer meetings. Imagine that I am Ned; what are you going to say to me?"

Interlocking. — If the pastor is able to give any attention to the committee work of the Juniors, that attention should be given to the lookout committee. The same thing is true of the Sunday-school superintendent, the teachers of the primary department, and the president of the Mothers' society. The work of the Junior lookout committee affects in many ways these different interests. Especially should the officers whose business it is to superintend the admission of children to the church take an interest in the work of this lookout committee, for they are more likely than any others to understand the true spiritual condition of the young people.

Dividing Them Up. — By far the most satisfactory method of carrying on the work of the lookout committee is to divide the membership of the society among the committeemen, a portion to each. At the consecration meeting, each member of the committee will notice the presence or absence of his own particular division, and will hunt up the absentees, reporting at the next meeting of the lookout committee what he has learned. These divisions should remain constant during the life of the committee, in order that each committeeman may become perfectly familiar with the voices, faces, and circumstances of his particular charges.

An Unknown Lookout Committee. — Select from your Juniors five of the most faithful and earnest Christians. Divide up among these the names of the members. All that the look-out committee is expected to do for the whole society, each of these five is to do for his division of the society. They are to give no public reports, however, and their work is not to be known to the society. The superintendent meets monthly with the five, asking for reports of what they have been able to accomplish in this quiet way; praying with them also, and suggesting new endeavors.

Gaining New Members. — For the winning of new members, it is not a bad plan occasionally to make a thorough canvass of the town or the neighborhood, though this canvass may be merely imaginary, the committee thinking over in their meeting the houses of the town, street by street, inquiring whether there are in each house children who ought to belong to the society, and making a list of the doubtful houses for future inquiry.

Your list of possible Juniors having been formed, send after each one the member of the committee who is best acquainted with him. If no member of the committee is acquainted, find some Junior who is, and let the committeeman go to the stranger with this mutual friend.

You can set your lookout committee to work most effectually if you give to each member a list of three or four possible Juniors, urging the committee to strive who can get the most to join, and do it in the shortest time. The superintendent will make the society more zealous in this particular of winning members if, at the time the new member joins, she make mention before the society of the Junior who was chiefly instrumental in winning him.

Utilize the Socials. — The society socials furnish one of the best fields for the work of the lookout committee. Teach them that at the social they have opportunities for coming in close contact with strangers, and interesting them in the work of the society. The social committee is chiefly occupied with the management of the social, and the lookout committee should be busied about this blessed task. Young people whom the lookout committee is trying to draw into the society they should take special pains to invite to the socials, introduce to the members, and make their evening a pleasant one.

Canvassing the Sunday School. — If you have a Sunday-school committee, the lookout committee should be in closest consultation with it. If your society lacks this useful committee, its duties will largely fall to the lookout committee. They should canvass the Sunday school for young people who should be in the Junior society but are not, and should in every way try to draw them in.

Empty Chairs. — If the lookout committee will see to it that beside each Junior of the society is placed an empty chair with the instruction that it is to be filled by a friend who is to be brought to the meeting, the plan will add greatly to the attendance and eventually to the membership. It can be seen at a glance what Juniors bring companions to the meeting, and the members will take pride in having their neighboring seats always filled.

Attend a While First. — Before any child is asked to join the society, the lookout committee should bring about his attendance at a few meetings, so that he may understand fully with what sort of organization he is to connect himself. If these visitors can be induced to take part in the meetings it will be a further test, and will tell the lookout committee a great deal about their spiritual life. This attendance of visitors will be increased if the Juniors, and the lookout committee especially, are urged to call for those who are not members, and take them with them to the meetings. Invitations may also be given out at school.

When To Vote In. — Though new members may be proposed by the chairman of the lookout committee at any time, they should be voted in and should take their first part only in the consecration meeting, and then with a little ceremony, which should be held at the very beginning of the hour This ceremony should always include the presentation of the Junior badge and of the society colors, if the society has such, together with the concert repetition of the pledge by the entire society, and some word of welcome. The secretary should at once place upon the roll the name of the new Junior, and call this name as he calls the other members.

Greeting the Newcomer. — When new members are received into the society, the president, of course, and the superintendent, say a word of greeting; but the Juniors themselves are necessarily silent until after the meeting is over, when this helpful duty is likely to be forgotten. Impress it upon the lookout committee that their first effort should be to make the newcomers feel that they are heartily welcome, and to put them at ease among the members. It is pleasant if the committee will not only speak its greeting, but write it out. A nice little note of welcome, written by the chairman and signed by all the members, will constitute to the new member a permanent assurance that the society members are glad to have him among them.

Keeping Track of Them. — It would be a good idea to make the member of the Junior lookout committee who proposes a new member to the committee and obtains his election to the society responsible for introducing that new member to the other Juniors, and for establishing him in the ways of the society. Teach your committee that their work is scarcely more than begun when the new members sign the constitution and pledge.

The Pledge First. — Above all committees, the lookout committee should emphasize the pledge. The superintendent should see that the committee themselves understand it, and are able to make others understand it. Before they propose any new member they should go over the pledge carefully with the candidate, and be sure that he not merely comprehends its provisions, but that he heartily agrees to them. Urge the members of the lookout committee to set before prospective Juniors, not the social advantages of the society, telling them how much fun they will have, or how interesting the meetings are, but simply the will of Christ, that in the society they will serve him, and will learn how to serve him better, and that the fun and the interest are to come in as side matters.

Pledge Meetings. — Meetings for the especial consideration of the pledge will aid the lookout committee in maintaining the faithfulness of the members. Juniors appointed beforehand to the task will read at this meeting little essays on the different divisions of the pledge. An open parliament may be announced at the preceding meeting on such a topic as, "How has the the pledge helped you?" or, "What part of the pledge do you find it hardest to keep?" or, "How can we keep the pledge more perfectly?"

A portion of the meeting should be devoted to confessions, the members telling how during the past month they have failed to observe the pledge.   Part should be devoted to prayer, asking God to help them keep the pledge in these different particulars.   There might well be a short talk from some older Endeavorer, telling from his longer experience how the pledge is helpful.   The United Society of Christian Endeavor publishes a Bible-reading on the pledge that may be used at this meeting, and the Juniors will like to select beforehand from the hymnal songs that are appropriate to the different portions of the pledge, which may be sung after the essays considering those portions.

Progress. — Urge the members of the lookout committee to make themselves models in all respects regarding which they are themselves to oversee the Juniors.   Urge them to advance in their society work, taking part in more and more difficult ways, not resting satisfied merely with reading a verse ; and set before them as one of the objects of this advance that they then will be able consistently to teach others.

The members of the committee keep careful account of the way in which each Junior takes part in every meeting ; utilize this account.   It is a good plan for the committee to make for each member a written monthly report, stating how many times he has taken part during the month, and in precisely what ways, with possibly a comparison with former months, a word of commendation for progress or of warning for retrogression.

A similar report should be made before the whole society without mentioning names ; and the work of the society along the lines of prayer-meeting participation should be carefully summed up, — as that, during the month, so many had taken part by praying, so many by testifying, so many by verse reading, so many by repeating verses.   Compare this record with the totals for the preceding months, and praise the society if it has improved and advanced.

The Record. — Furnish each member of the lookout committee with a little blank-book, fitly ruled, in which he may keep a record of the members of his division.   He will note their attendance at each meeting, and the way in which they take part, using simple contractions, such as a vertical stroke for attendance, P for prayer, V for verse read, R for verse repeated, T for testimony, and so forth. These books should be brought to all committee meetings, and a summary of their contents will furnish the principal portion of the monthly report of the committee.

Stars and Hearts. — The lookout committee may use this method of encouraging the Juniors to take part in their meetings : Upon a blackboard are written the names of the active members, followed by five spaces for the four or five meetings of the month. The members of the committee divide up the active members among them, and note what part, if any, they take in the meeting. The record is placed on the board in the following manner. Absent members receive a black star ; those that were present without taking part have a black heart placed after their names ; those that recite Bible verses receive silver stars ; and those that pray, or express their own thoughts on the topic, get gold stars.

A Warning. — A little thoughtfulness before the consecration meeting is better than a great deal of painstaking afterward. At the previous meeting, the committee should remind the society of the consecration meeting coming next week ; and during the week it would be well to speak in private to the few Juniors who experience has taught the committee are most likely to be unfaithful to the pledge at this meeting.

Investigating Absences. — The Junior pledge does not contain the provision of the older societies regarding three consecutive absences from the consecration meetings. The Junior lookout committee should watch cases of unfaithfulness with far more promptness than this would imply. It is best, if a Junior is absent for two of the weekly meetings without excuse, at once to look up the matter. The best way is, of course, to call upon the delinquent. Under no circumstances should the absences be allowed to accumulate without investigation ; and whenever the investigation is made, the superintendent should be notified of the result.

Looking Them Up. — It will pay the lookout committee to look after its absent members in the following thorough fashion. At the close of each meeting the superintendent makes out a list of active members who were absent, and hands it to the chairman of the lookout committee. This chairman makes out a written notice for each absentee, and these notices are divided among the members of the lookout committee to be distributed. They are so divided that the members can distribute the notices at school. This plan will do much to keep up the attendance.

Work with Trial Members. — Repeatedly tell the members of the lookout committee that much of their work lies with the trial or associate members. In every way they are to seek to lead these into full membership. This may be done by earnest private conversations. Often the prayer meetings may be so turned as to influence them. Occasionally let the lookout committee tell in open meeting why they are active members, and what good it has done them, asking the other Juniors to give similar testimonies.

It is a good plan for the superintendent occasionally to review, in lookout committee meetings, the entire list of associate or trial members, and set the members of the committee at work in their behalf. Sometimes it will be best to divide these trial members among the committee as the active members are divided, each committeeman to make a special effort toward the admission into the active list of his own charges.

New Year's Letters. — Such anniversaries as New Year's and Christmas furnish the lookout committee an opportunity to bind the society together, and to add to the zeal with which the society work is performed. In no way can this better be done than by writing little letters, to be distributed the Sunday before Christmas or New Year's. These letters will have a word about the approaching holiday, a wish for the happy enjoyment of it, and a bit of exhortation regarding faithfulness to the pledge in some particular wherein the committee sees that the members need spurring.

Helping Each Other. — It may sometimes happen that the members of the Junior lookout committee, in their search for new members, will come across young people who should join the older society. A similar discovery may be made by the lookout committee of the older society; and so these two committees should work together, the chairmen frequently consulting each other.

The necessity of graduation from the Junior to the older society furnishes an additional reason for this close co-operation. A joint meeting of the two committees should be held occasionally, both that the Juniors may learn the methods of the older committee, and that the older Endeavorers may come into closer touch with the best workers among the Juniors.

Look Them Up. — Other hints regarding the work of the lookout committee will be found in chapters of this manual that deal with cognate subjects, such as those on the pledge, the consecration meeting, the attendance, and the daily readings.

CHAPTER XVII.

THE ATTENDANCE AND RECORDS.

A Warning. — There is danger in this keeping of records. Sometimes the superintendent and the society depend too much upon marks on paper. Personal appeals are needed to keep any society up to the highest efficiency in any direction. Both the superintendent and the lookout committee should be earnest in hunting up absentees, and winning them to faithful attendance; in speaking to those who have been tardy, and urging upon them promptness in the future.

Let Them Keep the Record. — Whatever method of recording the attendance of the Juniors at the meetings the superintendent may adopt for her private convenience, the Juniors themselves should be set to keeping a record also. This work is easy and definite; and it will help them to appreciate the need of promptness and regularity, and to feel their own responsibility for the success of the society along these lines.

Simple Marking. — Teach the members of the lookout committee, if they keep the record of attendance, this simple way of marking. If a Junior is absent, make no mark opposite his name. If he is present, make a straight mark. If he is present and takes part, change the straight mark to a cross. If he is present and does not take part, draw a circle about the straight mark at the conclusion of the meeting.

Utilize Them. — Though the keeping of a record of attendance is a valuable training in itself, yet the superintendent should count it a great loss if she makes no use of these records after they have been made. Frequently she should speak to the Juniors about their progress in the matter of regularity, summarizing their attendance for the past week or month, and comparing it with the attendance for former periods. Facts regarding the attendance should always be put in the report, and the superintendent should be as hearty in her praise of regularity and promptness as she is earnest in her reproof and exhortation if there is any defect in this matter.

The Higher Motive. — In all your strivings after improved attendance, urge upon the Juniors the higher motive. I should offer prizes for regular attendance seldom, if ever. Teach the Juniors the reason for good attendance, showing them how habits of regularity, formed when they are young, will remain with them and strengthen all their future life; how their example will lead others to become faithful; how much they are losing if they remain away even from a single meeting; and above all urging upon them the one great motive, that Christ wants them to be there, where they can come closest to him.

As They Come In. — I do not approve of the plan of calling the roll at every meeting. It soon becomes monotonous, and the superintendent is unable to take up new plans. A roll-call once a month, at the consecration meeting, is sufficient, though of course the attendance should be regularly recorded. If none of the methods elsewhere spoken of are adopted, the superintendent should herself record the attendance as the members enter the room, not trusting to her memory to mark her book after the meeting.

Personal Record Cards. — Some Junior superintendents will like to use personal record cards, on which the Junior records for himself his attendance during the Sundays of the month. The following is a sample. The fifth space, of course, will not be filled except when there is a fifth Sunday in the month.

MY RECORD

AT

JUNIOR CHRISTIAN ENDEAVOR SOCIETY.

For the month of...

1st SUNDAY.	2d SUNDAY.	3d SUNDAY.	4th SUNDAY.	5th SUNDAY.

Say whether present or absent. If absent, why?

Name...

Hearts and Stars. — A Massachusetts superintendent has originated this ingenious method of recording attendance and participation in the prayer meeting. On a large piece of pasteboard she writes the names of her Juniors. Following each name are thirteen spaces, one for each week of the quarter. If any of the Juniors must be absent, but sends a verse or a message, or if he comes and reads his own verse, a blue heart is stuck in the place opposite his name. If he has prepared his verse so well that he is able to recite it, a red heart is pasted on instead of the blue. If he makes any original remarks, gives any testimony, or offers a sentence prayer, he has a gilt star. This record is made during the meeting by some one who sits behind the children so that their attention is in no way diverted, and at the conclusion of the meeting it is brought before the society.

Attendance Prizes.— Many Junior workers find it helpful to offer a small prize for regular attendance at the Junior society. The pastor of a Methodist Junior Christian Endeavor society gives each child a fifteen-cent Junior silver badge for attendance at ten meetings in succession. When the Junior comes twenty times in succession, the fifteen-cent badge is returned, and a twenty-cent blue enamelled badge is received in exchange, the first being used for some one else. The Sunday school or the older Christian Endeavor society pays for these badges, and they find that it pays them.

Junior Circles. — Quebec Juniors have adopted what is called the "circle plan" of keeping track of the attendance on their meetings. The entire membership is divided into groups or circles of from eight to ten each. These circles are numbered, and one member of the lookout committee is placed in charge of each group. Every member of the group is furnished with a card which contains the names of all the members of his group. With this card each member of the circle keeps account of the attendance of all the other members, recording also the way in which each takes part in the meeting. It is sought thus to interest each member of the group in every other member, so that all will seek to find out the reason for the absence of all absentees, and in helping the indifferent to take part in the meetings.

Thorough — It may seem a rather stern method; but some Junior superintendents have found it advisable for the secretary to sit in front of the society with a list of the members, marking each one present, crossing this mark as each takes part, and crossing it again for each prayer. At the close of the meeting the names of those who have not taken part are read, and at the end of each quarter the names of those who have been present and who have taken part in each meeting are read.

Attendance Badge Records. — A spur to faithful attendance may be made by utilizing the ribbon badges in the following manner: When the Junior is present at every meeting of the month, paste on the badge a gilt star. If the Junior is absent any Sunday of the month, leave the space for that month vacant. This plan necessitates new badges, probably every year.

A Peg Record. — The Juniors will take pleasure in keeping their own record of attendance. Let them do it after the following fashion: Obtain a pine board of appropriate size, and make in it as many holes as you have Juniors, with a few extra for future growth. Write above each hole the name of one of the members. Below the board, which is fastened near the door of your society room, place a small basket swinging by a ribbon. This basket is to contain pegs, which fit into the holes of the board.

Each Junior as he enters stops at the board, takes a peg, and places it in the hole under his name. The membership of the society should be divided among the members of the lookout committee, and at the close of each meeting the committeemen stop and examine the board to see if the Juniors belonging to their divisions have been present. If any hole is empty, the Junior thus designated is hunted up during the following week.

Self-Recording. — An excellent method is reported by one of the State Junior superintendents. Write the names of all the Juniors upon a large chart. After each name leave a space for every Sunday in the year. Before the meeting, place this chart by the door, and put a pencil near by. As each Junior enters, he is expected to mark his own attendance with a cross in the proper space. If he is tardy, he writes a T in this space.

At the end of three months a silver pin is given to each Junior who has not been tardy, and has been present at every meeting. If he is similarly faithful for the next three months, he returns the pin, and receives a better silver one. At the end of a year of equal faithfulness this second pin is returned, and a gold pin given the Junior, which he keeps.

A simpler method is this. Place in the vestibule a pencil tablet with a pencil, and instruct the Juniors to write their names on this as they enter. For a large society it would be necessary to have several tablets, in different places.

CHAPTER XVIII.

SOMETHING ABOUT ROLL-CALLS.

Roll-call Variations. — Do not call the roll of the society yourself. This is something the Juniors can do, and so they should be taught to do it. See that the officer who calls the roll uses a strong voice and enunciates distinctly. Maintain quiet in the society while this exercise is going on. An admirable plan for a variation in the roll-call is for each chairman of the committees to call the roll of his own committee, the secretary noting at the same time who are present.

" Faithful." — Some Junior superintendents have found it a good plan to call the roll at each meeting, the responses from the Juniors being with either the word " Faithful," or the word "Present." The former response is used by those alone who have kept their pledge by reading their Bibles every day. At the monthly business meeting of the Young People's society, there is read the roll of honor from the Junior society, this roll of honor containing the names of all who have answered "Faithful " at every meeting during the month.

One Verse a Month. — Many societies call the roll of the Juniors at every meeting, the Juniors responding with the repetition of Bible verses. Sometimes this verse is the same during the month ; and at the consecration meeting a new verse is repeated, which is the verse chosen by the Junior for the coming month.

The Record. — If you wish at some time to emphasize the good or bad attendance of each Junior, let the secretary call the roll, each member responding " Present," while after each response the chairman of the lookout committee states the number of times the responding member has been absent during the past month, making the same statement, of course, in the case of absent members.

Train Their Eyes. — Whenever you form a roll of the society, to be placed on the blackboard or hung on the wall, let it be most carefully written or printed, the letters distinct and clear, and sufficiently large to be read without straining the eyes. Make everything of this sort as pretty and tasteful as you can. Remember that all such things form a decided though unconscious training of the children's artistic sense. If you are incapable of this work, get some good draughtsman to help you. Make tasteful use of colored chalk, colored ink, paints, gilding, and of colored paper cut out to form pretty silhouettes. When you have occasion to make a new roll, form it on a different plan from any you have set before the Juniors previously.

A Merit Roll. — The best form of a merit roll consists of two parts. One is a large wall roll for the names, opposite each name being placed a star when the Junior has accomplished work of a certain kind. These stars should be of different colors. By the side of this large roll hangs a smaller one which is the key to it. It contains stars of each color, opposite the star being written the work which that star signifies. The following is the full list sent in by one society that has tried this plan : —

Books of the Bible,
Ten Commandments,
Ten verses containing promises,
Five verses containing commands,
Twenty-five names by which Christ is called,
The Beatitudes,
The Lord's parables,
The Lord's miracles,
The Twenty-first Psalm,
The Thirty-fourth Psalm,
His favorite chapter of John,
The twelve apostles,
A short story of the life of each apostle,
A short story of the life of Christ,
A short story of the life of Ruth for the girls, and of David for the boys.

I advise superintendents to make use only occasionally of honor rolls, merit rolls, and similar devices. Appeal to the Juniors on higher grounds, whenever you can, making it their desire to do good to please God rather than to be seen of man.

The Roll. — Probably most superintendents will not find it advisable to tie the meeting down to a roll-call, however valuable this exercise may be as an occasional feature. The roll, however, should always be kept accurately by the secretary. The secretary should note the attendance of visitors, as well as of the members, keeping a separate list for these.

For other points regarding the use of the roll, see the chapter on the consecration meeting, and also that on attendance.

CHAPTER XIX.

THE DAILY BIBLE-READING.

The Daily Verse. — The little books in which the United Society of Christian Endeavor prints the daily readings for the Juniors are very attractively printed and bound. They cost $1.50 a hundred, or three cents each, and they should be in use in all Junior societies.

Daily Reading Thoughts. — Once in a while ask the Juniors to bring, each one of them, a single thought which they have gained from some one of the daily readings of the week. This will be their contribution to the coming meeting. To vary this method, ask the Juniors to write out one thought on each of the six daily readings. These papers are to be brought to the meeting, and all the Juniors will read them. First the Juniors will read their thoughts on the daily reading for Monday, then for Tuesday, and so on. Possibly the Juniors might be asked to vote which day had given the best thought. For a large society, of course, this plan would have to be modified, the daily reading for only one day, possibly, being taken.

An Advance Reading. — It might not be a good plan for every week, but occasionally, at least, go over the daily readings for the coming week with your Juniors at the meeting, to show them how they bear upon next Sunday's topic, and to show them also how they may obtain from the daily readings thoughts on the lesson, and how they should read their Bible, keeping the coming Christian Endeavor meeting constantly in view.

Daily Reading Songs. — The Juniors will like once in a while to select songs that are appropriate to the daily readings. Ask them a week beforehand to do this, and then at the next meeting let the Juniors recite the daily readings one after the other, singing after each the appropriate hymn.

Daily Reading Illustration. — Let the Junior superintendent occasionally prepare some illustration for each daily reading of the week. It may be an original drawing, or some picture cut out of some paper or magazine, or it may simply be an object. Passing these around among the children, ask them to tell which daily reading is illustrated by which drawing, and then suggest that the Juniors talk about these illustrations in the course of the meeting.

Daily Reading Leaders. — Occasionally appoint seven leaders for the prayer meeting, one for each daily reading of the week. Ask these different leaders to speak each upon his own daily reading, showing how it illustrates the topic. A variation of this method is to appoint one leader and six assistant leaders, who may be called "followers." After the main leader has spoken upon the topic, these six may speak, briefly and in order, on the daily verses for each day of the week.

10-9-8. — For encouraging faithfulness in Bible reading, let the secretary call the roll every Sunday, requesting those who have read their Bibles every day of the week to respond 10, those who have missed one day to respond 9, etc.

His Favorite Verse. — It inspires new interest in the daily reading, if occasionally you ask the Juniors, telling them your plan at the preceding meeting, to repeat each of them from the daily readings of the week the verse he likes best.

In the Meeting. — Sometimes, at least, let the superintendent begin the meeting by asking, "Will some one please repeat Monday's daily reading?" A Junior rises and repeats the verse, which is in turn repeated by the superintendent, slowly and with emphasis. The superintendent then explains carefully the meaning of the verse, and shows the Juniors how it bears upon the topic of the meeting. Tuesday's verse is then given by another Junior, and treated in the same way, and so on through the entire seven verses. The whole exercise does not occupy more than ten minutes.

A Gain. — One of the advantages possessed by the laborious plan of writing out the daily readings on slips of paper, which are given to each Junior, is this: that the lookout committee may be set to giving these slips to each absent member, thus reminding the absent members of the society meeting to come, and interesting the members of the lookout committee in looking up the absent.

Special Bible-Readings. — Junior Bible-reading will be greatly promoted if, in addition to the regular Bible verses laid down in the uniform topics, the superintendent occasionally assigns for the week some special Bible work, such as the reading of the shortest chapter in the Bible, Ps. 117; the reading of the longest chapter, Ps. 119; the reading of six parables, six promises, six prayers; or the following lesson in Bible arithmetic: addition, 2 Pet. 1 : 5–7; subtraction, Rev. 22 : 19; multiplication, 2 Cor. 9 : 6–10; division, 2 Tim. 2 : 15; profit and loss, Mark 8 : 36; bookkeeping, Mal. 3 : 16, 17.

Study One Book. — For extra work in Bible-reading, in addition to the daily readings, the Juniors may be set to reading — all of them — the same book of the Bible for a month. At the end of the month the pastor may be called in to question the society as to the author of the book, and the book's particular teachings.

The Best Time. — A wise superintendent will instruct the children as to the best time of day for reading in the Bible. Usually, of course, this will be the morning. If, however, for any reason, the parents are not likely to be at leisure in the morning to explain the verses when they need explanation, the evening is a better time. Teach the Juniors not only to get help from their parents, but to think over the verses by themselves, and above all to pray over them when they cannot understand them.

Rainbow Bookmarks. — The Juniors will appreciate rainbow bookmarks, and these will help them to attend to their daily readings. Strips of baby ribbon of different bright colors are fastened to a single brass ring. One color is to be chosen for each day. The Juniors will place scarlet, for instance, in Monday's Bible reading, green in Tuesday's, and so on. The fixing of these bookmarks in the appropriate places in the Bibles may be made an occasional exercise in verse-finding in the Junior meetings.

Badges and Bible-Reading. — An Illinois Junior society makes ingenious use of its society colors to promote Bible-reading at home. The colors are pink and white. Any Junior that completes the reading of the book of Matthew receives a pink ribbon badge, and for the reading of any other additional book of the New Testament a white star is printed upon the badge.

Daily Reading Stars. — A Kansas Junior superintendent has had little cards printed, bearing a large gilt star composed of many smaller stars. There is one star for each day in the month. Every day the Junior performs the Bible-reading assigned, he thrusts a pin through one of the small stars. The Juniors themselves might be set to making these cards, and they will serve as useful records and faithful reminders.

Another Record. — Some Presbyterian Juniors of Pennsylvania use, in order to promote fidelity to the daily-reading clause of the pledge, a pretty little card showing a large C. E. monogram, the E bearing the legend, "For Christ and the Church," and the C, " I promise to read the Bible every day." About the outer edge of the C are thirty-one white dots, one for each day in the month ; and as the Junior is faithful to his pledge he pricks one of these dots with a pin. Such cards are soon to be sold by the United Society.

A Calendar Reminder. — An admirable reminder of the daily Bible-reading is a year's calendar printed in small type, on a card of convenient size to be kept in the Bible. Tie at the top of each card a tiny bow of baby ribbon, and stick a pin in it. As the Junior each day fulfils his pledge of Bible-reading, let him punch out the date. In this way unfaithfulness will speak for itself.

A New Card Each Week. — If the superintendent has a duplicating apparatus and the necessary time, one of the best ways of emphasizing the Junior daily readings is to print, by means of the duplicating apparatus, the daily readings for each week upon a piece of card-board, giving these cards out to the Juniors every Sunday. The boys and girls will place these cards where they can be seen daily, and will thus be led to remember their duty.

Diaries. — Some Junior superintendents spur their Juniors to daily Bible-reading by giving to each active member at the beginning of the year a diary. These diaries are brought to the weekly prayer meeting and placed on the desk of the secretary. During the opening part of the meeting this officer copies in the diaries, from *The Junior Golden Rule*, the daily verse references for the week, and then quietly distributes the diaries to their owners. This plan, of course, is practicable only in a small society, and must be modified in a large one. Each day the Junior looks up and reads the Bible reference, and copies the verse in the blank space of the diary.

A Reminder. — To stimulate the daily Bible-reading of the Juniors, at least one hard-working superintendent prepared for each Junior a round of card-board, on the circumference of which was placed as many gilt stars as there were days in the month, with a big gilt " C. E." in the centre. Beside each star, pointing toward the centre, the superintendent carefully wrote the reference to be read on that day. The whole was hung up with a loop of blue ribbon. On each day the Junior was to prick with a pin the star for that day, provided the reference was read ; and the whole was to be returned to the superintendent on the first Sabbath of the next month.

CHAPTER XX.

THE SOCIETY AND THE SUNDAY SCHOOL.

The Sunday-School Committee. — Much of the work of the Junior Sunday-school committee is along the same lines as that of the older society. For example, they should be on the watch at the church services for children who are strangers, that they may invite them to come to Sunday school with them. They are to seek new scholars for the Sunday school among their acquaintances and friends throughout the town. These new scholars they should call for in person, introduce to their class and teacher, and in every way make them feel at home in the school.

It should be the especial pride of the Junior Sunday-school committee to help the superintendent carry out all his desires, and to assist the teachers of their own classes. They should set an example of orderliness before their associates. They should be prompt in attendance, and the superintendent should place it upon their consciences in every way to be models to their mates in Sunday-school work.

This committee should see that notices of the Junior society are given to the superintendent, wherever it is the custom to read these notices from the Sunday-school desk. There are certain classes of the Sunday school with whose teachers they may well co-operate — the primary department and other classes of Junior age.

If the teacher desires such assistance, this committee should hold itself in readiness to visit the scholars that have been absent and that are sick. They should report to the superintendent the causes of absences. It is well to divide the Sunday-school committee, assigning one or more to each teacher who desires their assistance.

New Juniors. — One of the most important duties of the Sunday-school committee will be to keep on the watch for new members that may be obtained from the children of the Sunday

school.   Each might canvass his own class, and obtain canvassers in classes that are not represented on the committee, reporting all names, of course, to the lookout committee.   In
some cases it has been found advantageous to issue, solely to
Sunday-school scholars, special invitations to the Junior meetings, neatly printed on a manifolder.

A Sunday-School Record. — The Junior Sunday-school
committee may keep a record of the attendance of the Juniors
at Sunday school, the society being proportioned out among the
different members of the committee who are in various classes.
This attendance may be reported at the monthly business meeting of the society, those Juniors who are present every Sunday
being reported as perfect.

A Sunday-School Social. — An Ohio Lutheran Junior society once found it a joy to give a social to the entire Sunday
school of their church.   Many a strong Junior society would be
glad and proud to do this.   For the smaller societies, however,
it would be a sufficiently laborious undertaking to give an occasional social to the Sunday-school scholars of their own age
alone.   If the lookout committee is active at the social, not a
few new members may be gained for the Junior society.

Getting New Scholars. —It is an excellent plan for the
Sunday-school committee occasionally to distribute among their
friends of the same age pieces of paper upon which may be
written the names of children who do not attend any Sunday
school, and who may be persuaded to go to theirs.   The Sunday-school committee will then hunt up these boys and girls,
and give them a pressing invitation to connect themselves with
their school.

Music and Flowers. — The Junior choir may be utilized in
the Sunday school and may help greatly in the singing.   The
entire Junior society may occasionally practise Sunday-school
songs, and may help very much in the process of learning new
pieces.   On occasions when such music is to be practised, the
superintendent should get her Juniors to be present themselves
at the rehearsals, and to see that other scholars are present.
The flower committee of the Junior society may well take upon
itself the decoration of the Sunday school, sending flowers to
the sick of the Sunday school, just as the flower committee of

the older society performs the same offices for the sick of the church.

At the Close of the Sunday School. — It is a good idea, if the society is small, to call the Juniors together for a moment at the close of the Sunday school, giving them a thought regarding the coming Junior meeting, or a question bearing on the topic, which each is to answer. Of course this could be done at the meeting before, but the matter is far fresher in the minds of the children if a moment after Sunday school is taken for this purpose.

The Primary Teachers. — The Sunday-school teachers that are over the younger children, those of Junior age, should co-operate most heartily and closely with the Junior superintendent, not merely in the Bible work, but in all other respects, helping to find new members for the Junior society, and speaking often in the Sunday school of the Junior Endeavor work and its advantages. These primary teachers should be frequent, and welcome visitors at the Junior prayer meetings.

CHAPTER XXI.

AT WORK FOR MISSIONS.

A Missionary Assistant. — Missionary work among the Juniors deserves enough care and attention to occupy the time of an assistant superintendent who is responsible alone for this branch of the work, thus relieving the superintendent, and adding to the interest the Juniors will take in missions. If there is no assistant superintendent, possibly the superintendent may get some enthusiastic missionary worker of the older society to relieve her of this part of her duties.

Country Leaders. — One Junior worker urges that the Junior missionary committee consist of a boy or a girl for each country that is to be studied. These are to be the leaders of the different missionary meetings, and each is to select members of the society to help him in studying his country and in carrying on his meeting. The entire society is thus to be divided.

Each of these leaders is furnished with a little blank-book, in which, under the direction of the superintendent, he is to write easy questions regarding his missionary country. Each of these question books is to be of a different bright color.

After the country has been studied in the society, these questions upon the study are to be read by the member of the missionary committee for that country, at any meeting when the superintendent may call for them. They furnish a useful review.

The Committee Responsible. — If possible, place your missionary meetings entirely in the hands of the missionary committee. This responsibility will make them more faithful to their work. The committee might also be empowered to select the leader for that meeting.

The Next Meeting. — Always announce at the end of your missionary meetings what will be the next country studied, and ask the Juniors to keep on the watch for interesting items about that country, showing them where these may be obtained.

Let each be asked to bring such items to the next missionary meeting. It pays to look as far ahead as possible in this work.

For a Year. — A list of the missionary meetings arranged even for a year ahead, and hung up in the meeting room, will teach the children to take long thoughts, and make plans for coming studies. This list should state what country is to be studied each month, and who is to be the leader of each meeting.

A Shrewd Move. — Kill two birds with one stone by occasionally giving out to the Juniors some bit of home work in the study of missions, in the accomplishment of which they will have to ask the aid of their parents. In this way you will plant the seeds of missionary enthusiasm in many older minds.

Helping their Elders. — Why not obtain from the older Endeavorers an occasional invitation to the Juniors to assist them in their own missionary meeting? The Juniors will be very proud of the responsibility thus laid upon them, and will be sure to astonish the older Endeavorers by the zest and ability with which they accomplish their task.

A Missionary Reading. — Ask the worker from the older society who looks after the Junior missionary committee to meet these Juniors one afternoon in each month and read missionary articles to them, for the purpose of inspiring them with greater zeal, and of giving them a fundamental knowledge of at least the missionary stations of their denomination.

Note-Books. — Missionary note-books should be given to all the Juniors, and they should be required to write in them the most important missionary facts, those you are especially anxious to have them learn. The very act of writing down these facts will help to fix them in the memory, while the note-book will constantly be referred to.

One Thing Thoroughly. — You cannot teach the children everything about the many mission countries; but you can teach them thoroughly a few things, and then let them grasp what they can of the rest. Choose some one or two subjects, and familiarize the Juniors with the facts along these lines. For example, throughout one entire year spent in the study of mission countries, take as your main theme the houses of the people, or the condition of the women, or the customs regarding children, or the fashion of dress, or study one great city in each country — anything, in fact, so as to get a standard of comparison and a line of continuity.

Utilize the Day School. — Do not forget that your children are studying in their day schools the geography, history, and natural history of the mission countries. Do not fail to make the story of missions more vivid to them, and to knit together their school with their church work, by frequently asking, in the course of your mission studies, questions that will bring out what they have learned in school. At the same time, for instance, that you teach them where missions in China began, teach them what part of China sends us our Chinese laborers, as well as a large portion of our tea. At the same time that they learn where Carey worked, ask them questions about the Ganges River and Calcutta. When you are studying the life of Paton, bring out facts concerning Oceanica.

Poems and Songs. — Obtain all the poems on missions that you can find, not forgetting, of course, the great missionary hymns. Have the children commit these to memory, and use one at least for every missionary meeting. Special missionary music may also be provided, and thus the music committee will be set to work as well as the missionary committee.

Mottoes. — Missionary mottoes may well be painted or drawn, and framed for hanging before the society in the meeting room. Such mottoes as Carey's famous sentence, " Attempt great things for God ; expect great things from God ; " or John Eliot's, " Prayer and pains through faith in Jesus Christ can do anything ; " or again Carey's, " I cobble shoes to pay expenses," — will, if their story is told, do much to keep the missionary ideal before the minds of these young Christians. In addition, it would be well to have some of the Bible rules for giving, such as, " The Lord loveth a cheerful giver ; " or, " He that giveth to the poor lendeth to the Lord ; " or, " To do good and to communicate forget not," — hung in different parts of the room.

Pictures. — A missionary picture book is easily made from the beautiful illustrations to travel articles that appear in such abundance nowadays in our popular magazines, as well as in many of the missionary monthlies. It is best to form a portfolio of separate leaves, the pictures being pasted on stout cardboard, so that they can be separated and passed around among the Juniors.

As Fractions. — A helpful article on Junior work, by " V. F. P.," suggests the vivifying of missionary information by the use of fractions, diagrams, arrangements like arithmetical sums, etc. She gives the following examples : —

Do you want to show a good reason for giving to missionaries ? There hangs the map of the world. You show the United States as one-tenth of the area: in the corresponding tenth live the Chinese.

We have   65,000,000 people.
They have   400,000,000.

They have $\dfrac{1 \text{ missionary to}}{250,000 \text{ people.}}$

We have $\dfrac{1 \text{ minister to}}{500.}$

In each $\dfrac{1 \text{ knowing Christ}}{250 \text{ never have heard of him.}}$

Write these things as the children have examples at school, fractions, equations : —

India = United States east of Mississippi.

Siam $\dfrac{1 \text{ missionary to}}{300,000 \text{ people.}}$

South America $\dfrac{1 \text{ missionary to}}{600,000 \text{ people.}}$

Brazil = United States or one-half South America in area.

In all South America one-third the work done in
$\overline{ \text{Philadelphia.}}$

The Chinese = one-quarter the world's population.

Suppose you are talking about the need of home missions in the United States, and wish the children to comprehend the many diverse nationalities that make up this country. Get the Juniors to write them upon the board in a long column, and see how much more impressive it will be.

English,	French,	Italian,	Norwegian,
Irish,	German,	Spanish,	Chinese,
Scotch,	Dutch,	Russian,	Japanese, etc.

Flags. — Do not forget to use little flags, placed upon pins so that they can be fastened in the map, and inscribed with the names of the missionary heroes about whom you have been talking, or the modern missionaries of your church. Helpful exercises may be devised by means of these flags. The superintendent, for instance, may ask, "Where shall I put Carey's flag?" or Bishop Thoburn's, or John Paton's; or, "Here is a flag belonging to the first missionary our denomination ever sent out. Where on the map of the world shall I fasten it?" These flags may be, also, of different colors, one color being reserved for your own denomination. For some uses it will be better to buy little circles of gummed paper, which may be obtained in different colors. These can be stuck on the maps in different places.

Missions and Postage Stamps. — Junior workers might well imitate the ingenuity of a missionary worker of whom I have heard, who utilizes the passion for stamp-collecting which she finds in her charges. Distributing foreign stamps, or taking advantage of the collections the Juniors have already made, she has them learn as much as they can about each country from which stamps are obtained, and then tell what they learn in the missionary meetings that deal with those countries. The fact of actually possessing a bit of paper that has come from these distant regions helps greatly to give vividness both to them and to the missionary work.

Junior Essayists. — Short articles on some heathen country will add much to the interest of missionary meetings. These articles should deal with the customs of the people, their manner of living, their dress, their religion, etc.; and pictures may well be brought in, illustrating the points that are made.

A Missionary Paper. — A missionary paper may be edited by the Juniors, and will add great interest to the monthly missionary meetings. It may be called *The Junior Missionary Review*. It should be prepared by different Juniors each month, and will contain news from the missionary fields, interesting items regarding the strange people among whom the missionaries work, clippings from papers, and extracts from books. If it is not thought best to make it a missionary paper always, the idea may be applied to a general paper, in which the Juniors will take delight.

Be Loyal to the Boards. — In some denominations the central missionary authorities object to special causes, and wish all the money contributed for missions to go to one centre, by them to be distributed among the different missionary fields, home and foreign, as they think best.   Other denominations appeal to their constituents along precisely opposite lines, assigning missionaries to groups of societies, by them to be entirely supported, and calling for special contributions from their Endeavorers for the building of home mission churches, or the support of " Christian Endeavor missionaries " in foreign lands.   Whatever may be the policy of your denominational secretaries in this particular, rest assured there are wise reasons for it in the constitution of your church, and loyally follow out their plans. The essential thing is to raise the money, and you can trust the consecrated secretaries of the mission boards to put it to the best possible use.

Don't be Narrow. — Be sure, however, that the thoughts and interests of your Juniors are widened to reach out beyond their own especial denomination, and take in the lives of the great heroes of missions who may have belonged to foreign countries or different bodies of Christians.   The work of such men as Judson and Carey, Gilmour, Henry Martyn, Patteson, Morrison, Mackay, Harrington, Moffat, Livingstone, and the like, your Juniors should surely know about; and the knowledge will add to rather than detract from their zeal for the missions of their own branch of the great church universal.

Juniors and Mission Bands. — Some, who have much at heart the work of the mission societies among the children, are suffering under an ill-founded fear that the Junior societies, springing up in so great numbers all over the country, will injure the progress of the mission bands.   We commend to all these doubters the following earnest and sensible words from Miss Laura Wade Rice, that well-known missionary worker among the Lutherans, the editor of *The Children's Missionary*, who speaks as follows, in the *Lutheran Missionary Journal:* —

" A mission band stands for a pledged endeavor to raise money for missions, and to stimulate interest in them.   An Endeavor society stands for a pledged endeavor to do "whatever Jesus would like to have " its members do.   Certainly he would not like any mission band to relax its interest in missionary work because it has become a Junior society. Nor need it do so, provided the superintendent chosen for the Junior work be in sympathy with the missionary movement. To let that interest flag is a step backward, and at utter variance with the true Endeavor spirit, which is onward, forward, upward, in its every tendency.

A Junior Endeavor society with mission-band attachment is far in advance of the old " one Sunday a month missionary meeting " for children. The true Endeavor training on the other Sundays will make the members more interested in the band meeting on the one Sunday of the month, will have developed them in prayer, in self-sacrifice, and in readiness to take part, besides providing them with a permanent engagement for Sunday afternoons, which will make their band attendance more certain.

For some time it was a problem with me how to combine the two; as it was evident that, as matters now stand, two constitutions would have to be adopted, for in order to be auxiliary to our Women's Home and Foreign Missionary Society it is necessary to adopt the band constitution provided by them. A very few unimportant and yet necessary changes were made in each for the society which we wished to form, the children voted on both, and our Junior Christian Endeavor society and Junior Christian Endeavor mission band was born. (The verb is singular, for they are one.) It all lies with the leader or superintendent. If she desires to have both, the matter is very simple; but she can make it an impossibility if she be uninterested in missions.

Two Missionary Sundays. — One society of which I have heard does not think it disproportionate to give two Sundays in each month to missions, the first Sunday being devoted to foreign and the third to home missions. In answer to the roll-call on these Sundays, each member is requested to give some item of missionary information appropriate to the theme of the meeting.

Home and Foreign. — It may be hard to maintain among your members equal interest in both home and foreign missions. The fault will lie largely in your own partiality for one of these fields. Remember, however, that God's work lies in one place as much as in another, and teach the Juniors as faithfully about the home as the foreign fields, equally dividing the money they contribute, and if possible giving an equal amount of time to the study of each.

Each with His Own Missionary. — Missionary work can be made very vivid to the Juniors if to each Junior is assigned the name of some missionary, preferably of his own denomination, whose work he is particularly to keep in mind in his prayers, to study about in the missionary magazines, and report to the society at the missionary meetings. In the sentence prayers at the missionary meetings, these distant workers may all be remembered by name. A helpful occasional exercise is a roll-call in which the Juniors, instead of responding "Present," reply to their names by giving each the name of the missionary who has been assigned to him.

Missionary Correspondence. — One of the best ways of inspiring interest in missions among the Juniors is through personal correspondence with children who are under the care of missionaries. In one Ohio society, for example, two boys and two girls of the society had a tintype group taken, each getting a picture, the total cost being fifty cents. Each one then selected from a picture of a mission school in Africa one of the pupils, and wrote to that one a friendly letter, enclosing their picture. The letter told about their home life, their duties, their school, their plays, etc. In due course these Juniors received a splendid letter from the four little Africans, entirely original, and written in their peculiar dialect. Those letters gave that society quite an impulse toward better missionary work.

Letters from the Field. — Cultivate missionary correspondence. If in any way you can put your Junior society in connection with some active missionary, so as to have a letter, if only once a year, coming from the very midst of heathendom, by all means do so. Remember, however, that missionaries are very busy people, and do not expect them to write many letters just for your society. It is a good plan for all the Junior societies in the district belonging to the same denomination to obtain letters in this way from a single missionary, and pass them around.

Adopting a Missionary's Girl. — Some Juniors I have heard about have "adopted," as they call it, a little girl of a missionary on the frontier. They have chosen her a member of their society, and sent her a Junior pin. She sends them in return an occasional letter for the consecration meeting, and in this way those Juniors are kept in touch with home mission work, much as other Juniors, by their correspondence with children in foreign lands, maintain their interest in foreign missions.

A Little Missionary Library. — A genuine missionary aid for the Juniors is a collection of missionary leaflets. Your denominational board will furnish you, at slight cost, or none at all, with a large supply of these; and there are other sources from which the collection may be enlarged. These leaflets should be covered with brown paper, numbered, and catalogued. The society librarian should be appointed to take charge of these, and loan them to the members. An interesting spur to the reading of these will be to have the Juniors report at the next meeting upon the number of their family who have read these leaflets, or heard them read.

Magazines and Tracts. — Every Junior worker should, of course, take the missionary magazine of his own denomination. He should also obtain some of the many bright missionary journals published for young people. The articles intended for older readers should be condensed and simplified by the superintendent before they are presented to the children. Most of the missionary boards publish very helpful missionary stories in tract form. These are of the highest value for reading in the missionary meetings, and to be handed around for home reading.

Missionary Envelopes. — Set your missionary committee to collecting missionary scraps, and keeping them in sets of envelopes, appropriately labelled. There may be one envelope for city missions, another for home missions, and one each for all the foreign missionary lands. If the Juniors are interested in any special missionary and his work, an envelope may be set apart for him also. When a missionary meeting is to be held, produce the appropriate envelopes. Gather the missionary committee — or the society, if it is a small one — around a table, and study the items that you have collected.

"Fuel for Missionary Fires." — This little book, by Miss Belle M. Brain, though written primarily for the missionary committees of the older societies, yet is packed full of bright suggestions for Junior workers. Every Junior superintendent should have it. It is sold by the United Society of Christian Endeavor for fifty cents.

Two Funds. — Every Junior society should have two treasuries, carefully kept distinct. One should be for the current expenses of the society, and the other for missions. It should never become the practice of a society to take from a single treasury all it needs for topic cards, hymn-books, socials, and the like, giving what may chance to be left for the service of the Master.

Their Own Treasurer. — Though all the committees of the society may well have their own secretary and treasurer, as well as their chairman, this is especially necessary for the missionary committee, and above all when the society carries on some form of systematic giving.

Work and Interest. — Your missionary meetings will be much more interesting if the Juniors, during the month that precedes, do some work for the missionary country or the mission field which is to be studied at the coming meeting.

Lay By Each Week. — Though, in reporting the practice of many superintendents, I speak in this chapter of special collections, monthly collections, and the like, yet I want it understood that I myself believe in collections at every meeting. The Juniors can in no other way be taught definite, systematic giving, and a small sum given each week will prove far more educative than the same, or even a larger sum, given occasionally.

Something Every Sunday. — If for any reason you do not find it advisable to take up a collection for missions at every meeting, see if you cannot induce the children to bring to every meeting at least something to give away, even if it is nothing but an apple or orange for the relief committee to give to the poor and the sick. It is not so much the amount that the children give as it is the drill in regular habits of giving, that will count for the cause of Christ when the children grow up.

Self-Denial Week. — In addition to the regular gifts of the children, special seasons of self-denial are helpful as calling attention afresh to the needs of the heathen lands, and to the comparatively little we are already doing in proportion to our opportunities and abilities. These special times of self-denial may be the week before Christmas, New Year's week, or the week that closes with Christian Endeavor Day, the latter being preferable, as it is the time chosen by most societies, and as the annual missionary thank-offering comes on that day.

The Fulton Plan. — The Fulton plan for giving to missions, so-called because it has been chiefly pushed by the Rev. Albert A. Fulton, a Presbyterian missionary to China, is that in accordance with which each Junior promises to give two cents a week to missions, this to be divided between the home and foreign fields. The United Society of Christian Endeavor has for sale blank-books to be used in connection with this system. These will be found helpful, though they are not absolutely necessary.

A Penny a Week.— The Fulton pledge plan may thus be modified for the Juniors. The pledge should read: "I desire to give, if possible, one cent a week through our Junior society, to help in sending the good news of the Saviour's love to those boys and girls who have never heard of him." This pledge is engrossed at the head of the roll of honor by a skilled penman, and all the members who will are got to sign it.

It is a good idea for the missionary committee to permit the Juniors to make at one time larger contributions than a penny, crediting them with as many Sundays in advance as their contribution will cover, and reminding them if they do not again begin their penny contributions when this time is up.

In some of the Western States pennies are not common, and in one church this plan is used. The chairman of the Junior missionary committee sits at a table at each meeting. To this table the Juniors bring their money, and the amount is credited in a little book. While this money lasts each Junior can receive from the missionary treasurer, every Sunday, a little envelope containing a penny. This envelope is placed by the Junior in the contribution box.

A Good Beginning. — One useful method of teaching the Juniors early to make a wise division of their money between themselves and the cause of Christ, is to ask each to keep a private record of his spendings, setting down in a blank-book just what he spends for toys, candy, and the like, and in another part just what he gives to good causes.

How Earned. — So far as I know, a Canadian Congregational society originated the excellent plan of wrapping up the money given to the missionary collection in pieces of paper, on which each Junior has written the way in which he earned the money.

The collection being received, the superintendent unrolls these slips and reads them aloud. " Helping mother," " Being up in time for breakfast," " Saved from car-fare," thus run the interesting records.

A Processional. — A missionary processional is a good plan for interesting the Juniors in giving. A missionary plate is placed on the leader's table each week. At the close of the exercises of the hour, the Juniors are arranged in a circle, the organist plays, " Hear the Pennies Dropping," the circle starts, and they all march by the plate, dropping in their pennies as they pass.

An Offering Hymn. — It is helpful to set the children to singing while the collection is being received. The following beautiful hymn has been written for this purpose by Rev. S. Winchester Adriance, a former general secretary of the United Society of Christian Endeavor. It is to be sung to the tune, " Jesus, keep me near the cross."

Take the gift, O Saviour, King,
Here I come presenting ;
With my love the gift I bring,
All my heart consenting.

CHORUS.

Cheerfully, willingly,
Here I bring my off'ring ;
Use it for thy service, Lord,
Banish sin and suffering.

Send thy gospel far away
To the lands of sorrow ;
Let the light of God's sweet day
Bring a glad to-morrow.

For our own home-land we pray,
Blessed by thy great kindness ;
May thy gospel have full sway,
Conq'ring darkest blindness.

Bless the little store I give ;
Make it tenfold greater ;
Grant me grace to thee to live,
Who art my Creator.

Fifty-Two Cents a Year. — One of the best methods of collecting the pennies, when the members pledge one cent a week for missions, is to give the Juniors a thick pasteboard card having places for four pennies cut in it, with a fifth hole in case the month has five Sundays. Printed or written on the card should be the pledge of systematic giving. The pennies are to be fastened into the holes with strips of gummed paper. At the end of the month the Juniors hand in their cards, the pennies are taken out, and the cards returned to be filled up again.

A Card=Bank. — A missionary offering card will prove of service in teaching the Juniors habits of systematic beneficence. This card has, pasted to the back, ten little envelopes, each designed for five cents, either in pennies or in a single coin. After each envelope is filled, it is to be sealed by the gummed flap. On the face of the card is the Junior pledge, with a space for the name of the Junior and the society, together with the superintendent's certificate that the money is given by the Junior. This card, which has been put to the test of practical use and found very helpful, is sold by the United Society for $3.50 a hundred copies.

Mite Boxes. — The use of mite boxes is a very great help in stirring up the Juniors to give systematically and regularly. These boxes may be obtained from most of the mission boards at a very slight cost. Appropriate Bible verses may be printed on three sides of the boxes, and in front the name of the church and society.

A Tithing Company. — The children will delight in the following method of missionary giving. Organize an association to be known as the Christian Tithing Company. Make the assistant superintendent the cashier, and one of the older boys receiving teller. All the Juniors who agree to give to the Lord's work one-tenth of the money they call their own become depositors in the bank.

Upon their first deposit they receive a small bank-book, of which they will think a great deal. In this book their account is strictly kept. The teller has a large book in which he keeps an account for the bank.

This money does not belong to the society, but the general fund is accessible for all the Christian giving of the Juniors.

At the first meeting of every month the bank is open. At that time deposits are received, and the Juniors can draw from their accounts.

A boy, in a society that tried this plan, once succeeded in making quite a profitable sale, and his mother's testimony was: "Indeed, that child derived more pleasure from the fact that he could make a large deposit in the bank than from any benefits that came to him personally."

Missionary Quilts. — Some Juniors desiring to increase the amount of money in their treasury, made a quilt of twenty-five blocks, each being stamped with some pretty design, and outlined in silk by the members. Other Juniors got their friends to pay five cents each for the privilege of writing their names on blocks, which were then outlined in silk and quilted together. The money was sent to missions.

Missionary Barrels. — One Junior superintendent in Illinois got a great deal of money for missions by distributing through the society little barrels, and requesting each holder to put in his barrel one cent a week for home and foreign missions. At the end of the year a missionary social was given in which the barrel-holders alone were permitted to take part. Those that held these barrels were not asked to contribute to the regular Sunday collections.

Definite Objects. — It is helpful to the Juniors, even more than to their elders, to have definite objects for which they can save their missionary money. Systematic giving is in this way most effectively promoted. Here is a sample card which was used in one society: —

I PROMISE

𝔗𝔬 𝔰𝔞𝔳𝔢 𝔢𝔞𝔠𝔥 𝔪𝔬𝔫𝔱𝔥 . . .

> *Two cents for Good Will Farm.*
> *Two cents to help educate girl at Pleasant Hill,*
> *Tennessee.*
> *Two cents for boy in Turkey.*
> *Two cents for support of our society.*

Total, eight cents. . . *CONSECRATION SUNDAY.*

Signed...

One to One — If you wish to interest Juniors in giving for any special mission school, either home or foreign, obtain if possible a list of the names of the scholars, with their ages. Assign each scholar to one of your Juniors of the same age and sex, telling his name, or hers, and letting the Junior know that his gifts, whatever they are, are going to help that particular boy or girl. Sometimes the Juniors can be interested in sending little presents to these special scholars.

Their Special Care. — When the older missionary society sends a box to home missionaries, the Junior superintendent should always inquire whether there are not some little children in the family whose outfit may be undertaken by her Juniors alone.

A Missionary Contest. — A method of stimulating giving among the Juniors is to choose two captains, who divide up between them the membership of the society, each striving to have all the members of his side bring pennies to the meeting. Account is kept to see which group of Juniors is most faithful to this duty.   Another plan is to choose a captain for the girls and another for the boys, the contest being divided along these lines.

Practical Work. — If your society has not yet done any practical missionary work, sent a barrel or a box to some missionary or his children, or in some such way worked with their hands as well as given money, you are missing a very important part of missionary training.   The children can be set to making little things that will be helpful in many a missionary home ; and they can be set to finding in their homes garments quite as good as new, that can do excellent service in the mission field.   There is no reason why boys, as well as girls, should not learn to sew ; and one of the most successful Junior workers I know has found that her boys take up the work of sewing for missionaries with as great zeal as the girls, and are even more faithful.

What They Want. — There is sometimes a bit of carelessness in sending gifts to missionaries, both in the home and foreign fields.   Before you pack a barrel or make similar offerings, take pains to find out directly from the missionary just what will most be needed, and fill your barrel accordingly.

Mission Maps. — One of the very best helps for Junior missionary meetings are small hectographed maps.   Merely the outlines of the different countries should be given, so that missionary stations and other localities, as well as figures and facts, may be inserted as the meeting proceeds. The Juniors should each be given one of these maps and a pencil, and it is astonishing how much more vivid the lesson may be made with the help of these simple and easily manufactured aids. If these maps are made of uniform size, the Juniors will be glad to preserve them, and bind them together into a book that they will call their missionary geography.

Maps. — You should keep hanging before the society all the time a map of the world. Let this be sufficiently inexpensive to permit pasting colored stars here and there to indicate the centres of your denominational missionary work. For filling in the minor details, use the outline maps just mentioned. The children will like to make for themselves also rough clay or putty maps of the different lands.

Sand Maps. — A sand map will add much interest to your Junior meetings. Fit a low rim to a large, square board, and obtain the cleanest and brightest sand you can. Bits of looking-glass, of course, will answer for lakes and seas. Coarse blue yarn will do for rivers. Blocks of wood will represent cities. For the mission stations, light little candles, and stick them up in the sand. If you make this map while the children are looking on, and talk about the different features as you form them, the Juniors will remember far better, and be doubly interested.

A Missionary Social. — Missionary socials may occasionally be given. In these, each Junior should be dressed in the costume of some missionary country, as nearly as that costume can be imitated. If, as is the best plan, each of your Juniors has chosen for himself a country which he will make peculiarly his own in the course of the year, to study about and pray for, then he should appear at this social in the costume of that country. At the social, each Junior should be expected to present some interesting item from the country of his choice.

It will be helpful, also, to have one Junior at least who will be a returned missionary, — one of the well-known missionaries of your denomination, — who will speak in the first person, and give an account of what has been taking place in his field. An interesting feature of such a social is missionary contests. Each

of the countries will select some Junior to speak for it.   There is
to be a jury; and the country whose representative, in its opinion, makes the best speech, is to receive the collection that is
taken at the social.

Missionary Matches. — After the Juniors have spent some
time in the study of a mission land, they will be prepared to
carry on a missionary match, and they will greatly enjoy it.
Leaders are to be appointed, who will choose their sides.   Two
of the oldest Juniors will prepare the questions.   Let it be one
boy and one girl.   The sides stand facing each other; and the
questioners propound their problems, first the boy and then the
girl asking a question.   The sides answer as a whole, any one
on a side being permitted to reply.   If neither side can answer
the question, the questioners ask each other.   The side is
counted victorious that answers the most questions.

Post-Office Meetings. — Post-office meetings will get the
Juniors to studying about missions.   To carry out this meeting,
each Junior will write a letter to some other Junior, pretending
that the writer is a heathen child.   Having selected his pre-
tended home, the Junior will study up about it, find out the
customs of the children and the children's surroundings, and
incorporate in this letter whatever he learns.   He will tell his
friend how he lives, and as much as possible about his country.
These letters will be dated from the places the children are describing; and the sealed envelopes containing them will bear, if
possible, foreign stamps from the countries they describe.   The
letters will be collected as the members enter the room, placed
in a set of post-office boxes, and distributed by the superintendent at the opening of the meeting, to be read in order by the
recipients.

A Missionary Concert. — With a very little trouble any
Junior society may prepare a missionary concert that will be
worthy of presentation before an audience of the older people.
Select for the Juniors brief and pointed missionary anecdotes,
startling and valuable facts regarding missionary progress and
difficulties, and concerning missionary countries.   Teach these
to the Juniors, or have them read little slips.   Give them also
bright missionary poems, and instruct them in the singing of
earnest missionary songs.   Your pastor will be delighted to give

the Juniors an opportunity to present this concert before the older people, and the missionary zeal of young and old will be greatly increased thereby.

A Missionary Alphabet. — An admirable plan for a missionary meeting is the following, which is sent me by a Connecticut worker. Cut from card-board a large number of letters, covering them with bright red paper. Number these letters upon the back, and pin them upon the Juniors, letting each know the number of his letter. In the course of the meeting, to illustrate different points, call out the numbers of the letters one by one, having the Juniors who bear the corresponding letters rise and come forward in such a way as to spell the words you wish to exhibit to the children.

Thus you will spell out the name of the country you are to study for the day, the towns where the different missionary stations are situated, the names of the missionaries, and any other fact you may wish to emphasize in this pleasant manner. You may also spell out little sentences, telling, for example, what the children might do for missions, such as pray, study, give. The children will enjoy this exercise thoroughly.

An Observation Party. — An observation party will add much to your missionary meetings. Arrange, back of a screen, or in another room, a table covered with all kinds of articles that come from the country under discussion — the fruits of that land, different food products in common use that are there obtained, articles of dress, manufactured products, images, jewelry, — everything, in fact, that you can beg or borrow, including, of course, photographs, plants, flags, and the like. Number these objects, and furnish the Juniors with slips of paper. Admit them to the room in sections, if necessary, and give them five minutes to name as many of these objects as they can. Afterwards write a correct list upon the blackboard, and have them compare theirs with it.

Missionary Journeys. — Missionary journeys will add zest to missionary meetings. To carry out successfully the journeys through the mission country you are studying, divide the route into sections, appointing one good worker to describe each section before the society. For example, if you are to study India, one Junior might be sent travelling in imagination from the

United States to Bombay; another might take up the journey there, and carry it on to the Punjaub; another from the Punjaub to Calcutta; and the fourth from Calcutta to Ceylon. These travellers should point out what missionary stations of their denominations they pass, and should tell, each of them, something about the characteristics of the country and of the people, describing as well the sights of the great cities.

Candles and Missions. — A skilful superintendent can make mission work in some of its phases very interesting to the Juniors by the use of candles. Set up before the Juniors a large number of candles to represent the different countries. Let them be large or small, and of different colors, to correspond with the condition of the countries. One, for instance, might be black, for Africa; one yellow, for China; one red, for the Indian tribes of North America; one brown, for the Malays.

As you talk about the countries, you may show how the Light of the world came to the United States from Europe by making the European candle light the United States candle. You can show how the United States passes the light on to China, India, Africa.

You may show how a small candle can light a large candle as well as a large candle could. Show them how the candles, though they are of different color, yet give the same light, so that it makes no difference what may be the color of one's skin, he can shine as well for Christ. Many other truths can be illustrated brightly by this means.

A Question Meeting. — One of the best ways of arranging a missionary meeting is by way of question and answer. Let the superintendent prepare a set of questions, numbered, giving to the Juniors the answers, correspondingly numbered. If these questions and answers are used for several successive missionary meetings, the facts stated therein will become familiar. The superintendent may test this by asking the questions, without furnishing the Juniors with the answers beforehand.

Another excellent plan that is similar, is to distribute, one week before the meeting, little slips of paper containing a set of five or six simple questions on the country to be studied, giving no clew to the answers. If the children cannot find the answers themselves, they go to the superintendent or to some member of the missionary committee, or to their parents and friends. At the missionary meeting the superintendent asks the questions, and the members give their various answers.

Missionary Trees. — A missionary tree will teach the Juniors about the missionary work of their denomination. It should be drawn upon a large sheet of paper, or on the blackboard. There should be as many roots to the tree as the denomination has missionary and benevolent societies. The branches of these roots represent local societies. The tiny rootlets of these branches represent the Juniors, and all who give to the work of the denomination. Each one is pouring into the roots, and so into the tree, the nourishment of his gifts.

The branches of the tree are the fields of work, which should be marked — the different lands, the different races, and different enterprises. The fruits of the tree are the Christian lives of the converted. The trunk is the gospel. These parts should not be named; but the Juniors should frequently be reviewed on the matter, being required to name the different parts as the superintendent points to them.

Chairs and Missions. — In many bright ways the arrangement of the chairs in the Junior room may be made to contribute to the interest and profit of missionary meetings. For instance, if you are studying for the day missions that lie in the islands of the Pacific, arrange your chairs in groups, each to represent an island where your church has missionary work. If you are to study some country, let the groups of chairs represent the missionary stations of that country, which will be situated usually in the important cities. Be sure to place these groups of chairs at the proper distances from each other, and in the right directions.

In the case of islands, the superintendent can instruct the chairman of the missionary committee to pass from island to island, representing the course of a missionary ship.

An ingenious leader will get much good out of such an arrangement as this. Little banners should be fastened to the backs of the chairs, bearing upon them in clear letters the names of the islands or of the cities. Questions about the missionary work in each district should, of course, be referred for answer to the children occupying those districts. A map of the country under discussion should be placed before the children. To each group of Juniors should be given some fact about the station they are representing, and at the end of the exercise they should be asked to rise and repeat these facts as a review.

A Flag Exercise. — Effective missionary lessons may be based upon the flags of the different countries. A sample of this method has been sent me by Ohio's zealous Junior superintendent, Miss Mary C. Merritt.

Holding up the flag of the United States, for instance, the superintendent asks such questions as, "What flag is this?" "When was it adopted?" "How many stars were at first on the flag?" "How many stars has it now?" "When do they make the change?" "By what names is the flag called?" "For what does the red stand? the white? the blue?" "For what do the stars stand? the stripes?"

Here the superintendent will give some instances of heroism connected with the American flag; some Junior may recite Whittier's poem, "Barbara Frietchie;" another will tell about the little coat in which Washington was baptized, which is still preserved by Miss Lewis of Woodlawn, Va. It is made of white silk, lined with red silk, and trimmed with blue ribbon.

Going on from this, the superintendent may continue her questions: "Does this flag represent a Christian country?" "Are all who live here Christians?" "Have we any real heathen among us, who worship idols?" "What other people among us need to be taught about Jesus?" And so the questions may lead to a review of the home missionary work of the church.

At the close of this exercise, two boys should come forward and each take hold of the flag, stretching it out so as to receive the money which the Juniors come and drop in. Each Junior, if there is time, will recite a verse as he lays his offering in the flag. When all have contributed, a short prayer will be offered, asking for God's blessing on the gift; and then a national song will be sung while the money is being counted, that the sum may be announced.

This is a sample of the way in which the flags of all countries may be treated; and it will readily be seen how the superintendent's ingenuity, supplemented by much study of books, will produce an exceedingly effective and helpful drill.

CHAPTER XXII.

TEMPERANCE WORK FOR JUNIORS.

Facts ! Facts ! Facts ! —The Junior superintendent should see to it that the temperance meetings are packed as full as may be with temperance facts. At least one fact each meeting should be impressed upon the minds of the Juniors so distinctly that it cannot be forgotten; for example, the number of drunkards in the country; the number that die every year; the number of saloons, the number of schoolhouses; the number of saloon-keepers, of ministers, and of teachers; the amount of money spent each year for intoxicating liquor, and the amount spent for schools, for missions, for bread, for meat; the number of States that have adopted prohibitory laws.

Such facts as these, taken one at a time and thoroughly committed to memory, will make earnest temperance advocates of your Juniors almost before you know it. There are many magazines of such facts, among them, *Handbook of Prohibition*, published by Funk & Wagnalls, New York City, 50 cents; *The National Temperance Almanac*, published by the National Temperance Society, New York City, 10 cents; the various tracts of the Woman's Christian Temperance Union, and the weekly issues of *The Union Signal* and *The Voice*.

The Memory. — There are many magnificent temperance poems with which the children's memories should be stored; and they will like to recite them, either singly or in concert. The temperance problem was not much of a problem in Bible times and in Bible lands; so that the Bible does not abound in temperance texts, however undoubted is its stand on the side of temperance and purity. Therefore it will be possible for your Juniors to commit to memory all of the temperance passages in the Bible. Make that your aim, and have them frequently recite these texts in concert. They will enjoy forming themselves into two temperance brigades, which will fire back and forth at each other temperance texts.

Temperance Experiments. — A little study of the temperance physiologies, now so often used in schools, will teach the superintendent some excellent experiments that may be made, that will demonstrate to the Juniors the injurious effects of alcohol upon the tissues of the body. These experiments will produce upon the Juniors an ineffaceable impression.

The Great Societies. — One temperance meeting might well be devoted to the study of the great temperance organizations, such as the Woman's Christian Temperance Union, the Y's, and the National Temperance Society. The date of organization should be learned, the important accomplishments of each, the work each is now doing in many directions, and the prominent workers connected with them.

Biographical Meetings. — No more inspiring theme for a temperance meeting could possibly be chosen than a study of temperance heroes. Get different Juniors to write brief biographies of Neal Dow, John B. Gough, John G. Woolley, Francis Murphy, Frances E. Willard, Lady Henry Somerset, and such heroes of the temperance cause. Have their pictures to show, and be prepared with interesting anecdotes to supplement what the children say. At the close, give some time to questions the Juniors may like to ask, and review the whole yourself by questioning.

" Water is Best." — For a temperance meeting, set half a dozen of the Juniors to telling Bible stories of the events in which water served good purpose, such as the miracle at Cana, the water drawn from the rock by Moses, Naaman's recovery from leprosy, and the like.

Story Skeletons. — The Juniors will develop unexpected talent in the way of original story-telling, and temperance meetings may be enlivened in that way. One writer suggests that a series of words be given the entire society, and each Junior asked to construct therefrom a short temperance story. A sample of such a series is, " boy, man, bottle, city, fire, baby." The Juniors will be interested to hear one another's efforts.

Current Events. — At least one temperance meeting in every year should be devoted to the study of the current events bearing upon temperance. The Juniors are not too young to be interested in the great struggle that is going on for the preservation of the home. If any temperance laws have been passed in your State or are proposed for passage, if anywhere in the Union the elections have been significant regarding temperance reform, if important conventions have been held or anniversaries observed, if you have any remarkable temperance speeches to which attention should be called, if any of the heroes of the temperance cause have recently died, these events, and such as these, will make up an interesting and profitable hour, and will do much to make your Juniors feel that temperance is not merely a great question in theory, but a practical and stirring problem on which live men and women are actively engaged.

A Temperance Alphabet. — Mrs. Scudder has kindly sent me the following temperance exercise for Juniors, which she has rearranged for this manual: —

A stands for Alcohol, a fluid of fire
Which often brings death to the seller and buyer.

B stands for Beer, sometimes sold by the barrel,
And most men who love it, love also to quarrel.

C is for Cider, which goes to the head,
And makes men appear as if they were dead.

D stands for Drunkard; oh, help him who can
To reform, be converted, and live like a man !

E stands for Eggnog, called an innocent drink;
Made of milk, eggs, and brandy; is it innocent think?

F stands for Fight, which is easy for those
Who of brandy and beer take a liberal dose.

G stands for Gutter, and also for Gin ;
Who use much of the latter, the former fall in.

H stands for Hops, a vine much abused;
By those who make ale, beer, and porter, it's used.

I is for Idler, to work he won't go.

J is for Jug, his companion and foe.

K is for Kindness ; how little is shown
To those who through liquor have desperate grown.

L is for Loafer, who after much drinking,
Stands on the corner apparently thinking.

M stands for Maniac, his reason all gone,
His dear ones heart-broken because he did wrong.

N is for Night, the time of dark deeds.

O is for Outcast, who on the husks feeds.

P stands for Pipes, which you often will find
Full of tobacco which injures mankind.

Q questions whether 'tis prudent and wise
To handle a drink wherein such evil lies.

R is for Rum, an enemy to all,
For those men that use it are certain to fall.

S is for Station-house, where, in sad plight,
Poor drunkards are frequently taken at night.

T is Tobacco, used in various ways
To rob men of strength, and shorten their days.

U stands for Usury, which adds to the woe
Of those who through drink to the pawnbrokers go.

V is for Vine; its innocent fruit
Is forced to help man sink below the poor brute.

W is for Whiskey, a very mean drink,
For all those who like it to ruin soon sink.

X's one, two, and three are used to describe
A drink which hundreds of drunkards imbibe.

Y stands for Youth. Oh, be wise and beware!
Yield not to the tempter, to die in despair.

Z stands for Zeal, which will help us to win
Many souls from the power of Satan and sin.

Swearing. — The subject of swearing is not inappropriate to be considered in connection with our temperance topics. Temperance committees should be set to doing work to guard the Juniors against this sin, and to suppress it when it exists.

Singing. — Temperance songs have a large part to play in Junior temperance work, and the Juniors should have many of them in their *répertoire*. Both the W. C. T. U. and the National Temperance Society publish little books of children's temperance songs from which you may teach many bright and stirring melodies to the Juniors.

From the Newspapers. — Set the children themselves to making a temperance scrap-book, the material for which will be gathered from the newspapers and other periodicals, by themselves, with the help of their parents.   Widen the scope of the book to include not merely the evils wrought by strong drink, but those of gambling, smoking, bad literature, and possibly of theatre-going.   Under these different heads will be pasted newspaper clippings showing the evil things that have been done by men under the influence of strong drink, and all other facts that may tend to make the Juniors stronger for temperance.

The Superintendent's Scraps. — Besides the temperance scrap-book kept by the Juniors and accessible to them, the superintendent will, of course, have a temperance scrap-book of her own, or, better still, a temperance envelope, in which she will keep little poems suitable for the Juniors to learn, and all kinds of temperance facts and illustrations.

The Sinews of War. — The temperance committee can do a great deal of helpful work by the circulation of temperance tracts and other literature, if they can obtain a little money to buy it.   This will not be a feat difficult of accomplishment if the committee circulate a subscription paper with this written at the head : " We, the undersigned, are glad to give ten cents apiece for promoting the temperance work of the Junior society of —— Church."

Drinking Fountains. — So much good can be done for the temperance cause by the erection of drinking fountains, that this is one very appropriate bit of temperance work that may be undertaken by Junior societies.   I have heard of one temperance society on the Pacific coast that raised money enough to put up a drinking fountain in front of the church.   Why should not every church preach in this way? and why may not every Junior society take up such a beautiful task ?

From the United Society. — The temperance committee supplies published by the United Society of Christian Endeavor, though intended primarily for the work of the older society, are yet in several cases entirely suited to the Juniors, and will always prove suggestive to Junior workers.   Among these are three temperance exercises, each of which costs $2.00 a hundred; two leaflets, — " The Temperance Committee at Work," 3 cents, and " Why Sign the Temperance Pledge? " 2 cents; temperence pledge cards, 50 cents a hundred; and pledge books, 3 cents each.

Temperance Literature. — The temperance committee can do a great deal by lending temperance stories, papers, books, and tracts among the members of the society, seeing that they are returned, and passed on again to others. Following a method spoken of elsewhere more fully, temperance stories may be placed in envelopes, numbered and catalogued, and circulated as a little library among the Juniors.

From the National Temperance Society, New York City, you may obtain a very large number of most excellent tracts that cost very little. They also publish temperance papers for children, as does the Woman's Christian Temperance Union, whose headquarters are The Temple, Chicago. The temperance committee will do a good thing, too, if it procures the insertion in the Sunday-school library of an occasional new temperance story.

Two Helpful Pamphlets. — A suggestive book is published by the National Temperance Society, 58 Reade Street, New York City, entitled *Temperance Arithmetic*. Its examples teach the children, after the fashion of the public school, important moral lessons. A sample problem is the following: "If Mr. B takes three glasses of whiskey a day, and his wife three glasses of beer with her meals, how much money will they drink up in the course of a year?"

This same society publishes a pamphlet giving the recipes for the making of all kinds of intoxicating liquors. Of this the superintendent may make effective use, showing the Juniors what is the poisonous and hurtful character of the substances that enter into these abominable compounds.

A Strong Pledge. — Here is a form of temperance pledge your Juniors may like to use. "Trusting in the Lord Jesus Christ for strength, I promise him that I will drink no intoxicating liquor, that I will use no tobacco, that I will use no profane language, that I will never listen to or repeat an impure story, that I will pray each day that the saloon may be banished from our land, and that, just so far as I know how, I will work for what I pray, and will do all in my power to kill King Alcohol."

Another Good Pledge. — Here is a Junior temperance pledge sent us by some Baptist Endeavorers. Other societies may prefer this form. "I promise that I will never drink anything that makes men drunk, never use tobacco, never swear, and I will ask God every day to help me keep these promises."

A Rhymed Pledge. — The following temperance pledge was sent me from the Congregational Juniors of Slatersville, R. I. Other Junior societies may like to see it.

> " A pledge I make, no wine to take,
>   Nor brandy red, that turns the head ;
>   Nor whiskey hot, that makes the sot ;
>   Nor will I sin by drinking gin ;
>   Hard cider, too, will never do,
>   Nor fiery rum, that ruins home ;
>   Nor brewer's beer that makes poor cheer ;
>   Nor sparkling ale my face to pale.
>   To quench my thirst I'll always bring
>   Cold water from the well or spring ;
>   And here I pledge perpetual hate
>   To all that can intoxicate."

Miss Willard's Pledge. — You will like to make use of this rhymed pledge, whose author is no less a person than Miss Frances E. Willard.

> " I pledge my brain God's thoughts to think ;
>   My lips no fire or foam to drink
>   From alcoholic cup, nor link
>   With my pure breath tobacco's taint ;
>   For have I not a right to be
>   As wholesome and as pure as she
>   Who, through the years so glad and free,
>   Moves gently onward to meet me ?
>   A knight of the new chivalry
>   Of Christ and temperance I would be,
>   In nineteen hundred ; come and see."

Ribbon Reminders. — Present to the Juniors that sign the temperance pledge a little bow of red ribbon to wear, telling them at the same time something about the work of Francis Murphy. They will appreciate this badge, and it will help them to remember their pledge.

A Pledge Book. — A temperance record book with the pledge written on the first page, followed by the names of all the young people you can get to sign it, will be a valuable possession for the society. Let all who sign this pledge book sign also a separate pledge card, which they may retain, and keep in some place where they can frequently see it.

A Wall List. — Some Denver Juniors once did some excellent temperance work among the young people of the Sunday school. They gathered signatures to the pledge, and after they had obtained all they could, placed the pledge and signatures in a frame to adorn the walls of the Sunday-school room. Similar work should be done in every society among the Juniors themselves. Have a pledge beautifully engrossed, obtain as many signatures of the Juniors as possible, frame it handsomely, and keep it as a permanent memorial upon the walls of the society room.

CHAPTER XXIII.

GOOD-CITIZENSHIP WORK.

Coming Citizens. — Junior superintendents may do much to arouse in the Juniors an interest in better citizenship, and so put them in line to do noble work in that revival of better citizenship which the present decade is witnessing.

The boys may be got together occasionally outside of the society meetings, and given practical talks on how they are governed. They may be set to holding debates regarding patriotic subjects. They will like to conduct elections, especially on election days, going through with the form which a regular voter must use. They will enjoy, during campaign seasons, campaign rallies, when Junior representatives of the different parties may be permitted to speak each for his own side.

The superintendent may do much by directing their reading in the public libraries to noble patriotic books. Portraits and statues of distinguished Americans and noble patriots of other countries may be exhibited occasionally in the Junior meetings, and the superintendent may talk briefly about their magnificent achievements. If there are scenes or buildings of historic interest accessible to your society, you might take your boys on occasional pilgrimages to them, and ask them afterward to write essays connected with those themes.

Teach them patriotic songs. Bear in mind historic dates that are famous for noble achievements, and remind the boys of them in connection with your Junior talks. Commemorate Washington's Birthday, Decoration Day, the Fourth of July, and Lincoln's Birthday, in some suitable way, if only by five or ten minutes spent appropriately in your Junior meetings. Encourage patriotic recitations. Get flags for the Juniors, which they may carry on stated occasions.

Many other ways will suggest themselves to the superintendent who is genuinely patriotic, and eager that his young charge shall have the same love for country that he has himself.

Training in Citizenship. — The superintendents of our Junior societies are, by a large majority, women. They will need to watch very carefully to see that they do their full duty along the lines of training in Christian citizenship. To teach the young voters their duty to their country, they will need themselves in many cases to make special study of that duty, which to them is largely unfamiliar.

A Junior superintendent should know the names of the prominent rulers of country and State. She should know when election times come. She should keep up with the prominent current events in this land and in foreign lands, and should be able to turn to account, for the inspiration of patriotism, all of these occurrences and seasons.

No boy that is old enough to join a Junior society is too young to be taught what constitutes a good ruler, and what are the duties of a good citizen. Few lines of study, moreover, are more helpful to the Junior superintendent in holding the boys than that of history. Many noble and inspiring illustrations may be drawn from the history of our own land; and in few better ways, if any, can man's noble and ignoble characteristics be illustrated before the society.

In this way the superintendent will win the boys and help them for all their lives; and if, as seems not unlikely, the girls themselves are to be added to the force of coming voters, then this training on the part of the superintendent is doubly necessary.

A Rally. — Junior unions have held good-citizenship rallies, and why should they not? Appropriate exercises at such rallies would be a flag drill by the Juniors, patriotic songs, also by the Juniors, together with patriotic recitations, and bright talks about the duties for which these young citizens-to-be should be preparing. Much should be made at such a meeting of appropriate decorations, banners, and the pictures of eminent patriots.

Good-Citizenship Pledges. — I do not see why the Juniors may not with profit follow the example of many older societies, and sign good-citizenship pledges. These should be written in a very simple way, but should contain the following, in substance: " I promise Christ that I will study about this good country that he has given me, and that I will pray for it; that when I grow up I will vote for good men, and will try in every way to make this nation such as Christ would approve."

Good-Citizenship Committees. — The older Christian Endeavor societies have good-citizenship committees; why should not the Juniors have them too? These Juniors will soon become citizens themselves; and it is time they should learn, under Christian auspices, how to perform a citizen's duty. It is the work of these good-citizenship committees to take the especial superintendency of all patriotic meetings, and under the superintendent's direction to inspire the Juniors with a more hearty and intelligent patriotism.

CHAPTER XXIV.

JUNIOR SOCIALS.

Its Chief Task. — The main work of the social committee is not to hold socials, but to welcome strangers, and make them feel at home in the meetings, to care for the shy and timid members, to call on children that are newcomers in the town or Sunday school, and in every way to promote genuine sociability and friendship in the society. Show them that this is their true and most Christlike work, and that the holding of pleasant socials must always have this as its main end.

Finding and Testing. — Interest the members of the social committee in the search for novel and pleasant games. Their bright wits will learn many a pleasing entertainment, and they will be capable even of devising others. It is best, before any of these new games are tried by the society, to have them tried by the members of the social committee themselves. The chairman of this committee may well gather the members at her home on some week-day evening, and spend the entire evening in playing new games, becoming familiar with the processes, and deciding on which shall be proposed at the next social.

No Clannishness. — Teach the social committee that one of its main duties is to break up the sets and cliques that are formed even among the unceremonious children. Children are clannish; and by them a stranger, or some one against whom they chance to form a dislike, is quite certain to be left out in the cold, unless an earnest Christian social committee remedies the evil.

Use Their Help. — The superintendent will make a mistake if she does all the work of preparing the refreshments for the Junior socials. The Juniors themselves will like to assist her. For example, you may ask each Junior to bring a cup to drink lemonade from. You may appoint certain Juniors to squeeze the lemons, some to cut them, some to cut the cake. Appoint others to pass these articles. Appoint others to attend to the arrangement of the chairs and benches.

A Second Social Committee. — Some Baptist Junior Endeavorers have two social committees. One is the ordinary social committee; and the other is a social committee for prayer meetings, whose duty it is to make strangers who attend the meetings feel thoroughly at home. In a large society this additional social committee may very well be formed, though in a small society one social committee should perform both lines of work.

Admission Tickets. — People value much more highly what it has cost them a little pains to get. This rule applies to children as well as to grown folks, and to Junior socials as well as to other meetings. It will pay you to use little admission tickets to your socials, and to make these tickets somewhat different in the cases of the Juniors themselves and of the friends they may wish to invite.

One may read: "Member's Admission Card. Admit ...., a Junior Endeavorer, to the Junior social held in ...., on ...., 189....., at .... P. M. This card should be presented at the door."

The other card reads: "Complimentary Admission Card. With the approval of the society, ... (the Junior's name) cordially invites .... (the visitor's name) to attend the Junior social," etc. The remainder of the card will be like the first.

Picnics. — In the summer months a Junior picnic held once a month is a most helpful feature. If the picnic is held at certain regular intervals, the children look forward to it with more eagerness than if it comes at uncertain times and without a long notice. The Juniors will like to meet at the church with their lunch-baskets, and march in line to the picnic grounds, possibly with drums and trumpets, and with flags flying. The parents should be invited to attend whenever it is possible; and the best time for these picnics is, of course, on Saturday afternoon.

Summer Joys. — Mrs. Hageman, Indiana's Junior superintendent, suggests for Junior meetings during the summer that they be held often in a dooryard, or in some grove. Let lawn socials be held once a month during the summer. In all these pleasures, however, don't let the Juniors forget the primary object of their organization.

A Treat. — One Junior superintendent of whom I have heard greatly endeared herself to the hearts of her Juniors one summer by making for them on hot days ice-cream, which two or three of the Juniors took around to the different homes in a little cart and sold by the dishful, thus realizing a neat sum for the Junior treasury.

A Junior Walk. — An occasional walk with the Juniors through the woods and across the fields will be a great help, if the superintendent is willing to take the trouble. Let him point out the beauties of the natural world, telling, as they move on, interesting things about the rocks and the birds, the flowers and the trees. Children have an innate love of all the beautiful objects of nature, and will almost worship one who opens to their eyes nature's wonders.

Teas. — Committee teas are capital affairs for bringing the superintendent into close contact with her Juniors. Once a month she may have to tea with her some special committee. During the evening they will talk over their committee work.

Together. — It is an excellent idea for the Juniors and the Young People's societies to hold occasional socials together. In this way both gain an inspiration.

A Visitors' Album. — It will be pleasant for each Junior society to keep a visitors' record book, in which to preserve the autographs of all its visitors. The Juniors will greatly enjoy this, and the book will make a valuable record.

Get them Photographed. — If there is a camera obtainable, by all means take a picture of the Juniors. They will treasure these, and the sight of the society together will inspire a spirit which will be very helpful.

Junior Squirrels. — A nut-hunt is a pleasant feature of a Junior social. The nuts are scattered everywhere, and the Juniors are set to hunting them, the one who gets the most in a certain time being counted the victor. An interesting variation is to hide nuts of two kinds, say peanuts and walnuts, permitting the Juniors to hunt for the peanuts first without disturbing the walnuts they may come across, and then, after this contest is decided, permitting them in a similar way to seek out the walnuts.

J. S. C. E. — Miss Jessie Norton, of Cleveland, Ohio, wrote the following poem. It was used by one of the Cleveland societies in a military drill given at a birthday social. Fifteen boys took part, and at various stages of the march they formed the letters " J. S. C. E." As each letter in turn was formed, the boys halted, and repeated together the verse appropriate to that letter : —

> " J " is for Junior ; though young, we are strong,
> And mean to fight bravely against sin and wrong.
> Our lives hid in Christ, we shall conquer each foe,
> Stand firm for the right, and learn to say " No."
>
> " S " for Society ; in strength there is might ;
> With the breastplate of faith and the banner of light
> Then onward we'll go, and triumphantly sing,
> For Christ is our Saviour and Captain and King.
>
> " C " is for Christian ; oh that we may be
> So full of sweet trust and of true purity,
> That naught that we do will ever bring shame
> To the dear Lord himself, who gave us his name.
>
> " E " for Endeavor ; let's work while we may,
> Till the trumpet of God sounds forth the great day ;
> Then, clad in his brightness, we'll march through the gates,
> Right into the city where Christ ever waits.

Social Souvenirs. — The socials will make a strong impression upon the Juniors if you give to each Junior a little souvenir at the conclusion of the entertainment. Pleasant souvenirs will be little dolls made of peanuts or English walnuts. Cards either pretty or comic, Japanese napkins which the Juniors will pass around among themselves for autographs, cradles made of egg-shells, little pictures, or dainty booklets, will all be appropriate souvenirs, and will indefinitely extend the memory of a pleasant hour.

A Christmas Pie. — For a Christmas social for the Juniors, a Christmas pie is an admirable feature. Fill a large pan with sawdust, mixing up with it the presents which the Juniors have made for each other, or, if you do not wish to run the risk of invidious comparisons, simply place in the pan sticks of candy wrapped in tissue paper, or some other inexpensive gift, one for each Junior. Blindfold the Juniors in turn, and permit them to grope around in the sawdust until each has found a present. The sawdust pie should be covered with paper, pricked so as to make it look as much like a crust as possible, and with a slice cut out. It will add to the amusement if the Juniors draw slips of paper each containing a number, and put their thumb into the pie in the order of these numbers.

May Baskets. — A happy idea for a May Day prank comes from Massachusetts. Some Juniors of a certain society there concocted some dainty baskets, filled them with candy, flowers, or fruit, and, slipping in the names of the babies, the dear old grandfathers or grandmothers, or of those who were sick, they slyly hung the baskets on the door-knobs of the parish when it began to grow a little dark.

Childish Games. — Do not neglect the simple games so dear to the hearts of little children, such as jumping rope, bean-bags, drop the handkerchief, puss in the corner, tag, " button, button," feathers, come-see-come, blowing a feather, hunt the ring, going to Jerusalem, and a long list of others.

Speaking Books. — A very bright form of Junior entertainment, quite easily prepared, is the following : Dress the Juniors so as to represent books of various authors. Prepare large frames reaching from their shoulders to below their knees. Cover these frames in such a way that they shall appear like books, binding them and lettering them to correspond with the character assumed by the Junior.

When done, the book will be a hollow box open at top and bottom, with two bars across the inside which the Junior's hands may grasp, thus supporting the book. The Junior should be attired in appropriate costume, at least as to the head and that part of the body that shows below the book. If representing Shakespeare, for instance, a classic head-dress and dress should be worn. If representing Dickens, some famous character of his may be personated. If representing James Whitcomb Riley, a sunbonnet and rough shoes would be appropriate.

On the evening of the entertainment, each Junior is to come forward in turn and repeat some carefully memorized extract from the works of the author he represents. Music and songs chosen from the works of the authors, or in some way connected with them, may be interspersed ; and the whole will make a very enjoyable evening's entertainment.

A Rainbow Social. — The Juniors will rejoice in a rainbow social. It is conducted in this way : Decorate tables with the different colors of the rainbow, and assign to each its waiter ; these tables being placed at the side of the room, and the provisions set forth upon them. Arrange the chairs in the centre of the room in sections, each chair being tied with a bow of bright ribbon, all the chairs in one section being of the same color.

As the Juniors enter, present each with a card tied with a ribbon of the same color as one of the tables and the corresponding seats. A Junior whose duty this is will then usher the Juniors to the section corresponding with the color given them, and refreshments will be served them by the waiter from the table of the same color. Planned in this way, there is no confusion, and all are served.

Junior Gymnasts. — When the Junior meeting is not held on Sunday, the superintendent can very profitably keep the Juniors for half an hour after the prayer meeting for a drill in light gymnastics, if she or some friend is able to give it. One superintendent of whom I have heard utilizes this gymnastic drill in giving an annual gymnastic exhibition with her Juniors. This work will, of course, delight the boys especially.

Interest all Summer. — One of the best devices for retaining the interest of the Juniors during the summer is to prepare for some entertainment early in the fall. Assign the parts before the summer begins, and before any of the Juniors have scattered with their parents upon their summer vacations. Be sure that all the Juniors have some part in the entertainment.

During the summer, hold regular meetings for rehearsals. It is well to hold these meetings once a week, even though, as will probably be the case, you will not have all the Juniors who are to take part at any single meeting. The time and place of these rehearsals should be unvarying.

It will be surprising to see how anxious the Juniors will be to make a success of their entertainment, and at the same time, all unwittingly, of their summer Junior Endeavor society. The entertainment should be given the week before or after the fall term of school opens.

A Good Programme. — An enthusiastic Junior superintendent from Ireland has sent me the programme of a recent social of her society, which contains, among others, these suggestive items: Testimony from applicant for membership. Reception of the same, with reception hymn. Address of the chairman of the social committee. Solos. Readings. Temperance dialogue. A paper on the pledge. Recitations. Duet. An action song. A blackboard talk. Refreshments. Rallying hymn. "The prayer that Christ taught his disciples."

A Sweet Social. — A candy social will please the Juniors. All the members that can are requested to furnish home-made candy. This is sold during the social.

A Butterfly Social. — A form of social that will delight the Juniors is the butterfly social. Slight refreshments are to be served, and the waiters are to be dressed with butterfly wings made from delicately colored paper. The napkins on the table should be folded in butterfly designs. In a room near by, paper articles may be for sale; the attendants at the table, and the Juniors everywhere, as far as possible, being arrayed in butterfly costumes. A musical programme with songs by the Juniors will fill out a very pleasant evening.

Good Socials. — Here are some pleasant children's socials suggested by Mrs. Slocum: A China party, where Chinese games are to be played, the refreshments being cocoanut cakes, little cookies, and lemonade. A berry party. An "others" social, each member bringing some little delicacy for the sick.

A Jerusalem social, each Junior learning something about Jerusalem to tell at the social, the Juniors also forming a model of the Holy Land in a great pile of sand. For this the lookout committee will bring mirrors for the lakes and ponds, the prayer-meeting committee silver cord for the rivers, the missionary committee moss for the mountains, while the boys will whittle buildings for the cities. Each member will bring a contribution for missions in Jerusalem, or for some appropriate object.

A Dorcas social, the Juniors to bring cloth, which they will sew into garments, even the boys helping. A picture party, the members bringing cards and pictures to send to foreign missionaries for use in their work. A book social, the members bringing books and magazines to help the Sunday-school library, or the Endeavor library, or for other good causes. At this social there should be little talks and recitations and essays on books.

A barrel social, for the packing of old clothes in barrels to be sent to missionaries. A patchwork social, the members bringing blocks they have made at home, which they put together into a quilt.

A Field Day. — The boys especially will delight in athletic field days, to be held once a year; and there is no reason why they should not be made attractive also to the girls. A committee on games should be appointed from the older society, with possibly one representative from the Juniors. There should be careful rules strenuously insisted upon. Prizes may be offered, and gold and silver Junior badges are the best.

It will take away any sting of defeat if these prizes are given, not immediately after the games, but on the next Sunday at the Junior meeting, the superintendent, in presenting them, making appropriate remarks along the line of 1 Cor. 9: 24, 25, Paul's description of the athletic games that Christians carry on in their living. If possible, get some energetic and consecrated Christian athlete to make these remarks. Attach to each prize a card bearing the name of the winner and an appropriate text of Scripture.

A picnic may be arranged in connection with the field day, the Juniors bringing their luncheons. A Baptist Endeavor society that has tried the plan arranged the following events and rules : —

EVENTS.

For the boys: 50 yard dash; running high jump; swimming race; tub race.

For the girls: 50 yard dash.

For both: 25 yard backward dash; potato race; running broad jump; egg and spoon race.

RULES.

I. Handicaps shall be arranged in accordance with the judgment of the athletic committee.

II. Entries shall close at the time specified.

III.   The committee shall judge in regard to the number of events any contestant may enter.

IV.   Disputes shall be referred to the referee.

V.   Judgment of unfairness shall debar any contestant so convicted from further participation in the games.

A Review. — Either by itself, or in connection with the "Junior field day" just described, a review may be held of all the societies of a union or a district.   A commander-in-chief should be elected, with a staff, to be made up of one representative from each society.   These officers should lay out the plan of the day, and plan for the games, if any are held.

Let there be a flag-raising, and then the general review of the societies, the Juniors to be drawn up in martial array, and to march past a grand-stand where are standing the commissioned officers, the pastors, and guests.   The society that has the largest number of members in the parade, and shows the best discipline, should be given the honor of raising the flag, and of carrying it during the Christian Endeavor rallies for the next year.   As the flag is raised, the entire company should join in singing some patriotic song.

This review might be made the occasion of large ingatherings to the Junior society.

Shadow Pictures. — One very pleasant feature of a California Junior social was a set of shadow pictures, illustrating scenes from "Mother Goose," the children guessing with each picture what rhyme was represented.

A Giving Social. — On Thanksgiving Day a Kansas Junior society held a "giving social," when each Junior brought clothing or good things to eat to give away.   After their songs and recitations, the Juniors were divided into little companies, and carried all these things to seven different families who were sick or in need.   This is a social which might be held at any time of the year.   Of similar nature are "pound parties," the Juniors descending in force on some very poor family, each bringing a pound of some food or other useful article.

Game Socials. — Occasionally have a social to which each child is requested to bring some game for the entertainment of the others.   Fill the room with little tables on which the games may be played.   Appropriate amusements for Junior socials will be Jackstraws, Tiddledy Winks, Checkers, Halma, Go-bang, Dominoes, letter games like Logomachy, such games as Parchesi, Crockinole, Table Croquet, Tiddledy-Wink Tennis, and puzzles, such as Pigs in Clover.

A Bubble Social. — A bubble party will furnish one of the prettiest of amusements for a pleasant afternoon social that may be held on the lawn. Furnish each Junior with a bowl of strong soapsuds, re-enforced with glycerine to make the bubbles last, and give them also clay pipes. Many games may be played with these bubbles.

First institute a contest as to who can blow the largest bubble without its bursting, then as to whose bubble shall float the longest, then as to whose bubble shall rise the highest.

Give each Junior a fan, and divide the Juniors into sides. Let some one stand in the centre between the two lines, and blow a large bubble. The Juniors will then use their fans, each trying, while he remains in his place, to fan the bubble over to the other side and keep it there until it breaks. Another contest is for each side to send at the same time a bubble into the air, and try, by blowing upon it, which side can keep its bubble floating the longest time.

Basket Socials. — A basket social is thus arranged. Each girl belonging to the Junior society will bring lunch for two, daintily put up in a pretty basket. Attached to each basket will be two button-hole bouquets, to be worn when the basket is purchased. These baskets are to be ranged upon a table; and after the opening exercises and the games, some comical genius from the older society will sell the baskets. These are to be bought by the boys, who are not to know the owners of them. After each basket is bought, the purchaser will hunt up the owner and eat lunch with her.

A Mother Goose Social. — A Mother Goose entertainment is easily prepared. The children are to be dressed to represent the characters of the immortal nursery rhymes. One of the brightest women in the church should represent Mother Goose. The children should appear upon the stage one by one, each repeating or singing the rhyme he represents. To represent some of the rhymes, more than one Junior will be needed. At the close of the presentation there may be a Mother Goose march in which all the Juniors take part, and the evolutions may be as complex as the leader is able to design.

Scrap-Book Socials. — Scrap-book socials occupy the time very pleasantly and at the same time usefully. Leaves of cambric are to be cut beforehand of uniform size, and the Juniors will bring to the social a large supply of bright pictures of all kinds. The girls may be set to working the edges of the cambric leaves with bright worsteds. The boys will trim the pictures, and paste them neatly upon the leaves as they are finished. The girls will then bind the whole in handsome covers, and they will be taken or sent to the nearest children's hospital.

A Washington's Birthday Social. — A Washington's Birthday social will interest the Juniors. Decorate the room prettily with flags, bunting, and pictures of Washington, with other patriots. Present each person on entering with a little pasteboard hatchet, appropriately decorated and inscribed. Have a short patriotic programme made up of recitations, brief talks, with possibly a tableau or two, or a flag drill. Dress the Juniors in costumes resembling those of the Revolutionary times, and have them serve tea in memory of the Boston Tea Party, and little cakes baked in the shape of a hatchet.

A Doll's Fair. — An excellent entertainment for a Junior social is a doll's fair. As many dolls may be exhibited as can be obtained from the younger Juniors and their friends. Some may be made by the Juniors, and these should be placed in a separate section. There should also be a paper doll booth. The dolls may be arranged in attractive groups, such as a wedding party, a tea party, a school, a " babies' table," or " an old woman in the shoe." There will be a table for curious dolls, or, maybe, for dolls of other nations. There may be a hospital for cracked dolls and broken dolls, laid out in little beds, with doll nurses in white caps bending over them. It will add much interest to the affair if a set of rhymes is prepared for each Junior who is in charge of a booth. The Junior may rehearse the lines descriptive of her exhibition. An interesting side-show is an exhibition of live dolls, to which an admission fee of five cents may be charged. These dolls are children, made to look as much like dolls as possible. One of the Junior boys will wind them up and exhibit them. If a small admission fee is charged, and especially if there is an auctioning of the dolls, quite a large sum may easily be realized.

A Babies' Photograph Social. — The social committee will collect, for this social, photographs of all the Juniors taken at as early an age as possible. These pictures are fastened on the wall encircling the room in which the social is to be held. Number the photographs in order, and give to each Junior at the social a pencil, and a slip of paper containing the same numbers. Opposite each number the Junior is to place his guesses at the names of the persons to whom the photographs belong. The social committee, after examining these slips, will give some honor to the person who has made the most successful guesses.

For a variation of this idea, try a reception given by the Junior society to the members of the older Christian Endeavor society. A series of pictures will be hung on the wall, the photographs of the older Endeavorers when they were of Junior age. These photographs are to be obtained without the knowledge of the persons they represent. The pictures of the girls are all to be numbered, and the young men of the society are each to escort to lunch the girl whose number is given him — first finding her!

" Social Evenings." — Junior workers will find a great many hints for Junior socials in a book entitled *Social Evenings*, by the author of this manual. It is published by the United Society of Christian Endeavor, and sold for thirty-five cents. It contains a hundred and forty-two pages, with more than one hundred and fifty games and entertainments, many of them simple enough for the Juniors, and some of them especially prepared for their use.

CHAPTER XXV.

THE BIRTHDAY COMMITTEE.

The Birthday Committee. — The chief duties of the birthday committee are to make a list of the birthdays of the members of the society, arranging them in the order of their occurrence throughout the year, to announce at the beginning of each meeting the names of the Juniors whose birthdays fall on the coming week, to keep the birthday boxes in which are placed the birthday offerings, to remind the Juniors whose birthdays are to be celebrated on next Sunday of those offerings, and to keep these Juniors in special remembrance in their prayers during the entire week. Besides the birthdays of the Juniors, the society will do well to remember, in some pleasant way, with gifts or otherwise, the birthdays of their pastor, of his wife, of the Sunday-school superintendent, and of the Junior superintendent. Christmas is Christ's birthday; and it would be pleasant, if the committee is able for the responsibility, to place the Christmas meeting in its especial charge.

On the Board. — The birthday committee will find it very helpful to put on the blackboard each Sunday the names of the Endeavorers whose birthdays fall during the coming week, the superintendent at each meeting requesting the Juniors to offer especial prayers for the happiness and spiritual welfare of these Juniors. The names, being before the Endeavorers during the meeting, are firmly fixed on the memory.

Birthday Pennies. — Often the Juniors give to the society, on their birthday anniversaries, as many pennies as they are years old. In some societies the members stand and sing a birthday prayer, while the member whose birthday is observed comes forward and drops his pennies into the birthday box. It is a good idea to keep this money apart, and use it either for the benefit of sick members who are poor, or for Christmas, which is Christ's birthday, when the money may be spent in making presents to needy ones, who will thus be given a happy Christmas.

A Birthday Hymn. — Choose a birthday hymn, such as No. 51 in " Gospel Hymns No. 6," " I belong to Jesus," and have this hymn sung on every occasion when a Junior's birthday is remembered.

A Birthday Celebration. — An impressive way of celebrating the birthdays of the Juniors is this : Let the birthday committee report the name. The Junior rises and stands while the children sing one verse of the hymn, " God will take care of you," No. 52, in " Junior Christian Endeavor Hymns." The superintendent then offers a short prayer for the Junior, committing him and all his interests to the Saviour. After this the Juniors sing the last verse of the same hymn.

Another Birthday Observance. — Some Juniors of Baltimore have this interesting observance in connection with their remembrance of the birthdays of the different members. At each meeting prayer is offered for those boys and girls whose birthdays occur during the week ; and all the Juniors are requested to think of these members on their birthdays during the week, and to pray for them. It is surprising how many do thus pray for each other.

A Birthday Chair. — A pleasant bit of ceremony is to set apart a particular chair draped with flowers or ribbon by the birthday committee, which is to be occupied during the meeting by the Junior whose birthday is to be celebrated. In some societies, this fortunate Junior is presented on this anniversary with a copy of the New Testament. It is always appropriate for the superintendent to give him, before the society, a few earnest and loving words of advice for the coming year.

A Personal Letter. — A personal birthday letter sent by the superintendent in her own handwriting will be greatly appreciated by the Junior who receives it. It may contain a pretty birthday card with a suitable verse of Scripture, and the Junior may be asked to make that verse his motto for the coming year.

CHAPTER XXVI.

THE SUNSHINE COMMITTEE.

The Committee Work. — The work of the sunshine committee is quite impossible to define, because it depends almost entirely upon the surroundings of the societies and the Endeavorers. This committee is to do any good Samaritan work that suggests itself, anything that is helpful, and cheering, and Christlike. Their special care is the poor of the congregation and of the neighborhood, and, of these, chiefly the children. They are set to minister to the sick, and should work with the flower committee in their beautiful ministry. They should co-operate with the relief committee of the older society, who should ask the Juniors of the sunshine committee to go with them in their calls upon poor families where there are children.

The pastor should keep in mind this branch of the Junior work, and make the chairman of this committee one of his active helpers. The doctors who belong to the church will be able to tell the committee who are sick, if they themselves cannot find out from their parents or their friends. The church officers, also, will be glad to direct the Juniors to families where their Christlike helpfulness will be appreciated.

A Home Committee. — Above all things, the sunshine committee is a home committee. Teach the children that while the Juniors are all bound by their pledge to make home as happy a place as kindness, love, helpfulness, and unselfishness can make it, yet the members of the sunshine committee are in a peculiar manner committed to such endeavors. The superintendent cannot talk too often about the little foxes that do so much to spoil the home vine — peevishness, fretfulness, crossness, the hasty word, the sluggish spirit, the willingness to impose upon the good nature of others. All these things the sunshine committee should be set to conquering in themselves, and should be taught that this conquest must come before they can successfully bring sunshine into the lives of others.

" And Co." — Members of the sunshine committee may well work in couples, or even in trios. For instance, one boy belonging to a Junior society of which I have heard was sick, and was visited three times a day by the Juniors, one member reading to him, another taking him delicacies for his dinner, while a third ran in to tell him the news.

Worth Remembering. — The following excellent sunshine committee motto is used by one Presbyterian Junior society. I commend it to others. " I expect to pass through this world but once. Any good thing, therefore, that I can do, or any kindness that I can show to any fellow-being, let me do it now. Let me not defer it nor neglect it, for I shall not pass this way again."

In Their Hands. — One superintendent of wide experience makes it her rule to accompany her Juniors on their first visits to the sick and others under their care. Afterwards, however, she seldom goes with them, and labors to make the Juniors feel their individual responsibility. This trust they appreciate, and are faithful to it.

To the Old and Infirm. — The ministry to the aged of the congregation and neighborhood is one of the most beautiful ways in which the sunshine committee can be helpful. The superintendent may ask the Juniors to volunteer for this service, or the superintendent may appoint certain members each week to do this delightful work. They can read many books for those whose eyes are failing. They can tell the news. They can sing their merry songs, and in other ways can carry the freshness of childhood into the lives that too often are desolate and lonely.

Serenades. — The sunshine committee will sometimes give much pleasure by an out-of-doors serenade on some aged person, or some " shut-in." They should get together the singers of the society, and, after practising one or two bright songs, should go to the homes they may select and sing them.

Shut-In Work. — The Juniors will be especially interested in the work of the Shut-In Society, whose secretary, Miss Monroe of Ashland, Mass., will be glad to tell any superintendent about its workings. The Juniors will write letters to these shut-ins, and send them pictures and books.

A Constant Reminder. — A Tennessee Junior society does not save its consecration basket for the consecration meeting, but sets it by the door at every meeting. The Juniors, as they come in, drop into it all sorts of good things and useful things; and at the close of the meeting the sunshine committee examines the contents of the basket and decides to which of the objects of their care these gifts shall go.

Practical Charity. —In no way can the beauty of charity be so clearly shown the children as when they are brought into actual contact with the recipients of their gifts. Thanksgiving is an excellent occasion for this. Some societies are in the habit of collecting from the Juniors money with which fruit, candy, and nuts are bought for children in families that would probably be too poor to afford such luxuries on Thanksgiving day.

A Thanksgiving committee is appointed, whose members meet at the home of the superintendent, fill their baskets, and go about among the homes of the poor the day before Thanksgiving, distributing these presents. This Thanksgiving committee reports at the next business meeting of the society.

A Merry Christmas. — Do not let Christmas pass without interesting your Juniors in making Christmas presents for poor children who will get none in other ways. Among the articles they can make are comforts, scrap-books, mittens, dolls' dresses, etc.

Some Noble Fun. — A way of distributing gifts to the poor that will especially commend itself to the fun-loving Juniors is the leaving of baskets of good things upon the door-step. Let the Juniors ring the bell and then scurry away, watching from some hiding-place the results of their beneficent stratagem.

A Food Store. — Your Junior society may like to establish a food closet, a sort of storehouse of canned fruit, flour, and similar articles of food, from which they can draw for the relief of cases of need that come to their notice.

No Pharisees. — In the sunshine committee work that is done for the poor, the Juniors should be carefully taught by their superintendent to exhibit nothing but a spirit of the ten-

derest sympathy. No feeling should enter their hearts that they
are better than the poor people whom they help and cheer.
The superintendent will do well to show his charges how much
of the world's poverty is due not to fault but to misfortune.

Child Ministries. — If your Juniors belong to a large city,
you should certainly interest them in the children's hospitals
and orphans' homes. Take them occasionally with you to visit
the unfortunate children, and see that they do not go empty-
handed. They will like to carry their presents and give them
in person, tell stories to the children, and play games with
them, and sing to them, before they go, some beautiful song
like, " There is sunshine in my soul."

After several visits from the children a Junior society may be
organized in the institution itself, which will furnish a fresh tie
between the favored and the unfavored young people.

If this cannot be done, at any rate these hospital children
should always be given an invitation to become members of the
Junior society on their recovery. Some very happy acquisitions
have thus been made.

A Lesson In Kindness. — When your Juniors have picnics
or other social gatherings, invite to join with them some of the
children of orphans' homes or similar institutions that may exist
near by, and teach the Juniors to make the little strangers have
a pleasant time.

A Hospital Visitation. — A hospital service for Christmas
time will be a great pleasure to the Juniors, and will furnish
them with an initiation into practical Christian work. Teach
them a supply of sweet Christmas carols. Give them sprays of
evergreen or holly tied with bright red ribbon, each spray bearing a card on which is written or printed a Christmas Bible
verse or a bit of helpful poetry. Carrying these to the cots,
wishing each sick one a Merry Christmas, and singing their
happy carols, the Juniors will pass through the wards, leaving
behind them brightness and good cheer that will last for many
a day, and carrying away with them a thoughtful spirit and a
truer appreciation of what Christmas means.

Comfort Sheets. — The Juniors will be greatly interested in
the making of comfort sheets, which at the same time will do
much good. Let the scrap-book committee get sheets of bristol

board in some pretty tints. These can be obtained more cheaply from a printing-office than from a stationery store. Cut them in stripes five by six inches, and divide them among the members of the committee.

Let these paste neatly upon them beautiful poems suitable for tired workers, weary watchers, patient sufferers, mourning friends, or for the aged or sick. Upon the back let bright, cheery pictures be pasted, or let some flower or pretty scene be painted. These comfort sheets should be distributed by the sunshine committee to the many who will be helped by them.

Hospital Screens. — A good thing for Juniors to make for the hospitals is a screen, for weary eyes to look at, and for the interception of the sun's brightest rays. These screens should be ornamented with bright pictures, especially with funny ones.

Story Envelopes. — Story envelopes for hospitals are easily prepared, and will be of the greatest service. These consist of stout manilla envelopes, each containing three pleasant stories.

Hospital Committees. — Some societies have hospital committees. The main purpose of this committee is to gather all the maimed, crippled, dilapidated, and otherwise disabled dolls, which the boys glue together and make solid, while the girls furnish them with fresh dresses. Then they are sent to the children's hospitals. Sometimes this hospital committee makes scrap-books, or covers separate leaves of paper with bright pictures, the latter being more easily held in the hand, decorates fans with funny or pretty pictures, stuffs pillows with bits of paper and covers them, and in many other ways cares for the pleasure and the comfort of the poor children in the hospital.

About Christmas time the Juniors should be made to feel that their own Christmas is incomplete unless they have helped to furnish a merry Christmas to those who otherwise would have a sad one. Fruit and clothing, toys and books, with the loving messages of the Juniors, and their own sunshiny faces when they can present the gifts in person, will do good like medicine.

A Good Present. — A nice Christmas present that the Junior society may give to the Sunday-school superintendent, the pastor, or any one they wish to honor, is a neat linen table scarf, on which each Junior's autograph has been outlined in silk. The corner should contain the Junior badge, embroidered in pretty colors.

Printed Helps. — In *The Junior Golden Rule* a great deal of sunshine committee work is suggested each month. Little prizes are offered, for instance, for the best-decorated fan that is sent in for the children in the hospitals; for the best-dressed doll, this to have the same destination; for the neatest and prettiest scrap-book, and the like. Moreover, the letters from the children, as well as the reports of Junior work given in the older *Golden Rule*, are full of suggestions.

CHAPTER XXVII.

THE SCRAP-BOOK COMMITTEE.

Junior Scrap-books. — Every Junior society should have a little library of scrap-books for the use of the different committees, and of these the scrap-book committee should have charge. The material will come, of course, mainly from *The Golden Rule* and *The Junior Golden Rule;* and it will be well for the society to have two copies of each, for clipping articles that may appear on opposite sides of the same leaf.

Each committee should have a scrap-book, which may he kept by the chairman of the committee. The material for filling the book, however, will be collected by the scrap-book committee, sorted, and the appropriate clippings given to each chairman for pasting in his book. The missionary committee might well have books for the different missionary countries, one in charge of each member of the committee; and to these books should flow a constant stream of bright anecdotes, useful facts, and helpful suggestions.

Hospital Books. — The scrap-book committee will find it a delightful, as well as a helpful task, to make large numbers of scrap-books, light and easily held in the hand, to be sent to hospitals. It will be a good plan to classify the material for these books. One may be a book of jokes, another a book of comforting poems, a third may contain nothing but helpful prose, and a fourth a collection of short stories. Picture scrap-books for children's hospitals, or scrap-books for the same institutions containing only poems and stories that the children will enjoy, may also be made. There may be a book of Brownie pictures, a flower book, an animal book, etc. In fine, there is here quite an unlimited field of blessed endeavor.

Scrap-Leaves. — Scrap-leaves are often better than scrap-books. These scrap-leaves are simply large sheets of paper or of cloth, covered with pictures. They should be of uniform size, and placed in a neat album whose sides can be tied together. Not only are these scrap-leaves easier for the sick children in the hospitals to handle, but they are better for the Juniors to make, because the Juniors are not so easily tired in preparing them as they would be in manufacturing each a large scrap-book.

A Scrap-book Evening. — Under the direction of the scrap-book committee the entire society may spend a happy evening once or twice a year. A large amount of material having been collected by the committee and sorted in different piles, near each of which is placed a large bowl of paste and a paste brush, the Juniors may be set to pasting these clippings in different scrap-books. One may have a pile of jokes for a scrap-book of jokes; another may make a scrap-book of poetry; another a China scrap-book, or a temperance scrap-book.

It is not necessary, by the way, to buy regular scrap-books for this work. Any well-bound book, part of whose leaves may be torn out, may be used for the purpose. Old government documents, patent office reports, and the like, are just the thing. For many purposes a light pamphlet will make an acceptable scrap-book, especially if the pamphlet, after being filled with scraps, receives a cloth or pasteboard cover.

Scrap-Envelopes. — Set the scrap-book committee to sorting all the scraps it can gather itself or obtain from its friends, placing them in a set of envelopes on which are written the different classes of scraps. Keep one envelope, for example, for helpful poems; another for bright stories; one might be a temperance envelope; another, a missionary envelope; another, an envelope for the sick; another, a Bible envelope.

These envelopes should be stout, so that they can be passed around from house to house. They should not contain so much that they cannot easily be read through in the course of a week, and returned on the next Sunday. This will make it necessary to have more than one envelope for many of the subjects. A wide-awake scrap-book committee can do much good by lending these envelopes to persons who can make good use of them.

A Scrap Prayer Meeting. — For an occasional variety, it is pleasant to invite the Juniors to be on the lookout for clippings bearing upon a certain topic, which should be appointed several weeks ahead. At the meeting when this topic is considered, each Junior will bring and read some scrap of poetry, or a little anecdote or fact illustrative of the topic. The chairman of the scrap-book committee might appropriately be the leader for this meeting.

Scrap-books as Presents. — If the society desires to make a present to the pastor, the pastor's wife, the Sunday-school superintendent, or others, it will find a scrap-book, appropriately made, very acceptable. Many a pastor, for example, would make good use of a large collection of helpful poems. Many a Sunday-school superintendent would enjoy a well-arranged scrap-book composed of clippings from *The Sunday School Times* and the denominational Sunday-school journals.

A Paper for Each. — In all this scrap-book work it will greatly simplify matters if each member of the scrap-book committee takes under his charge a single one of the journals from which the committee expects to get most of its material. In addition, the society should be canvassed, that the committee may learn what papers and magazines not accessible to any of its members are taken in the families of the other Juniors; and, as far as may be, those Juniors should be interested in gathering helpful clippings from those periodicals also.

The Superintendent's Scraps. — Every Junior superintendent should have a Junior scrap-book, in which should be placed clippings from *The Golden Rule* and other Christian Endeavor papers, as well as from Junior leaflets, and any helpful articles, poems, and the like. The scrap-book should be divided into appropriate divisions, such as " music," " missions," " temperance," " lookout," " prayer-meeting," " social," " general," " committee work," " Bible drills," " incidents," " the pledge," " boys," " business." The chapter heads of this Manual will furnish suggestions for the subdivisions of such a book.

Sometimes it will be better to use a set of stout envelopes, fittingly labelled, each large enough to hold such pamphlets on Junior work as the United Society may publish from time to time.

Besides these scraps regarding methods, keep scraps of all kinds of good literature. Nearly every Junior topic can be illustrated with appropriate poems, and you will find that Juniors delight in committing these to memory and in repeating them. If you bear in mind the topics for several months to come, you will find many poems suitable for their illustration in the current periodicals. These scraps also should be classified in envelopes marked with the main subject of the poems, such as "forgiveness," "kindness," "love," "animals," "Christmas," etc.

CHAPTER XXVIII.

THE FLOWER COMMITTEE.

Working Together. — The members of the flower committee should be those who are congenial; and this may be brought about without any pandering to the caste spirit, and without any fostering of cliques. The flower committee are frequently thrown together; and, if they like each other, their excursions over fields and through woods will be tenfold enjoyable.

Taking Turns. — There are few churches in which the older society does not carry on the beautiful ministry of flowers, decorating the pulpit on the Lord's Day. It will be best for the older society to share this pleasure and duty with the Juniors. Let the Juniors decorate the pulpit on one Sunday and the older society the next, alternating. In this way a not hurtful rivalry will be brought about, and each society will be less heavily burdened.

Co-operating with the Pastor. — It is not always that the flower committee need know the theme of the pastor's sermon in order that its decorations may be suitable. Occasionally, however, the decorations might be quite incongruous with the subject of his sermon, and at other times a changed order of decoration might greatly assist the effect of the sermon. At any rate, the superintendent should ask the pastor to let the flower committee know at any time when he wishes special kinds of decoration in order to allude to it in his sermon.

Special Decorations. — On Christmas, Easter, Thanksgiving, Children's Day, and similar holidays, let the Juniors join with the older Endeavorers in decorating the church. It will be a good plan if a certain part of the church be set apart for the Juniors to decorate all by themselves.

Decorate the Junior Room. — The work of most flower committees is expended, and very appropriately, almost entirely upon the church, the Sunday-school room also occasionally re-

ceiving a few flowers. It may be well, once in a while, to decorate the Junior meeting-room too. For special occasions, such
as graduation day and Christian Endeavor Day, this should
always be done.

For the Sick. — Whatever use of flowers the committee may
make, let them imitate the beautiful practice of the older committees and distribute the flowers, after they have served their
purpose, to the hospitals and to the sick of the congregation.
The Juniors may go in a body to the hospitals, and, when the
attendants permit, sing one of their songs in each ward, afterwards distributing the flowers. Scripture verses may be repeated, or the Lord's Prayer said in concert. It will be far
better if the Juniors themselves carry the flowers to the sick.
With each bouquet that is sent out, let a helpful verse of Scripture go. These verses should be written on cardboard, the
information being added that the flowers are the gift of the
Junior Society of ——— Church. The cardboard should be tied
to the bouquet.

Lending and Giving. — The lending of flowers will furnish
one of the helpful methods this committee may use. Many a
sick room could be brightened by a rose in full bloom, a lily, or
a hyacinth. The committee might also raise some of these
plants to give away. Instances have been known where the
coming of a plant into a poor and dirty tenement has worked a
complete moral revolution.

Birthday Flowers. — The flowers that are not needed for
the sick or the hospitals should be sent to the pastor's study,
and once in a while a particularly nice bouquet should be made
all for him. Similar delicate attention should signalize his birthday, and the birthday of the Sunday-school superintendent, and
the pastor's wife, and of any one else the society wishes to
honor. In this the flower and birthday committees should
co-operate.

Junior Horticulture. — There is no reason why the Junior
society, any more than the older society, should go to the large
expense of buying flowers that their own members might raise
with equal pleasure and profit. Let the flower committee see to
this. They might buy small plants, and distribute them among
the members to care for. The same thing might be done with

packages of choice flower seeds. It would be a pleasant plan for the flower committee to establish a flower garden, taking a corner of some yard offered to them, and working in it all together, or taking turns.

Variety and Simplicity. — It should be the aim of the flower committee to introduce as many novel effects as possible in the decorations of the church. Certainly the methods of decorating should be different on consecutive Sundays. Teach the Juniors the value of simple decorations, especially the use of large groups of flowers all of one kind. Show them that grains and grasses produce beautiful decorative effects, as well as ferns, autumn leaves, and any green foliage, and, in the proper season, almost any kind of fruit.

The Church Yard. — One of the most helpful things a Junior Christian Endeavor society can do, if it has an energetic flower committee, is to take charge of flower-beds about the church. These will serve the double purpose of beautifying the grounds and supplying flowers for the pulpit.

Flower Shows. — The flower committee may earn money for missions or for the general purposes of the society by organizing a flower show. This, of course, must be planned for many weeks beforehand, and the co-operation of the entire society will be necessary. The results of these weeks of careful tending are to be brought together, arranged on tables and shelves in attractive ways, the room being decorated also with tissue paper and similar adornments. If the affair is well advertised, and if the plants are auctioned off by a bright member of the older society, a neat sum will be gained.

Flower Meetings. — Flower meetings are very helpful in the Junior society. Ask the Juniors to bring flowers, accompanying each, if they can, with a Bible text about that flower. Or, if the flower they have to bring is not mentioned in the Bible, let them bring with it, at least, some flower text. The flowers should be given to the sick. The superintendent may talk about the flowers mentioned in the Bible. She may tell stories about flowers and their helpfulness. Some of the Juniors may recite flower poems, and songs about flowers can always be found.

These meetings may be named after the flowers that happen

to be then in bloom, and each Junior may come wearing one of the flowers after which the meeting is named. Thus there might be daisy meetings, violet meetings, lily meetings, rose meetings, aster meetings, or chrysanthemum meetings.

A Flower Salute. — For many public occasions a flower salute will make a pretty exercise, and of this the flower committee may appropriately take charge. The salute originated, I believe, with Rev. F. B. Everitt of New Jersey. The children stand in a row facing the audience, in their right hands small bouquets, and in their left handkerchiefs. The pianist gives the signals, playing merely the four chords in any key, and the octave chord. This is the salute: —

First chord, flowers to lips.

Second chord, flowers extended in the right hand as if a kiss were thrown, while at the same time the Juniors step forward on the right foot.

Third chord, flowers in position the same as before, the Juniors waving their handkerchiefs briskly with the left hand.

Fourth chord, the Juniors return to their first position, the flowers and handkerchiefs at the side.

Octave chord, all are seated.

CHAPTER XXIX.

COMMITTEE WORK IN GENERAL.

Why Junior Committees ? — I once read an article whose writer argued that committees are harmful in a Junior society. She urged various reasons. One is that the superintending of the committees is a severe drain on the superintendent's time. The answer is, that if it is too much for the superintendent, she should obtain helpers from the Young People's society. These aids would learn many a valuable lesson while overseeing the Junior committee work.

The second objection was that " if the children do efficient work upon committees, it is too great a tax upon them, added to their other duties. Add to the demands of their school work, the study of music or painting, their household duties, the running of errands, then the hour spent in the Junior meeting, besides Sabbath school and other church services, and they surely have enough without committee work." The response is that the committee work does for the child what none of these other duties can accomplish. It is the child's training in organized, practical religious work. Better drop something else, if need be, than relinquish this. But in reality this work. if rightly conducted, becomes as interesting and enjoyable as play.

The third objection was that " the committees, if we have them, should be trained to do thorough work ; for what is worth doing at all is worth doing well. The lookout committee is considered a very important one, but to my mind it is unwise to put children on this committee at all. We well know how carefully and prayerfully our older ones have to do this work, and even then there is danger of doing harm. It is a delicate matter to speak to others about being derelict in duty, and children are very outspoken. Then it has seemed to me that a good deal of the Pharisaical spirit may be developed by watching the other members in a criticising way, to see who have not done their duty."

In reply, let it be said that the child's outspoken way is, more often than not, the Christlike and best way. A wise superintendent will need, of course, to guard against the Pharisaical spirit; but her work will not be in half so much danger from it as it would be if her flock were older. The earlier children are taught that they are their brothers' keepers, the more likely are they to grow up loving, helpful, frank, and sympathetic men and women.

The final objection was couched in these words: "There is danger that the committee work may come to seem the important part of the society, while the spiritual should always be first. We have older Christians that are ready to do work that can be done with the hands and head and feet, but stop when it comes to the heart work, or spiritual part. When the children enter the Young People's society they can be placed on committees with older ones, and there be trained for this part of the work." The misconception of committee work shown here is the fundamental difficulty that led to the writing of the article. The writer does not see how profoundly spiritual committee work in a Christian Endeavor society is. If it is done merely with the hands and head and feet, and not with the heart, it is a failure, in Junior, Young People's, and Senior society alike. It is in the committee work of the Junior society that the prayers are made vivid, the Bible verses brought in touch with life, the joy of service disclosed, the spiritual life at the same time drawn upon and quickened. It gives added zest to the society, practicality to its theories, and adds works to its faith. It is not the chief essential to a successful Junior society, but it is an essential.

Each on a Committee. — If it is necessary, in a Young People's society, to place every member on some one committee, how doubly necessary is it in a Junior society? These wide-awake youngsters differ conspicuously from their elders in the fact that they are miserable unless given something to do. There is one committee on which, after a liberal allowance of members to the other committees, all remaining members may be placed; that is the sunshine committee. There is infinite scope for their ministry of loving words and deeds.

Novel Committees. — A consecrated ingenuity, however, will be forced to this "lumping" only in the largest societies. The superintendent can invent committees, temporary committees, changing their names and purposes with the changing needs of church and society. There may be "surprise committees," to do pleasant little needed things for the church and society, and bring them out as jolly surprises. There may be "pastor's aid committees," to do little tasks under his direction, or the direction of the pastor's wife. There may be "sewing committees" among the girls, to make useful things to give away. There may be "hospital committees" among the boys, to mend broken toys to be sent to children's hospitals. There may be "scrap-book committees," to get up bright and entertaining scrap-books for the same purpose. These and other novel committees are fully described in this Manual. Every member on some committee — that's an essential to the highest success in a Junior society; and it may be brought about.

How to Appoint. — How should we appoint our committees? One interesting method has lately been proposed. Let the superintendent call for volunteers, naming each committee in order, and asking who would like to serve on that committee, getting a boy and a girl alternately. Possibly this is as good a way as any to set the ball rolling; but when once the committees are formed, it would be well to have a regular rotation of service in them. Why not? The Christian Endeavor idea is to get as many people as possible to work for Christ in as many ways as possible, and it is a great mistake to keep the best members always on the most important committees. Both best members and worst members need the stimulus of new work, and it is hard to say which need it most. One of the most important things in determining the composition of a Junior committee is to see that you have placed upon it some very timid members as well as some who are bold and enterprising. Look very carefully to the balancing of your committees.

On New Committees. — Matters should be so arranged that at the end of the term each Junior should enter a new committee, and one, if possible, on which he has never served before. Of course, no one would advocate the bodily transference of the lookout committee, say, into the work of the prayer-meeting committee. That would keep the same set of workers together, and would be a bad thing for the social spirit of the society. All that is urged is that each Junior should be assigned, if possible, to a new committee at the end of each term of office.

With this method there can be no complaint at the assignments made by the superintendent, because each member will understand that all kinds of work will come to him in his turn. The officers will remain, to be nominated by the superintendent and elected by the society, as before.

Many Committees. — Put every member of the society upon some committee, but do not have the committees so large as to be unwieldy. Effect this object by having a good many committees.

Be the Silent Partner. — Though the superintendent may meet with the committees of the society, and, indeed, should so meet as often as possible, yet the chairmen of those committees should conduct the meetings, even when she is present, otherwise they will not feel half so much responsibility as they should. In fact, the great danger of committee work is that too much of it shall be done by the superintendent, and too little of it by the children themselves. Learn to trust the powers of the children. The more you learn of their bright brains and ready zeal, the more you will confide in them. It is your part to plan, advise, direct. You must show them just what to do and how to do it, and this work will often be more laborious than to accomplish the tasks of the committee yourself. The purpose of the Junior society, however, you must remember, is not to get work done, but to train workers for the tasks of the coming years. Make it your fundamental principle in committee work never to do anything yourself that you can, by earnest endeavor, get the children themselves to accomplish.

In Charge of Committees. — If you are compelled to be absent during the summer, and can in no other way provide for the continuance of the meetings, try the plan of giving the several meetings into the charge of the different chairmen of the Junior committees. You will be pleased to see how well they will respond to this responsibility, and how much strength they will gain from this courageous endeavor.

The Older Endeavorers. — The best plan I know of for

holding the monthly committee meetings is to put each under the special superintendence of some member of the corresponding committee from the older society. It is asking too much of any superintendent to expect her to be present at each monthly committee meeting of all her committees. The plan of committee meetings I think best is the following : —

After the consecration meeting, or after some other assigned meeting held at a regular point in the month, the society breaks into committee groups, which go to different parts of the room, or to different rooms, each with its member of the corresponding committee from the Young People's society to help and suggest. It is not a bad plan, after half an hour's discussion and consultation, for these committees to come together again as a united society. At this time the chairmen of the various committees will bring before the society any plan upon which the advice and decision of the entire society may be desired.

Older Chairmen. — I believe that it is almost always best to permit the Juniors to be chairmen of the Junior committees, at the same time appointing members of the older society to act as overseers, or committee superintendents. A plan proposed by Mrs. Scudder, however, may meet the need of certain localities ; and so I mention it. She advocates that these older Endeavorers be appointed chairmen of the various Junior committees, and act as instructors of the Juniors, and that the superintendent herself be the chairman of the prayer-meeting committee, as that is the most important.

Committees of Two. — It is better, in a small Junior society, to have very small committees and many of them, rather than few committees with a large number of members. A new society of which I hear starts with twelve Juniors, divided into six committees of two members each, one of whom is chairman.

Committee Sundays. — It is a good plan to set apart certain committees for each Sunday of the month, so that all the committees will have a regular Sunday for their monthly committee meetings. The names of these committees may well be printed on the topic card following the announcement of the leader.

Only Chairmen. — In small Junior societies it has sometimes been found best not to divide the society into committees, but to appoint simply the chairmen of the usual committees, requesting each chairman to consider the entire society his committee for the accomplishment of the work ordinarily assigned to him. When the missionary committee, for example, would have work to do, the chairman of that committee calls a meeting of the entire society, and so with all the other committees.

Prayer Always. — It is a good rule never to have a committee meeting without prayer. This point deserves a paragraph to itself.

All Ready for Work. — One little Junior of Washington, D.C., enthusiastically cried at her first Junior meeting of the year: "Oh, I should like to be on every single committee, and work just as hard!" That is the right spirit to show. Try to inculcate it in all the committee work your Juniors undertake.

Honor Them. — Our Junior societies should recognize, more than they do, honest work on committees. It is well occasionally for the superintendent to give a little prize for the best committee service, or in some other way to honor publicly the best committee workers.

Monthly Committees. — It is a question how long Junior committees should serve. Several societies have found it profitable to have a rotation in committee work once a month, especially in the lookout committee. The argument for long terms of committees in the Young People's society is that only thus is it possible to form and develop wise and far-reaching plans. In a Junior society, however, the conserving and continuing of effort is provided for by the existence of a continuous superintendent, and long terms of office in the committees are not so necessary.

Any experienced superintendent, of course, knows the relief which is felt when a committee has been developed to the point of partial or entire independence, so that it will do its work well without continuous oversight. It is a great temptation to keep such members in office for a long time; and, of course, they should be kept in office long enough to become thoroughly at home in the work.

But the growth of any society, as a whole and as individual members, depends on rotation of work — on dropping the easy and familiar tasks, and taking up new and difficult ones. And especially in a Junior society much of the interest depends on keeping the work fresh, and making things lively. It will almost always be found better to give a Junior a short term in lookout-committee work, and then a second term after an interval of some other work, than to keep him at the same work for a long time. The change will rest him, and enliven him, and he will come back to his old work with new zest.

From all these considerations it would appear wise to shorten the terms of Junior officers and committees, if not to one month, at least to a period shorter than the terms used in the older societies.

Committee Drill Meetings. — An occasional committee drill meeting would be very helpful to a Junior society. It may be conducted in the following way. All parts, of course, should be carefully prepared beforehand.

At the meeting let the different committees sit together. The superintendent, after preliminary exercises, calls on the committees in order. As she names a committee, the members of that committee rise. Then the superintendent questions them. "Lookout committee, what is your work for Christ and the church ?"

Says one Junior (these answers have been given out at the previous meeting), "To get new members for our society." Says her neighbor, "To explain, to all who would like to join, just what the pledge means." Say the other members in order: "To look after absent members, especially when they are absent from the consecration meeting." "To look after the members who seem not to be keeping their pledge." "To give invitations to outsiders to attend our meetings." "To urge the associate members to become active."

After all these have spoken, the committee repeats in concert a bit of Scripture appropriate to its work, such as Phil. 2: 3, 4, and then sits down. The superintendent makes a little talk about the duties of the lookout committee, the spirit in which it should work, and the spirit in which the other members should work with it, and receive its help. Then there are a few sentence prayers from the Juniors, asking God to help this committee, to give it wisdom, to keep it faithful, and to help the society to receive its words and warnings in the right spirit. Then a hymn is sung, appropriate to the lookout committee, like " What shall the harvest be ? " or " Will Jesus find us watching ? " In the same manner let all the other committees be treated.

It would be a capital plan to select some good, bright member from each of the corresponding committees of the Young People's society, and have him present, to say a few words of love and encouragement to the Juniors who are engaged in the same work. If your Juniors are at all skilled in talking, it would be a capital plan, after each committee has told what it is trying to do, to ask the society in general to tell what the society ought to do to help that especial committee.

Committee Reports. The Junior society that is not training its members to make regular written reports is preparing trouble for the Young People's society into which that Junior society will grow. It is very easy to get the Juniors to make reports, if you go about it in the right way; and that Sunday of the month when the reports are given will be looked forward to with great interest.

It will not be found advisable to seek the same kind of reports from all committees. Each committee, in fact, should have a unique way of presenting the results of its work. The sunshine committee, for instance, would soon become priggish if it reported in the ordinary way the good deeds done by its members.

Here is an excellent method for sunshine committee reports. Let each member of the committee write out, for the encouragement and pleasure of the society, in simple and reverent language, an account of the helpful deeds to which he has been prompted, during the month, by membership in the sunshine committee. It would be a good thing to add an account of one or two good deeds the member has noticed in others. As no names are to be mentioned, and as no one, not even the supertendent, is to know who writes these reports, these little histories can do no harm by developing a Pharisaic spirit. As the members come in, let them place their reports in a gilt ball, made to represent the sun, and called the " sunshine ball." From this the superintendent will take them, and read them out loud, making brief comments.

To aid the chairmen of the other committees in preparing their reports, the superintendent should write on sheets of paper sets of questions for each committee. These questions could be preserved for continual use. The answers to the questions, written in the children's own language, will make very creditable reports, if the questions are wisely worded. Here is a set for the prayer-meeting committee : —

1. How many prayer meetings have been held this month?

2. Who were the appointed leaders? Did they all serve? Have you any suggestions for future leaders?

3. What has been most helpful, do you think, in our prayer meetings lately?

4. Are the members becoming more faithful in offering prayer and speaking for Jesus?

5. Do you see any faults in the meetings? How can these faults be helped?

6. What are some of the difficulties the prayer-meeting committee has lately had to meet?

7. In what ways does the committee want the help of the members?

8. Has the committee any new plans to propose for the prayer meeting ?

Frequently let the reports be given in novel ways. For example, the monthly report of the lookout committee might be presented, for a change, in the following manner: Let a chart be prepared. On it are seven gold stars, for the seven active members received during the month, and three silver stars for three new associate members. Here is a row of blots — six of them — for six members who were absent from the last consecration meeting, and sent no message. Here are ten outline stars, for the ten new members that are wanted during the coming month. Who will set the committee on the track of them ? Here are three stars covered with a veil; you can barely see them. They are three Juniors who have not taken part in the meetings during the whole month, except by reading a verse. Won't they throw off the veil and shine out ?

If the superintendent is ingenious and persistent, she can bring it about that the reports of the Young People's society, when her Juniors get there, shall be among the most inspiring features of the entire work ; and that is very far from being the case now.

Bind Your Reports. — Junior superintendents will make a mistake if they do not insist upon written reports from the committees. These reports should be kept on file. If written on uniform slips of paper, they can be bound up at the end of the year, and make a volume in which the little authors will take great pride.

Who Give the Reports? — When you have committee superintendents appointed from the Young People's society, be sure, none the less, to have the report of the committee work prepared and given, not by the committee superintendents, but by the Junior chairmen of the committees, in order to teach the Juniors to do the work, and to hold them to their responsibility.

Visiting the Committees. — Ask your president and vice-president to drop in systematically upon the meetings of the different committees, so as to keep informed regarding their work. It would be well to arrange for their visits at a time when the superintendent cannot also be present.

Public Announcement. — Though the habit is one to be discouraged in the older society, yet in the Junior society it is not a bad plan to have the committee meetings, that are called for the week, announced by the chairmen of the different committees at some fit time in the Junior meeting, preferably at its beginning.

Committee Seats. — You can avoid the weekly calling of the roll, and gain many other incidental advantages, by adopting the plan carried out by a certain Canadian Junior society. In this society each member is allotted a certain chair; the members of the hymn-book committee, for example, occupying the outside chair of each row. As the Juniors enter, they distribute the hymn-books, and collect them again at the close of the meeting. At the other end of the rows sit the members of the lookout committee, each looking after the attendance of his row, visiting the absentees, and reporting. They have a committee called the kind-act committee, whose members occupy chair No. 5 in each row, and see that all the Juniors have Bibles. In the same way the other committees are seated, one member behind the other.

A Committee a Week. — It is a severe task for the superintendent to oversee all the Junior committees and come in close contact with each, but the matter may be easily managed if she plans an evening a week with some committee, the committees taking turns in coming to her house for the discussion of their work, and the formation of plans for prayer and Bible-study appropriate to their tasks. A helpful adjunct to this work is the requirement that the committee which thus meets with the superintendent shall be held especially responsible for the next week's prayer meeting.

Committee Ribbons. — Small bows of ribbon for each committee, these ribbons differing in color with the different committees, will be found helpful in giving the committees *esprit de corps*, and in reminding the little workers of their duties. The colors of the ribbons may be symbolical. The prayer-meeting committee may have white, for purity and holiness. The lookout committee may have blue, for the sky. The sunshine committee, of course, should have yellow. The social committee should have red, the color of the heart. The flower committee should have green, the color of leaves.

Committee Mottoes. — Bible mottoes for Junior committees are very helpful. The newly elected chairman may select them. Each member is required to learn the motto of his committee, and then promises to try to live up to it. The temperance committee of a Canadian society has for its motto Ps. 39: 1, and each child whom they persuade to sign the temperance pledge repeats this verse before signing. Mottoes of the other committees are: missionary, Mark 16: 15; sunshine, Eph. 4: 32; music, Ps. 66: 4; lookout, Ps. 119: 105; prayer-meeting, Col. 3: 17, etc. The officers should also choose their mottoes.

In connection with this you may establish a pretty ceremony. Call each forward in turn and have him say, "I will try to be faithful to my duties as president," or "secretary," "treasurer," etc., and recite his motto. The chairman and members of the committees will do the same.

Committee Outlines. — The following set of suggestions for the different Junior committees used by one superintendent will be found useful in many ways. They should be written out with the typewriter, and a copy of the appropriate set given to each committee chairman. A copy should also be given to each assistant from the older society. Spaces for fresh suggestions should be left on each slip.

The Prayer-Meeting Committee. —
1. Select leaders and topics for the prayer meeting.
2. Keep a list of the part taken by each member.
3. Help new and timid members by asking them to take some specified part in the meetings.
4. See that the meeting does not drag.
5. Pray for the meeting before coming to it.
6. Welcome new members and strangers.
7. Encourage members to be faithful to the prayer-meeting pledge.
8. Meet with the leader for a little prayer service before the meeting.
9. Always praying.

The Social Committee. —
1. See that every member is acquainted with every other member.
2. Welcome new members and introduce them to the old members.
3. Call on new members and newcomers.
4. Conduct occasional social gatherings.
5. Praying always.

The Music Committee. —
1. Lead the singing at the meetings.
2. Keep up the Junior choir.
3. Arrange to sing each week one song in which the others need not assist.
4. Encourage all to sing.
5. Praying always.

The Sunday-School Committee. —
1. Call upon the absent scholars.
2. Get new members into the Sunday school.
3. See that all the members of the society are members of the Sunday school.
4. Get new members into the society from the Sunday school.
5. Praying always.

The Missionary Committee. —
1. Assist the missionary societies of the church in any way practicable.
2. Arrange a missionary meeting at least every quarter.
3. Collect papers, fruit, and flowers for distribution in hospitals.
4. Collect clothing, fruit, flowers, and other things for the poor and sick.

5. Request that members bring some of these to each missionary meeting.
6. Get signers to pledges of money, and collect it once a month.
7. Praying always.

The Scrap-Book Committee. —

1. Collect pictures and scraps for books.
2. Make books of cambric, and paste in the scraps.
3. Distribute them to the poor and in the hospital, especially among the young.
4. Cut from *The Golden Rule* and *The Junior Golden Rule* suggestions for the Junior committees, and make a book of them for the superintendent and the committees.
5. Praying always.

The Sunshine Committee. —

1. Prevent quarrels among the members.
2. Assist in collecting fruit, flowers, and clothing for the poor, and distribute them.
3. Welcome strangers to the meetings.
4. Be pleasant to all whom you meet.
5. Make others happy in any way you can.
6. Praying always.

The Birthday Committee. —

1. Obtain the date of birth of each member.
2. Report each week the names of those that have birthdays during the week, and pray for them.
3. Obtain the date of the birthday of the pastor, and celebrate it if convenient.
4. Celebrate the birthday of the society.
5. Have a birthday box, and let each member put in one cent for each year of his age on his birthday.
6. Praying always.

The Book Committee. —

1. Distribute Bibles at the meetings.
2. Distribute song-books at the meetings.
3. Distribute tracts.
4. Erase any marks found in the books that should not be there.
5. See that those that come late have books.
6. Help build up the Sunday-school library.
7. Praying always.

The Good-Literature Committee. —

1. Get subscriptions to *The Junior Golden Rule.*

2. Get subscriptions to denominational papers.
3. In every way encourage good reading.
4. Praying always.

The Lookout Committee. —

1. Speak to those who are careless in keeping the pledge.
2. Be present every week, and mark the roll-call books.
3. Bring new members into the society.
4. Visit the absent ones, and report the reason for their absence to the superintendent.
5. Be first at the meetings, and first to take part.
6. Always praying.

The Flower Committee. —

1. Furnish flowers for the church.
2. Bring flowers to the meeting each week, and take them to the hospital, the sick, and the poor the next day.
3. Assist the missionary committee in distributing fruit and flowers.
4. Raise flowers for distribution.
5. Decorate the church for special services and entertainments.
6. Praying always.

A Thread=and=Needle Committee. — One Junior Christian Endeavor society in South Carolina has a committee with this odd name. The purpose, however, is perfectly manifest. It is a sort of Dorcas committee, and makes not only nice things for missionary boxes, and to be given away to needy families at home, but dresses dolls for poor children, and does all such delightful work.

Humane Committees. — One of the most important subjects upon which the Juniors should be instructed is the kind treatment of animals. The superintendent can do much by occasional talks, but more can be accomplished by the formation of a humane committee. The duties of this committee should be to gather items relating to the humane treatment of all living creatures, and turn them over to the scrap-book committee for a special volume; to report cases of cruelty; and to prevent, as far as possible, any that they may see.

A Sailors' Committee. — An English Junior society has a new committee called the "sailors' committee," which was suggested by a San Francisco Endeavorer who had crossed the water. The work of this committee is to send good literature on board steamers for the use of the sailors, and to do everything they can to make the voyage pleasant for them.

A Smoking Committee. — Forms of committee work that are especially appropriate to boys are valuable above all others. One odd committee of which I have heard is a " smoking committee." This committee keeps watch over all the Juniors, and reports to the superintendent any that may be seen smoking. Other vices to which the Juniors are more likely to be addicted may furnish motives for committees of different names. In the particular society that adopts a smoking committee, at the next meeting after the report to the superintendent, a special prayer is offered for the guilty Juniors.

Message Committees. — Message committees are found useful in many a society. The duty of this committee is to notice who are absent from the business meetings or the prayer meetings, and notify them regarding any special point of business which the interests of the society require them to know. Sometimes also the superintendent uses this committee to pass messages around among the members, informing them of special meetings, or matters of the sort.

A Postman Committee. — A postman committee of the Junior society will work very helpfully for the Young People's society if placed at the disposal of the proper officers, and set to delivering parcels or letters, or assisting the older Endeavorers in their religious work.

Information Committees. — It is a great inspiration to the Juniors to learn what other Juniors are doing. The older societies have their information committees and report at the beginning of each meeting, for five minutes, things that have been accomplished by other societies and new plans of work.

A similar committee would be especially enjoyed by the young folks. They might read papers written by other Juniors for the State conventions. They should consult *The Junior Golden Rule*, and find out from the letters there published the work in which other Juniors are engaged. Of course the news page of *The Golden Rule* contains frequent hints, all in the same line.

CHAPTER XXX.

WINNING AND HOLDING THE BOYS.

Vim and "Go." — If your society has few boys in it, some-thing is wrong with you, or with the society. It has been proved by many superintendents that this something, whatever it is, is discoverable and removable. Try to enter more thor-oughly into the likings of a boy, not catering to what is rude and careless in boy nature, but appealing to everything that is manly, and to all his innocent boy tastes.

Boys like noise, for instance. They like a great deal of vigor and vim in whatever they are connected with. They are pleased with novelty and with movement. If they are learning Bible verses, they enjoy them far better if they are divided into Com-pany A and Company B, and are permitted to fire Bible verses at each other, one division repeating one verse, the other imme-diately charging with a corresponding verse. Now and then you may vary this plan by the formation of temperance brigades, who will have a fusillade back and forth of temperance quota-tions from the Bible, with an occasional temperance song.

How to Appeal to Them. — In seeking to win the boys, adopt Professor Drummond's principle in his college work, and strike for the boy leaders. If you win them, you have won all of Boy-land. Show the leaders that you need them. They will learn after a while how much they need you and the society. Tell them of some of the definite lines of work that you have for them. If they feel that they will have some immediate occu-pation in the society, they will be far more likely to enter it. Place responsibility constantly upon them. Ask their advice and consult with them whenever you can.

Responsibility. — Lay upon the boys as many definite duties in connection with the society work as you can. Appoint one, for example, to care for your desk for a month. Appoint an-other to take charge of the society maps, pictures, and similar illustrative objects. Let the blackboard be the charge of a third, the hymn-books, possibly, of a fourth, the windows and ventilation of the room of a fifth. Let others see that the chairs are arranged in proper order, and changed, if you adopt the wise plan of varying the arrangement from time to time. Let others be chosen to pass the singing books and the Bibles. Assign to one each month the duty of reading the society notices, and seeing that the notices are given out in Sunday school. It is a good plan to have one of the Junior boys read these notices himself in the Sunday school.

By Themselves. — Pay a little especial attention to the boys occasionally, remembering how difficult it is to reach them and hold them. Invite them to remain for a few minutes, sometimes, after the Junior meeting. Hold with them a short prayer service, urge them to help you win the other boys of the Sunday school, and ask each boy to select another boy for whom he will pray and work during the coming months. This plan was instrumental in doubling, in a very short time, the number of boys in a certain Junior society of which I have heard.

Seek the Fathers. — Among the Junior workers there is none too much talk about the mothers, but there is far too little talk about the fathers of the Juniors. If we wish to win the boys, we must look more to the fathers to help. Get the men to drop into the Junior society once in a while. It will be harder to do this, because their business hours must not be interfered with ; but it may be accomplished now and then. Urge the fathers in all ways to show their boys that they approve of the Junior society, and believe in it thoroughly.

The Help of the Young Men. — You can never get the boys to join the Junior society and remain there without the co-operation of the young men of the older society. Let the boys see that the young men to whom they look up are interested in Christian Endeavor, and they themselves will be interested. Get the young men of the older society to take part in the socials of the Juniors, organize for the boys skating-parties, walking-parties, coasting-parties, and in all ways to try to make friends with them, and win them and hold them for the Master.

Forward — March ! — Boys like gymnastics and marching,

and there would be no harm in brightening your Junior meetings with many motion songs and similar exercises, being careful always to tie the exercise firmly to some gospel truth. For many reasons it is a good plan to drill your entire society, boys and girls, in marching. This accomplishment is especially useful in all union gatherings; and it tends to weld the society firmly together, as well as to increase the children's interest in it. Teach the Juniors the meaning of such military terms as "fall in," "right dress," "front," "at ease," "right face," "about face," "forward march," "mark time," "double quick," "column left," "single file," "column of fours," "right wheel," etc. Practise the Juniors in marching along aisles, up steps, and about the platform.

Let Them Know. — In answer to the question: "How do you manage to keep your boys?" one Junior superintendent gave the significant answer: "I just love them real hard, and *let them know it*." It is in the last four words that most superintendents fail, if they fail at all.

Manliness Wins Boys. — One of the most experienced Junior workers in the country has given me this plain and sensible hint: "So many Junior superintendents worry because the boys will not come to the meetings. The reason is plain. The Junior talks are given in such a childish, goody-goody way as to disgust older girls and all boys. Practical talks about the every-day happenings of life are what appeal to their better selves, and not some tale of a good little boy who never did a wrong act."

How She Won the Boys. — A California Junior superintendent has told how she was able largely to increase the attendance of boys on her Junior society. After Sunday school it was announced, with a little mystery, that the boys of certain classes were requested to meet her after the lesson hour.

Talking with them, she urged upon them membership in the Junior society, stating that it was not fair that the girls should monopolize all the good things; urging them to come in a body to the next Junior meeting, each bringing a friend; insisting, moreover, that they keep the whole affair secret, so that it should be a profound surprise. She got the boys to promise to do this by asking each one if he would do it if all the others did.

More can be done by a very brief talk with a lot of boys together than you will accomplish by a hundred times the amount of work with boys taken separately. If our Junior superintendents understood how to take advantage of the gregarious nature of boys, and their love for little secrets and mysteries — in short, if they would take more pains to understand boy nature — there would not be the dearth of boys that is now experienced by many Junior societies.

As the result of this little scheme I have just described, that Junior society, whose membership was almost entirely of girls, received such an accession from the boys that they now constitute more than two-thirds of the membership. More than that, they are good and faithful workers.

Military Drill. —There is quite a difference of opinion in regard to the advisableness of incorporating with Junior Christian Endeavor work the work of the Boys' Brigade, or anything of a military character. There is no doubt that the boys are strongly attracted by military drill, brass buttons, and uniforms. There is no doubt also that the reign of the Prince of peace will not be furthered by any appeal to the love of war. The use of military tactics, however, and of the manual of arms, has no essential connection with war, and will be retained, I believe, as an admirable discipline, long after all swords have been beaten into pruning-hooks.

No Junior superintendent, of course, will adopt military drill for his boys except with the full and hearty consent of the pastor and the church officers; and if, with this consent, military methods are in any degree adopted, let all care be taken lest the pleasure and exhilaration of them supersede the interest in the distinctively religious work for which the Christian Endeavor Society is established. Give enough of them to freshen mind and body, to train the children in order and obedience, to enlist in the work their physical and social natures, but not so much that the spiritual aims of the work are lost.

And especially, in all military drill, so train these young Christian soldiers that they shall see that the weapons of their warfare are not carnal, but that they are enlisted for life under the banner of the Prince of peace, that their strife is to be against war and anger and passion and all other evil things.

Some Junior superintendents form the Junior boys into what they call the " Boys' Brigade of Christian Endeavor." Others have simply "a brigade committee" of the Junior society. Others drop the word " brigade " altogether, and organize what they call " Christian Endeavor Guards," or " Christian Endeavor Cadets." With any plan, membership in the Junior society is an essential to membership in this military company.

Usually the military drill occupies the hour preceding the prayer meeting of the Junior society, — only, of course, when the prayer meeting is held on some week-day. At the roll-call the Guards respond with Bible verses. They also report attendance at church, Sabbath school, and Christian Endeavor society. Sometimes at this roll-call the Juniors are required to give the text of last Sunday's sermon, or the topic of the coming Christian Endeavor prayer meeting.

The Boys' Brigade constitution calls for a monthly missionary meeting and for a Bible study every fortnight; and this work would, of course, be done by the Junior society in the combination here described.

Squads of this military company could be detailed by their commander to do all kinds of Christian Endeavor work. A musical squad might be drilled in a choir. A relief squad would do the work of a relief or sunshine committee. A lookout squad would win new members, and watch over the faithfulness of the members already obtained. A White Cross squad would see that the boys' lips are kept pure from intoxicating drink, tobacco, and profane and vulgar language. This idea may be indefinitely extended.

A boy's cap, belt, and other equipments, including his wood-barrel gun, need not cost more than $1.80. Their uniforms may also be obtained very cheaply. A single entertainment given by the Guards would easily pay for the whole, or the boys' friends or parents would probably delight to fit them out.

As to the captain, it is by far the best plan to enlist in this service some young man from the older society, if a competent drill-master can there be obtained. In this way you hold the young men as well as the boys.

The Cadet Committee. — Junior societies that do not wish to take up the work of the Boys' Brigade may find a hint in the cadet committee formed by a certain Junior society within my knowledge. This society has more than one hundred boys. They are uniformed, and are given regular drills. They are taught that it is their special work to preserve good order in the society, to set an example of manly deportment, and to perform any helpful service they may be called upon to carry out.

Boys to the Fore ! — If you arrange the boys so that they sit next to the organ or piano, and the girls sit farther away, you will find that the girls will sing quite as well, and the boys will sing very much better. In this way, too, the boys will be brought to the front, where their behavior will be improved.

A Secret Name. — You will please the boys by giving them, all to themselves, some name which will be a secret between you and them, the initials only being communicated to the outside world. For example, they may be known as the " E. R's," " Ever Readies."

Boys' Clubs. — A boys' club will prove a useful auxiliary to any Junior society that can find a good superintendent for it. This club should have a room appropriated to its use, where games may be played, and debates and similar exercises held. The room should be opened especially during the evenings, and the boys should be at liberty to invite to it their particular friends. The young men of the older society should be inter· ested in the movement, and would be glad to take turns in superintending the room during the evenings. In no better way can the Christian workers of the church get a strong hold upon the boys, not only of the congregation, but of the entire neighborhood and town.

Debates. — Boys like debates, and it will do no harm now and then to spend fifteen minutes of your society meeting in a brief debate on some moral question ; one side, for example, urging the superior claims of home missions and the other side of foreign missions ; or the debate may turn upon the compara- tive needs of the different mission fields, or upon the best way of defeating the liquor power ; or the question might be, " Which does more harm, card-playing or theatre-going ? "

Well, why not ? — One wide-awake Junior superintendent — this was in Canada — won the boys to his Junior society by establishing a swimming-club.

Boys' Meetings. — Occasional boys' meetings will prove a success. They should be composed not merely of the boys of the Junior society, but of all their boy friends whom they can get to come.

A Banana Peel Committee. — One Junior superintendent I know of has organized a " banana peel committee " among the boys. The duty of this committee is to put out of the way of others banana peelings and cigar stumps. When the boys are shown what mischievous work is done by the waste cigar stumps that are collected and used over again, they will see the point of the latter portion of their work.

The Postman Committee. — It is well to have the postman committee consist entirely of boys, and brightness will be given to the work if the committee is changed each month by the superintendent. It is their duty to distribute letters with texts to learn from the leaders and from the prayer-meeting committee, during the week; to deliver for the superintendent messages to the members; to run errands for the pastor and older Endeavorers and the Sunday-school superintendent, and in general to make themselves useful after the fashion of postmen

CHAPTER XXXI.

BADGES AND BANNERS.

Wear Them. — Urge the Juniors to wear their badges all through the week. Remind them of the responsibility they are thus taking on themselves, and urge them not to disgrace the emblem. These badges will not only keep the Juniors from yielding to many a temptation, but they will advertise the society among the young people, and strengthen each Junior's loyalty to the organization.

A Variety. — The United Society of Christian Endeavor has quite an assortment of Junior badges, — the shield, bearing the "C. E." monogram, above which is the word "Junior." This is made of gold, costing $1.00, or in gold and enamel, whose price is the same. A silver and enamel badge costs 30 cents, and a silver badge 25 cents; Corinthian silver and enamel 20 cents, and Corinthian silver 15 cents. These are all pretty, well made, and serviceable.

A New Badge. — Emphasize reception into the Junior society always by pinning upon the breast of the new member, in the presence of the society, a new Junior badge.

Paying for Them. — Teach the Juniors to care for their Junior badges by requiring them to pay for their second one in case they lose the first. In most societies, probably, each Junior pays for his first badge also; but it is better that it should be an entrance gift from the society.

Paper Badges. — Superintendents may like to manufacture Junior badges out of pasteboard for special occasions. The Junior monogram may easily be cut out of paper of different colors, and hung from pretty bits of ribbon. This will furnish a pleasing badge for union socials and the like, those of different societies being of different colors, or, possibly, those of similar committees in the different societies being of the same color.

Junior Colors. — When a society cannot furnish each member with a pin or badge, it will be the next best thing to adopt Junior colors, and present each member with a ribbon badge of the same. Special emphasis should be placed on the faithful wearing of these badges at school. Here they attract attention, and often give opportunity for an invitation to the Junior society. Besides that, they serve as reminders to the Juniors themselves, and, when the same ribbon badge is adopted by all the societies of a local union, they introduce the members of the different societies to one another.

Junior Banners. — Your society needs a banner, if it has not one already. If you ever attend a convention in a body, you will want the banner to fly at the head of your marching column. If you have adopted the pleasant and shrewd custom of dismissing the Juniors by having them march in an orderly manner from the room, singing a marching song, you need a banner to lead the way. Let the smallest boy carry it.

Even when the banner is quietly hanging before the society in the place of meeting, it is of use in keeping before the society the fact that it *is* a society. Used year after year, a banner comes to have a great deal of meaning, and a glance at it is sure to bring up many pleasant memories.

The banner is to last for years. Make it, therefore, of tough material, and letter it handsomely. Adopt some characteristic emblem, as a crown, a cross, a shield, a star. Place on the banner the name and denomination of the church, as well as of the society and its location: "The Junior Society of Christian Endeavor, of the Third Baptist Church, Springfield, Ill."

Use also some good motto. "For Christ and the Church" should be on every banner, but you might adopt also a local motto.

Appoint, with your other officers, a standard-bearer. You will find the post a coveted one. Train the standard-bearer to be a good leader in the marching. If the design and motto on the banner are well chosen, they may be turned to much spiritual profit in the society.

Make the banner attractive in coloring, but not gaudy. Children should be trained in artistic sense as well as in higher things. See to it especially that the lettering is so distinct that it can be read across a large church. Such combinations as black on a blue background, or silver on a white background, are to be avoided. Let the banner be sufficiently simple to tell its story at a glance. Do not overload it with ornament.

Orders for society banners are filled, cheaply and promptly, by The Golden Rule Co., Boston.

Home-Made Banners. — Some societies cannot afford to have an expensive banner of silk, and other societies need special banners for special occasions. It is well for all Junior workers to bear in mind, therefore, how cheaply banners can be made. A Florida superintendent tells us of a beautiful banner which she constructed, whose total cost was seventy-three cents.

The foundation was a piece of cotton flannel of the requisite size. The standard was made of a slender stick, painted white. The ornamentation was of crêpe tissue paper, white, green, and gold. This beautiful paper, which is so much used, can be twisted and puffed and plaited in many different ways, and quite gorgeous banners can be fashioned quickly and effectively, as well as little souvenirs for special occasions.

Red, White, and Blue. — Much may be made by an inventive superintendent of the use of flags, especially in connection with Christian citizenship meetings. The Juniors will like to wave these flags during the singing of patriotic hymns, or to march, carrying the flags, or to talk about the flag and what it symbolizes.

Committee Shields. — It is an advantage to have the Junior committees seated together, and this is not always so easy of accomplishment as it might seem. One ingenious superintendent brought it about by making five shields, one for each committee. Upon these shields was the Christian Endeavor monogram, and each was differently colored. Each of these was placed upon a certain row of seats which the committee was to occupy during the meeting.

A committee meeting may easily be called by putting one of these shields in a conspicuous place. Once in one society, for example, it was desirable to hold meetings of all the committees at the close of the regular session. These shields were placed in the parts of the room where the meetings were to be held.

The organist played a marching song, and the committees took their places. When the time was nearly up they were called back by the organist.

Shield Contests. — A shield contest will add greatly to the interest of the society. Divide the society into companies, whose size will vary with the size of the society. Number them A, B, C, etc. Cut from heavy pasteboard a shield. Cover it with cloth, — light blue or any other pretty color, — and hang it by a neat cord. One of these shields should be for each company, and lettered across the top with the company's name.

The shields should be about two feet long. Cut from red paper the Christian Endeavor monogram, pasting it upon the shield. About this monogram are to be pasted silver stars as each company earns them. Set over each company a captain, whose business it is to keep his company in order, see that it is punctual in attendance, etc.

In dividing the members into companies, be sure to place in each company representatives of the different classes of children in the society as to age and character. Seat these companies together in the Junior meeting, with the shields hanging in front.

The credits are earned as follows: One silver star is given to each company who has every member present. If an absent member sends a verse, he is counted as present. Another star is earned when every member of the company brings his Bible. A gilt star is given to the company that brings in a new member. A silver star is earned by the company every member of which is in place at the time for the opening of the meeting. If each member of the company has prayed and read the Bible every day during the week, another star is earned. This schedule can be enlarged by the superintendent, according to the needs of the society.

Room should be made about the Junior monogram for, say, fifty stars, and a small prize may be given to the company which is the first to complete this number.

Junior Colors. — The society should by all means adopt a color, and this should appear not merely in connection with the Junior badge, as a little bow of ribbon, but, as far as possible, in all the decorations of the society room.

Mottoes. — A motto is an inspiration to any Junior society. Better have it in plain English. It may be chosen from the Bible, or from some author familiar to children. Tell the Juniors something about the author, whether sacred or secular. Get some good artist to make an illuminated copy of the motto for the society walls.

If the Juniors themselves can select an appropriate motto, so much the better. This motto may well be chosen afresh each year, though the society might also have a standing motto that it might call its society motto.

CHAPTER XXXII.

ORDER IN THE SOCIETY.

Keep Control. — It is important that the superintendent sit not merely where she can see the entire society, but where the entire society can see her. A warning glance or shake of the head will often preserve the order of the meeting. It is always best to remove a child who persists in creating a disturbance, rather than to allow the meeting to be spoiled ; and it makes no difference who the child may be. Do not forget that the devout spirit of the superintendent, made manifest in a reverent bearing and tone of voice, is almost certain to lead the children to similar reverence. Boisterousness in the superintendent will make a boisterous society, and it could hardly be expected to result otherwise.

Go to the Root. — If you are troubled with disorder in the society, see if you cannot remove the cause of the disorder. It may sometimes arise in the distribution of the books. Have them distributed before the meeting. Sometimes the smaller children may grow fidgety because their feet cannot reach the floor. They are compelled to swing them or press them against the seats in front. Provide them with smaller chairs. Sometimes the children are interested in watching the visitors. Seat them behind the society. Sometimes it is bad air that spoils the meeting. See to the ventilation of the room. Sometimes the children grow restless because they cannot hear what is said. Make the leader and those who take part speak more distinctly.

Seek the Best. — Here is a wise suggestion from an Illinois superintendent: " My rule for controlling restless and sometimes troublesome children is to study the lovable traits of such, which I can always find, and make the most of such avenues of approach to the heart of the child."

Time to Get Disorderly. — The fact that the children are allowed to gather in the meeting-room some twenty minutes before the time for the meeting is often responsible for the disorderliness that continues throughout the Junior hour. If the superintendent herself has a key to the door of the room, and does not open it until ten minutes before the hour, and herself sees to the preservation of order before the meeting, everything will move more smoothly.

Be on Hand. — Much of the disorder that arises in the Junior meetings has its source in the superintendent's tardiness. If she is present in the meeting-room before any of the Juniors arrive, this danger will be avoided. Some superintendents find it a wise plan to set the Juniors to singing as soon as **two** or three of them have gathered together, and to keep up the singing until it is time to begin. This would be a good opportunity for the practising of unfamiliar songs.

A Good=Order Committee. — Good-order committees are great helps in many societies. The most obstreperous boys in the society are organized into the committee, and their ringleader is appointed chairman! It is their duty to keep order in the meeting, and the effect is marked and immediate.

The members of this committee should sit in the back part of the room, making a note of the names of all offenders in the matter of order, and should report them to the superintendent, who will either talk with the culprits, or summarily dismiss them from the society, or put them on probation, as he may think best.

In some societies this good-order committee is a " committee of the whole," and is divided into as many parts as there are members, so that each Junior is chairman of a subdivision. The superintendent can therefore say, " Now, Charley, as chairman of a subdivision of the order committee, you ought to set a better example."

A Courtesy Committee. — A worker among the Juniors of Victoria, Australia, urges the establishment in every Junior society of a " guild of courtesy." This guild, or committee as we should call it, will seek to promote among the Juniors courteous habits, neatness, chivalry, personal cleanliness, and purity in all ways. The committee will have for its field of action not merely the society, but the school, the playground, the street, the table, the home ; in short, everywhere.

A Peace Committee. — An Illinois society has a "peace committee," whose work it is to prevent all quarrels among the Juniors and their friends, and in general to restore the peace wherever there is any trouble.

Toe the Mark! — If the Juniors are at all disorderly, a set of rules, carefully formulated and posted in the room, will be found exceedingly helpful in preserving order. Here is a sample set used in one society : —

1. When the meeting is called to order, each Junior must take his seat quietly.

2. Two Juniors must not talk at the same time.

3. There must be no changing of seats, talking, whispering, or misbehaving of any kind during the meeting.

4. Any one who breaks these rules will be taken from the room.

Shaking Hands. — The Juniors will like to shake hands with the superintendent as they go out. This little ceremony will aid the superintendent to maintain order as the society passes from the room.

Separating Them. — Some Junior superintendents who have found difficulty in managing unruly boys have solved the problem in this way. They have divided their societies into divisions by means of the different committees, one the missionary division, another the lookout, and a third occupied by the prayer-meeting and social committees. The assistant superintendents were placed each in charge of one division, and in each division was placed one of the unruly boys. The members of each division were required to sit together, and thus there was peace in the meetings.

Take Turns. — It is an excellent plan to have the boys and girls alternate in occupying the front seats, especially if there is any strife among the Juniors for the back seats, or for any special position.

Up Front. — It is a small point, but you will find it helpful not to permit the smaller members of the society to be hidden behind the taller ones in the meeting.

Caught! — If the talkative members of your society are in the habit of grouping themselves at the back of the room, a good plan to break this up is to get the prayer-meeting committee, before the meeting, to turn the rear seats around so that no one can sit in them, thus forcing the members forward.

Each His Seat. — It is an admirable plan to assign to each Junior a special seat in the meeting-room and expect him to retain that seat.   In this way the superintendent is able to separate the disorderly members and those who are inclined to talk and laugh together, and she can throw into companionship those who are able to help one another.

A Rest. — It helps to keep the Juniors in good order if, right in the middle of the meeting, when they are becoming a little tired, you have them rise and circle about the room, singing a marching song.   This rests them, and makes them fresh for the close of the meeting.

Thistles. — I have heard of a Junior society that is divided into three sections, the " pansy," the " primrose," and the " thistle " sections.   If a Junior becomes disorderly he is at once degraded into the " thistle section "!

An Occasional Visitor! — Sometimes the younger boys of the Junior society are especially disorderly.   One Junior superintendent has succeeded in quieting them by occasionally inviting one of the fathers of the Juniors to come in and sit among them during the meeting.

A Badge of Honor. — If the deportment of your Juniors needs improving, try this plan : Buy a gold Junior badge which you will call the badge of honor, and permit this badge to be worn at each meeting by some one whose deportment at the preceding meeting was very good.   Do not say that you offer it for the best deportment, because that will provoke invidious comparisons.   Show them that they all have a chance to wear it.

Ushers. — You will find the appointment of ushers a decided stimulus to order in your society.   Be sure not to call them " monitors."   They may hold office for one month, and two will usually be enough.   Their duties will be to attend to newcomers and strangers, seating them, and finding their places in the Bible and the hymnal.   They will watch that the doors are closed, and that the windows are open as ventilation is needed, that the chairs are well arranged, and all similar matters.

CHAPTER XXXIII.

THE BUSINESS MEETING.

Slowly and Systematically. — Do a little planning for the business meeting, keeping in mind the development of the Juniors' knowledge of parliamentary law. Make it your purpose to introduce one new principle, but seldom more than one, at each Junior meeting, and contrive beforehand how this may be done. At one meeting, for instance, you may have the society resolve itself into a committee of the whole to consider some point that requires informal discussion. At another meeting you may scheme to bring in the principle of an amendment to an amendment. At another, you may bring about the reconsideration of a vote, and so on.

Snap and Vim. — Strive to introduce into the conduct of the business meeting as much snap and acuteness as possible, taking care, of course, to avoid even the slightest approach to quarrelling and "smartness." Instruct the young president to insist jealously upon his rights. Let him refuse to recognize members unless they rise in addressing him, and on no account let him permit any one to speak without first obtaining permission of the chair. Let him put no motion unless it is seconded, and until the seconder has risen and obtained the floor.

Be Accurate. — It is a mistake to permit any slipshod method of carrying on the business meeting, or to think that, because the Juniors are young, carelessness in business methods may be overlooked. Remember, they are forming habits here that will last them through their lives. It is not necessary that these Juniors shall understand all the complex laws of parliamentary tactics, but it may easily be brought about that they shall understand the few simple principles that they will need to practise in the management of their business meetings. The superintendent herself should make a careful study of some standard book of parliamentary law, such as Roberts's *Rules of*

Order, or Cushing's *Manual*.   Either book is sold by the United Society of Christian Endeavor for fifty cents.

Criticise. — Encourage the children themselves to correct one another when errors are made, not in any spirit of unfriendly criticism, but solely in the interests of accuracy and for the good of the society.   Do not hesitate yourself, also, to correct the youthful officers and parliamentarians when they are in the wrong.

Let Them Recite. — An excellent plan to enliven the business meetings is to have the Juniors prepare recitations to be given at the opening and close of the meeting.   It will be well to have as many of these as possible bear on temperance and missions.

Sugar Coated. — If the Juniors are slow to come to the business meeting of the society, try the plan of holding socials in connection with those meetings.   This will bring them out.

Some Parliamentary Rules. — Do not be confused by the many rules of the manual.   Those that are essential are few and simple.   I venture to give the following list of the most important points : —

A motion to adjourn takes precedence of other motions.

A motion to reconsider a vote must be made by a member who voted with the majority.

When any member thinks that a parliamentary error has been committed he may rise and say at once, " I rise to a point of error," and then be seated.   If the president says, " State your point," he will again rise, and call attention to the error.

Any member may appeal from the decision of the chair, and this appeal must be seconded.   The presiding officer will then ask, " Shall the decision of the chair be sustained ? " and, after debate, will put the question.

By-laws may be suspended by a two-thirds vote, but not the constitution.

A motion to lay on the table requires a majority vote.   After it is passed, the subject under discussion goes over to the next meeting.

When one moves the previous question, and the motion is carried, the debate must cease, and the question be put at once.

Sometimes the most desirable way to avoid debate is to refer the matter under discussion to a committee, that is to report at the next meeting.

There are several ways of amending a motion. It may be amended by adding to it, inserting in it, striking out portions, or substituting portions.

The amendment may itself be amended, but the chain can go no farther.

The vote must first be taken on the amendment to the amendment, then on the amendment, and then on the original motion as amended, if it is amended; otherwise, as it originally stood.

Standing committees are the committees that are formed according to the regular rules of the society. Special committees are those appointed temporarily.

When the chairman or the society names a committee, the first person named is chairman. The committee may, however, if it choose, elect another chairman.

When the report of a committee has been given, it may be voted to accept it or adopt it. In this case the committee is discharged. When a committee, however, makes only a partial report, and this partial report is accepted, the committee is continued.

To pass into a committee of the whole is simply an informal way of discussing the matter. When a motion to pass into a committee of the whole is agreed to, the presiding officer names some Junior to act as chairman of the committee, himself leaving the chair. After discussion, it is moved that the committee rise and report. The president resumes his seat, and the chairman of the committee of the whole makes his report to the society.

A quorum, if there is no rule to the contrary, is always a majority of all the members.

Motions may be passed by general consent, the chairman simply saying, "If there are no objections, the motion is adopted." It may be passed by acclamation, the chairman saying, "As many as are in favor of this motion will say Aye; contrary minded, No." A motion may be passed by the raising of hands, or by a rising vote, or by yeas and nays, the secretary calling the roll, or by ballot, the president appointing tellers who collect the ballots and count them, one of them afterwards reporting them to the society. Finally, a motion may be made that the society instruct the secretary to cast the ballot of the society for it.

When there is a tie vote, the chairman may always vote. He may also vote whenever his vote would create a tie. In no case can he vote twice.

A good order of business for the Junior meeting is: Prayer, reading of the minutes of the last meeting, election of officers, election of new members, reports of standing committees, reports of special committees, unfinished business, new business, prayer, adjournment. Singing may be interspersed, and other exercises, at the discretion of the society.

For the election of officers, it is best to appoint a nominating committee at the preceding meeting. In this way the new officers can be more carefully chosen.

The minutes should contain an account of all motions that were passed, but need not trouble themselves with motions that failed to pass.

The reports of the committees should always be written, and should be placed on file with the secretary. A good report will contain an account of what the committee has been able to accomplish, of what it has hoped to accomplish that it did not do, and why it did not do it, together with its most important plans for the coming weeks, especially those in which the co-operation of the Juniors is needed. The report will also contain any suggestions that will be helpful in the general work of the committee.

CHAPTER XXXIV.

JUNIOR FINANCES.

Be Systematic. — The treasurer of the Junior society should have a little account book, and should be taught the little mysteries of debit and credit, and of balancing his books at the end of each month. The superintendent may act as the auditor. The treasurer should give careful monthly reports, and give occasional reports also to the older society, whose members ought to be interested in seeing that the funds of their younger brothers and sisters do not run too low.

Missionary money should be handed in to the treasurer, even if the missionary committee collects it. From him, whenever the society appropriates it by vote, the money should go to the treasurer of the church, to be by him sent to the designated object or board. The church treasurer should be careful always to say that the money comes from the Junior Christian Endeavor society of his church. In some societies it might be better, where there is a systematic plan of giving to missions, for the treasurer rather than the missionary committee to attend to the monthly collection of these gifts.

Cheerful Givers. — No Junior society should incorporate in its constitution any provision for regular dues. All gifts made by the Juniors should, in accordance with the well-known Christian Endeavor principle, be voluntary.

The Collection. — Inculcate in the Juniors habits of giving by taking up a collection *every* Sunday.

There is always more or less disorder while the collection is being taken. This may be remedied by having the Juniors sing a verse of a hymn during the taking of the collection.

Occasionally, at least, also have the Juniors repeat their Bible verses while the collection is being received, each saying a verse as he deposits his penny.

Quiet Giving. — Instead of passing around the contribution box, it is best to place at the door a basket in which each Junior, as he enters, will deposit his offering. In this way the poorer child can give his penny quietly, and not feel the contrast between it and the silver dime of the better-off. In every Junior society the children should be made to feel the significance of the story of the widow's mite, and the truth that God knows how much each is able to give, and judges the faihfulness of the giver rather than the size of the gift.

The Use of Envelopes. — One good way of taking up the collection is this, used by some Methodist Juniors of Canada. The treasurer, during the closing hymn, distributes collection envelopes. Upon these each member writes either his name or a number previously given each, putting in his offering, and handing the envelope to the treasurer as each passes out.

Junior Banks. — Toy banks are useful in Junior societies. They can be obtained at a cost of about five cents each, and will last indefinitely. In some societies, those who take these banks pledge themselves to put in them at least two cents a week for missions; more, if they desire. The banks are opened on special occasions, like Christian Endeavor Day, Christmas, or Easter Sunday.

A Mite-box Opening. — Mite-boxes are a helpful adjunct to any Junior society. They may be obtained, either free or at slight cost, from most mission-board rooms. They are kept in the homes, and not in the society room; and the occasion of their opening should be made a grand ceremony, accompanied with special exercises. The Juniors should come forward one by one, each presenting his mite-box, and reciting a verse about giving. The mite-boxes should then be emptied into a common receptacle before the money is counted, so that the poorer Juniors need not be chagrined by the smallness of their faithful gifts.

While the money is being counted, let the Juniors all stand and read Matt. 6 : 1-4, afterwards having a song service. After the amount of the gift is announced, let the Juniors, led by their superintendent, repeat after her a short prayer, asking God to bless the gift, and make it fruitful in his service.

Precise. — Definite pledges of money are always helpful. Here is one used by a Chicago Junior society: —

I will save each month
    2 pennies for a little girl at Erzroom, Turkey;
    2 pennies for a little Indian girl out West (South Dakota);
    2 pennies to find some Chicago boy a home;
    2 pennies for the expenses of our society.
Total, 8 pennies, to be brought each consecration Sunday.

A Source of Supply. — The honorary members of the Junior society will furnish one sure source of revenue. They should understand when they join that they are expected to contribute each year toward the expenses of the society with which they have connected themselves.

Their Very Own. — The average Junior society will need money for the purchase of topic cards and daily readings, pledge cards and constitutions, and *The Junior Golden Rule.* It will want also Junior song-books, badges, and banners, and money for the enlivenment of Junior socials, which are luxuries, rather than necessities. The Juniors will appreciate their topic cards and their other supplies far more if they earn the money they spend for them, and as near as possible this should be brought about, though the Juniors contribute only a portion of the necessary amount.

How to Earn Money. — Here are some ways in which the Juniors can make money. Give each five cents to trade with, having them report at the end of a certain number of weeks how much each has made by trading, and how the money has been gained. At the appropriate seasons of the year, young chrysanthemum plants, Easter-lily bulbs, and the like, may be given to the Juniors, to be cared for until they blossom; then a chrysanthemum or a lily show may be given, and these plants may be auctioned off to the church members by some bright and witty fellow.

A doll show will please the Juniors, and may be made to make money for the society. The Juniors could sell candy or popcorn from house to house. They may make by themselves stove-holders, table-spreads, quilts, and similar articles, which they may sell.

On the occasion of church suppers and the like, the Juniors may be permitted to have ice-cream stands, lemonade stands, etc., for the sake of adding to their treasury. If their minds are set upon it, they will find ways of earning money at home, as well as of saving from their own allowances.

Society Pictures. — Junior societies always make pretty photographs, especially if some taste is exercised in the grouping. These photographs sell well, and may be made to add money to the society treasury. Try the plan of grouping the Juniors upon steps, or upon a grassy bank, in the form of the Christian Endeavor monogram.

The Best Way of Spending. — An admirable lesson in the right use of money was given once by a Junior society whose superintendent presented each Junior with a penny. This penny was to be spent in the best way each could think of, and at the next meeting they were to tell how they had spent the money. The Juniors were then to vote and decide which was the best way to spend a penny, a little prize being given to the one who received the most votes. In this particular instance the prize went to the Junior who, with her penny, bribed a little girl to go to the Junior meeting!

CHAPTER XXXV.

JUNIOR LITERATURE.

Missionary Packages. — The good-literature committee should set itself, in co-operation with the similar committee of the older society, to gathering the helpful papers and magazines and books that can be spared by the members of the congregation, and sending these in packages to all persons who can make good use of them, especially to missionaries, and to Sunday schools in needy districts. It is a good plan to write letters with each package, and read to the society the cordial replies that are received. If this gathering is done at regular intervals, the harvest will be much larger.

Sending. — One of the best things that can be done by Junior good-literature committees is the lending of helpful books and magazines. They should especially keep watch to see what members of the society or their friends are forming a taste for vicious or weak literature. In this the superintendent should guide them, and should help them also in the choice of bright and valuable literature which may take the place of the poison.

Bits from Books. — Encourage the Juniors to bring to the meeting helpful bits that they find during the week in books and papers. As a safeguard, however, require them to show what they bring to their parents beforehand.

Barber Shops and the Like. — Christian Endeavor socie-- ties are doing everywhere a noble work in supplying the best papers and magazines to barber-shops, hotels, railway stations, prisons, and hospitals, and even fixing pockets on the backs of the seats in the parks, these being filled with useful and elevating tracts and journals. In this work, of course, the Juniors will wish a hand; and the older society should go into partnership with the Junior good-literature committee, assigning to it a certain portion of the field.

Helping the Sunday School. — What the good-literature

committee of the older society does for the books of the Sunday-school library adapted to the age of their members, the Juniors may do for their own class of Sunday-school books.   They may call the attention of the society to those that they themselves have found particularly attractive, and in every way may strive to promote the circulation, among their members, of the Sunday-school library books.

A similar service may be done for the books of the public library, if your town is blessed with one.   It is a good thing, too, to mention in the society meeting any helpful article, story, or poem, that the members of the committee have read in magazines that are accessible to many of the Juniors.

Subscription Agents. — Much good may be done by the good-literature committee if they will take in charge subscriptions to *The Junior Golden Rule* and *The Golden Rule*, as well as the denominational papers and magazines.   Juniors make capital canvassers, because they have so much time, and are not at all afraid to present the claims of the papers for which they are canvassing.   Let the Juniors find out from their pastor what papers and magazines will be most helpful to the members of the congregation and to him in his work, and then see how many subscribers they can gain.

The International Organs. — It has been suggested that one of the best prizes, if prizes are offered at all in connection with Junior work, would be a year's subscription to *The Golden Rule* or *The Junior Golden Rule*.   It has also been suggested that one of the pleasantest ways of putting the society in connection with children of foreign lands is to subscribe to *The Junior Golden Rule* for them, making this the means of opening correspondence.

Endeavor Reading Circles. — A Lutheran pastor of Pennsylvania started among his Junior Endeavorers what he calls an "Endeavor reading circle."   He made clippings from *The Golden Rule* and his denominational papers, selecting chiefly the stories that would be attractive to the young people.   Each of these was placed in a separate neat envelope, numbered and catalogued, as Sunday-school libraries are.

The envelopes are exchanged at every meeting of the Juniors. This operation takes but little time, as the envelopes are returned at the opening, new ones being given out at the close of the meeting. This plan has resulted in adding fully fifty per cent to the attendance of this particular society, besides teaching the Juniors to read helpful and elevating literature.

The Junior Golden Rule. — Superintendents and Juniors are loud in their praise of this, the international organ of the Junior movement. Few superintendents, however, know how to utilize the bright little paper in the society work itself. The following methods have been tested, and found practical and helpful in different societies.

The paper has many departments which are sustained by the writings of the Juniors themselves. There is an Open Parliament, in which the children express themselves on various topics of interest to them, such as, "What is your favorite Bible character?" "How do you intend to spend your next vacation?" "What is the most interesting thing you ever saw?" "What kind of minister do you like best?" and so on. A slight prize is offered for the best response each month. The Juniors of your society may like to write, each of them, a paragraph for this contest; the society voting which is the best, and sending that one as the society contribution, at the same time not debarring any one else in the society from sending his contribution if he wishes.

Another department is that of "Bright Sayings," in which the Juniors may report any funny saying of their friends, or any joke on which their eyes may fall that seems to them especially comical. A slight prize is offered for the best of these also.

In another department sets of Bible questions are asked each month, to set the Juniors to studying the Bible in new ways. Each month, also, the best letter received from Juniors of each separate denomination is printed in the paper. These letters describe the society work and its results. Junior badges are given to all the successful letter-writers.

One of the most helpful features of the paper is the department called "Something To Do." A little task is set the Juniors each month. Sometimes it will be to dress dolls for the children of the hospitals, sometimes to make games for them, to decorate fans for them, or to make for them scrapbooks. At other times the contest will be of quite a different character, to see who can patch a hole in the best way, or darn a piece of torn cloth, or whittle the most ingenious set of jack-straws, or make the best collection of tree buds, or of common minerals. Slight prizes give zest to these contests also; and the Juniors have, in addition, the satisfaction of helping other children, or of adding to their own information.

Besides these various features that interest the Juniors directly, the paper contains bright stories and poems and pretty pictures, articles from the best writers for young people, letters from the general secretary and the president of the United Society of Christian Endeavor.

Probably the most helpful feature of the paper is the page devoted to the weekly prayer meeting. Here are given a large number of classified Bible references, together with a helpful talk on each topic, and suggestions for Junior leaders.

The paper is abundantly worth its cost, which is only 25 cents a year where ten or more copies are sent to one address in one wrapper. For separate addresses, its cost is 35 cents a year.

The Golden Rule. — No Junior superintendent can afford to do without the International Christian Endeavor organ. The Junior page of *The Golden Rule* is entirely for superintendents. There is a department of Junior methods, and the weekly topic is treated in several different ways. One writer suggests plans for the superintendent's talk, and for the conduct of the meeting. Another writer gives an attractive chalk-talk. Still a third writes a little story, or gives some other illustration of the topic that the superintendent or the Juniors may use. There is also a set of simple questions bearing on the topic. These questions may be distributed to the Juniors for them to answer in the meeting.

The entire paper, moreover, is helpful to Junior workers, as well as to all Endeavorers. The department of " Ways of Work-ing," kept up by contributions from Endeavorers from all over the world, contains many a method that, though intended for older societies, may be adapted to the Juniors also.

Society Periodicals. — Every Junior society should take *The Junior Golden Rule*, at least one copy for the use of the leader; and the Juniors should also subscribe for one copy of *The Golden Rule*, that the leader for each week may have the advantage of its suggestions on the Junior topic, which are entirely different from those in *The Junior Golden Rule.* The society should also take one copy of the denominational missionary paper that. is best fitted to its use, and this should go to the leader of the monthly missionary meeting. A few cents may be spent each month for interesting temperance tracts and articles, or for a subscription to a child's temperance paper.

United Society Publications. — The United Society of Christian Endeavor either publishes or has for sale a number of books and pamphlets exceedingly helpful to any Junior worker. I have space to do no more than mention some of these. I have spoken of others in other parts of this Manual.

Foremost mention must be made of *Attractive Truths in Lesson and Story,* by Mrs. Alice May Scudder, a book of three hundred and thirty pages, costing $1.25. This is filled with helpful Junior exercises, stories to illustrate different truths, and suggestions for Junior superintendents.

Two books are especially useful along the line of object lessons for Juniors, and chalk-talks. One is *Little Children in the Church of Christ,* by Rev. Charles Roads, a book of two hundred and twelve pages, costing $1.00. The other is *Five-Minute Object Sermons to Children,* by Rev. Sylvanus Stall, D.D., also costing $1.00.

Books especially useful to blackboard workers are *The Blackboard and the Sunday School,* by Frank Beard, $1.25; *Plain Uses of the Blackboard,* by Dr. and Mrs. Crafts, $1.00; and *Pictured Truth,* by Rev. Robert F. Y. Pierce, $1.25.

Dr. McCauley's handbook of Christian Endeavor methods, entitled *How,* devotes six pages to Junior workers; and many suggestions may be gained from its chapters devoted to older Endeavorers. The same is true of Mr. Ogburn's *The Young People's Prayer Meeting and Its Improvement,* and of Mr. Bomberger's *Christian Endeavor Plans and Principles.*

A Christian Endeavor classic that should be in every Junior worker's library is *Ways and Means,* by Rev. F. E. Clark, D.D., the president of the United Society. It costs $1.25, and is filled with practical and helpful suggestions.

These are all books. Among the pamphlets and leaflets of especial value to Junior workers are *Meetings for Juniors and*

How to Conduct Them, by Mrs. James L. Hill; *Missionary Plans for Junior Societies*, by V. F. P.; *Scripture Illustrated*, by Mrs. Scudder; *A Live Junior Society*, by Rev. W. W. Sleeper; *Junior Christian Eudeavor Unions*, and other pamphlets by Miss Kate H. Haus, together with some bright exercises for special meetings; one, *An Evening with the Juniors*, by J. A. Shannon; another, *Let the Little Ones In*, by Mrs. James L. Hill; and services for anniversary, graduation, and the enforcement of the pledge, by Miss Kate H. Haus.

All of these books and pamphlets are to be obtained of the United Society of Christian Endeavor, whose price-list is sent on request. This price-list will also put the superintendent on the track of many helpful publications for older Endeavorers, whose methods can be adapted, with slight change, to the Junior society.

CHAPTER XXXVI.

THE TRIAL MEMBERS.

Trial Members. — Trial members are defined by the Model Constitution to be " those who wish to attend, and promise to behave when at the meeting. These shall have their names on the trial roll, but shall not sign the pledge, or serve as leaders for the meetings."

The term, " trial members " is, in my opinion, to be preferred to " associate members ; " because the latter recognizes a permanence in the arrangement, while the former, like the Methodist word " probationer," looks forward to a speedy advance from trial to full membership. And that is what we all want.

A Pledge. — This temporary nature of trial membership makes it seem best not to propose a pledge to trial members, for signing a pledge seems a bond of continuance. Nevertheless, not a few societies have associate members, and use some such associate members' pledge as the following : —

Junior Associate Membership Pledge.

As an associate member of the Junior Christian Endeavor Society, I promise to be present at every meeting, unless prevented by a very good reason. I promise to be orderly, and to do all I can for the society.

Name..

I am willing that.............................should sign this pledge, and will do all I can to help.................keep it.

Parent's name...

Residence..

A Harder Pledge. — Another form for an associate members' pledge is the following, which may approve itself to some superintendents: "As an associate member, I promise to pray to Jesus every day, to conduct myself properly in the meetings, to try to get some good out of every meeting, and to do whatever the superintendent asks me to do."

All Active ? — It is the strong opinion of many Junior workers that associate members, and even trial members, have no business in the society. "The object of Junior work," says an experienced superintendent, "is to take the boys and girls before they know anything else than serving Christ, as day by day and Sunday by Sunday he is shown them, and to bring them to manhood and womanhood without ever asking, 'Do you wish to serve Christ?' or, 'Do you believe in him?' There are few boys and girls who are not ready to join actively in the work when its aims are placed properly and understandingly before them."

Practical workers, however, will not share in this opinion. They know how varied are the states of religious development in children, and understand that it is especially confusing and discouraging to them to place on precisely the same level the earnest, well-instructed young Christian, and the boy or girl who has scarcely begun to comprehend who Christ is. Justice to the former, as well as care to stimulate the growth of the latter, would forbid this "lumping."

From Trial to Active. — How can you tell when the child is ready for active membership ? Children differ so widely that no rule can be laid down. Consider the child's knowledge of Christ, desire to please him, realization of his presence. Look at his faithfulness in Bible study and in society work. Test him on some committee. Let him try whether he can keep the Junior pledge for a month. Find out about his home life. Ask the advice of his parents. Inspire in him a longing for active membership, not for the sake of honor among his fellows, but for the sake of the activity in Christ's service. Sometimes all, sometimes only a part, of these tests can be met by one who is ready for active membership.

Not Leaders. — If, in the Young People's society, it is found best to establish an invariable rule that no associate member should lead the meetings, so, even more surely, it will be found best to confine the leadership of the Junior society meetings to those Juniors who are confessed Christians — the active members. Children especially need to see emphasized the difference between Christians and non-Christians. Besides, for most topics, the leader cannot do effective service without proclaiming in some way his love for Christ, that he may inspire others to do the same.

Not Chairmen. — It is, perhaps, equally important to reserve the chairmanships of the various committees for the active Juniors. There may be among the trial members a child who could get up interesting socials ; but you want to teach your Juniors to be " social to save," and you should not put a non-Christian at the head of your social committee. One of the trial members might direct the work of the flower committee with taste and skill ; but the higher service of this committee, the ministries to the sick, the choice of Bible texts to accompany the bouquets, the songs and prayers in the sick room, should not be in the hands of a non-Christian. Place the trial members on the subordinate committees in subordinate positions, but never as chairmen, and do not give them any position at all on the lookout, prayer-meeting, and missionary committees.

The Roll-call. — For the same reasons, jealous distinctions should be made at the consecration meeting between the two classes of members. Their names should be placed on a separate roll, and they should be called separately, if at all. They should be required to answer no more than, " Present ; " though they should not be hindered from making as full a response as they feel moved to make, and, indeed, should be encouraged to pray and testify at this meeting as soon as the superintendent perceives that they are ready for this step. The roll of trial members, when called, should come at the beginning of the meeting, to avoid an anti-climax.

Work Them In. — However, we must make good use of our trial members if we wish to lift them into active membership. They can safely be set to many tasks. Place them on the sunshine committee, the music committee, the flower committee, the book committee, the social committee, the postman committee. Get them to serve as ushers, to distribute singing-books, to copy verses for the prayer-meeting committee, to help you with the blackboard and in getting objects for your talks. Get their aid in all missionary work especially.

Show them how eager you are to receive them into full membership. Get the lookout committee to do the same. Pray for them and with them. Unfold to them with tender faithfulness the character and commands of the dear Saviour, and before many weeks you will be rejoiced by the manifest blooming of Christian character. Your trial members will have become active Christian Endeavorers.

CHAPTER XXXVII.

RECEPTION, GRADUATION, AND DISMISSION.

An Honor Roll. — To spur the Juniors to win new members to the society, an honor roll is excellent. This honor roll should be printed on a large sheet of paper; and a gilt star should be placed after the name of every Junior who brings in a new member, the star being doubled, tripled, etc., as more members are obtained.

Two by Two. — The two by two method is as helpful in getting new members into the Junior society as it is in any other form of Christian service. Divide the active membership into pairs, and set each couple at work to interest in the society some particular boy or girl.

Permanent. — When you give special inducements to the Juniors, asking them to gain new members for the society, do not fail to make it one of the requirements in the undertaking that the new members be *kept in* the society, as well as introduced to it.

Searching Questions. — It is a mistake to think that a child who is old enough to join a Junior society is too young to have had a Christian experience, and to know what it has been. The following letter and questions are given to each applicant for membership in the Junior society of a certain church in Belfast, Ireland. After each question is left space for a full reply.

MINERVA HOUSE

JUNIOR SOCIETY OF CHRISTIAN ENDEAVOR.

.... 18

Dear ....

We are very glad that you wish to join our Junior Society of Christian Endeavor.

You will not find the pledge easy or a pleasure to keep unless you are "trusting in the Lord Jesus Christ." Therefore we ask you to test yourself by the following questions.

Yours very cordially,

....

Superintendent.

1. Why do you wish to join our Junior Society of Christian Endeavor?

2. Why do you wish to strive "to do whatever he would have you do "?

3. When did you begin to want to please Jesus?

4. How were you led to trust in the Lord Jesus Christ?

5. What *does* "trusting in the Lord Jesus Christ" do for you?

6. What *will* " trusting in the Lord Jesus Christ " do for you?

(Signed) ....

A Reception Exercise. — A good service for the reception of new members must be short, earnest, and pointed. These requirements are well met in the following exercise by Miss Laura Wade Rice : —

(All members rise, while the Junior with a signed card comes forward.)

Supt. — What do you mean by bringing this card?

Junior. — I mean that I have made a promise to God.

Supt. — What do you mean by a promise?

Junior. — A promise means that I will do as I say, that I will keep my word.

Supt. — What have you promised?

(Junior reads pledge on card.)

Supt. — Let us pray.

After the close of the superintendent's prayer all the members join in the following prayer :

Dear Lord Jesus Christ, give us strength to keep our promise to thee, and may we help one another to be true to our pledge, Amen.

A Reception Service from Ireland. — A Junior society in Ireland finds it best to use a great deal of formality in the reception of new members. Test questions are presented to the Junior to answer in writing. These questions are so formed as to elicit evidence of conversion. The applicant for membership being retained in another apartment, the superintendent reads to the Juniors these answers, and the society shows its satisfaction with this testimony by raising hands.

If no objection is raised, a member of the reception committee goes to the other apartment, and brings in the person who is to be received. As these enter, all the Juniors rise and repeat in unison Num. 6: 24, " The Lord bless thee," etc. The applicant then takes his place near the secretary, at a small table that contains a pledge card and the roll book.

After a suitable prayer by the superintendent, the secretary hands to the new member the pledge card, which he reads aloud. On the completion of this reading, the active members, who have been standing, march around the table singing a reception hymn. At the chorus of the last verse, as the members pass, each one shakes hands with the new member, the chorus being repeated until all have done this.

In a Hollow Square. — One Junior Society of Washington, D.C., admits the new members in a novel way. The child who is to be received stands and answers questions about the pledge, these questions being asked by the superintendent. When this is satisfactorily completed, the active members take hold of hands and form a circle or a square about the new member. They then repeat the pledge together, and sing, " Consecrate me now to thy service, Lord."

Still One More. — Here is another good programme for the reception of members : Singing. Prayer by the leader. Concert repetition of the first Psalm. Responsive reading of the Beatitudes. New members called forward. Song, "Who will join our band to-day?" ("Junior Christian Endeavor Songs," No. 32). New members repeat the pledge. The society chants the pledge. Charge to the new Juniors by the superintendent. Charge to the old Juniors by the superintendent or some other Endeavorer. Song. Sentence prayers by the Juniors. Roll-call with verse responses. Song, "Blest be the tie." Mizpah benediction.

A Gift. — At some point in the course of the reception service, let the Junior president pin a Junior badge upon the new member, telling him that it is a gift from the society, a token of their interest in him, and of their hope and trust that he will always be true to the Christian Endeavor pledge. This should never be omitted, as the badge, so presented, will be greatly increased in value and influence.

Set Him at Work. — Be sure that the new member gets something to do the very first day of his attendance on the society. Have a verse ready for him to read, or get him to make a little prayer, or give him a question to answer, written out on a slip of paper.

Dismission Cards. — One Junior society of which I have heard gives to each member that leaves the society for another place what is called a " good-will card." This card simply states that the person has been a member of the Junior society, and commends him to the cordial fellowship of the Juniors where he may go. The form and name of these dismission cards may vary, but it is always pleasant thus to introduce the departing Junior to his new friends.

The cards should be granted by the society at a regular business meeting, on recommendation of the lookout committee. They should be signed by the president and secretary of the society, as well as by the superintendent; and they should be addressed to the secretary of the society in the church the Junior will attend, or, if this is not known, " to whomsoever it may concern."

If you can learn the address of any member (preferably the president) of the Junior society your departing Junior will join, be sure to write, telling that the new Junior is to be expected, and asking that she be called upon and cordially invited to join the society there.

Graduate Them. — It is a bad mistake to permit Juniors to linger on in the Junior society after they have reached the age and attainments proper for graduation. You injure the other Juniors, the younger of whom should be pushed forward to the responsible places the graduates would leave empty; and you injure the older society, that needs the inspiration of new members, and needs also to get hold of the young people before they have grown so wedded to Junior ways that it has become difficult for them to accommodate themselves to the methods of the older Endeavorers.

To be sure, the Junior has a naturally strong attachment for his old society, and somewhat dreads going among comparatively strange faces, and taking up work in which he cannot hope to excel without long waiting and working. If, however, the relations between the two societies have been such as are urged in this Manual, this reluctance will be minimized. For the good of both societies, then, keep constantly before your Juniors the thought of graduation, treating it as an honor to be won, and a happy privilege to be enjoyed,

When Shall They Graduate? — This question is debatable. The answer to it depends partly on the maturity of the Junior. Some children are further advanced at ten than others at sixteen years of age. The answer depends partly also on the condition of the older society, and whether it is large or small. Most Junior societies have fixed upon the age of fourteen as the best time for graduation, though this rule must be left flexible.

The superintendent must decide in each separate case whether the child is sufficiently well developed in Christian character, in ability to do Christian service, and in knowledge of the Bible, to make a good worker in the older society, and to pass with safety from her own close superintendence. If the older society is not too crowded, give the Junior the benefit of the doubt, and graduate him at fourteen, even if his progress has not been entirely satisfactory. Often the increased responsibility and more mature companionship of the older society will prove just the spur he needs.

Graduation Day. — Remembering the natural shrinking of the Juniors from entrance into the older organization, you will see how much better it is to graduate them in companies than singly. Let all whose fourteenth birthdays come within the year, and who are to be permitted to graduate, reserve their graduation till a certain day early the next year, — say New Year's Day, or Christian Endeavor Day, or, probably better, some Sunday in January when there will be no other interest to detract from this, and when an entire evening in the church may be devoted to the graduation ceremonies.

On this Sunday it would be well to arrange, if the season fits the requirements of the church, that the graduating Juniors who are not church members be received into the church. Surely, after all their years of Junior training, they will by this time be ready for this step, and will not wish to join the older society as associate members. Thus the day will be doubly blessed to the church.

The Graduation Programme. — Issue little printed invitations. Advertise the matter widely. Get a large attendance of old folks. This is a magnificent chance to interest them in the work of both societies.

Let the choirs of each society sing in turn, then antiphonally.

Have Junior ushers, as well as ushers from the Young People's society. Let the presidents of both organizations sit on the platform, with the Junior superintendent, pastor, and graduates. Either the Junior superintendent or the pastor should preside.

The programme will contain, as its main feature, short papers or addresses by each graduate. The themes should have a range as wide as the Christian life and experience. In assigning them, consider what kind of Christian work the Junior knows most about, and let that be his subject. The Junior president may

---

"FOR CHRIST AND   THE CHURCH."

DIPLOMA.

To whomsoever these presents may come,
  Greeting : —
  This certifies that..
because of progress in morals and devotion to Christ and his church, has been honorably graduated from the

JUNIOR SOCIETY OF CHRISTIAN ENDEAVOR

Of the Church of...

  ....*Junior C. E. Sup't.*

  ....*Pastor.*

  ....*Junior Endeavor President.*

  ....*Junior Endeavor Secretary.*

  ....*day of*............................18

---

give a history of the year's work of his society. The Junior superintendent will say good-by to the Juniors, and bid them Godspeed. The Young People's president will bid them welcome, in the name of the older society, at the same time pinning upon each the badge of the older organization. All the older Endeavorers will now rise and repeat with the new members (who should have been voted in at a former meeting) the Christian Endeavor pledge. Finally the pastor will address the graduates, telling them about the new kind of work that awaits them, and inspiring them to enter with zeal upon it. Then he will offer prayer for God's blessing upon the new bonds just sealed.

Intersperse throughout the evening bright songs and responsive readings. Have concert work by all the Juniors, but permit no Junior except the graduates and the president to take part upon the platform. Let the keynote of the entire occasion be " Consecration to higher service."

Diplomas. — Some societies like to signalize the graduation of their Juniors by the presentation of neatly printed diplomas or certificates, which may be prepared after the style shown on the opposite page.

CHAPTER XXXVIII.

THE INTERMEDIATE SOCIETY.

The Need. — The Intermediate Society is a recent outgrowth of Junior work, — too recent, in fact, to have developed any distinctive methods. Probably no distinctive methods are needed for the conduct of an Intermediate society, those of the older society, and those of the Juniors being appropriated in different degrees, according to local and varying needs.

The demand for Intermediate societies is greatest, of course, in large churches, where it has also been found necessary to divide the Young People's societies. In such churches it frequently happens that both Junior and Young People's societies are overcrowded, while yet a large number of Juniors are ready to graduate. The solution of the problem is to form an Intermediate society. In many churches already this plan has proved practically helpful, and it is destined to be widely adopted.

Ages. — The proper age for graduation into the Intermediate society must of course be variously determined in accordance with circumstances. Probably most churches will put into the Junior society children from six to eleven, into the Intermediate those from twelve to fifteen, and into the Young People's those from sixteen to one hundred, unless the church is fortunate enough to possess also a Senior society.

Officers. — Some churches have only one president for both Junior and Intermediate societies, this president being an Intermediate. There is, however, a treasurer and a secretary for each society. I should myself prefer separate presidents also; and over the Intermediate society should preside a separate superintendent. Each society should have a distinct ribbon badge and topic card. Scarcely any modifications need be made in the ordinary Junior constitution to fit the Intermediates, except the change of name.

The Committees. — As to the committees, in some churches they are union affairs, containing members from each society. I should prefer here also a complete separation. The Intermediate society will be able to devote more attention to committee work than the Juniors, and the work it undertakes will be of a more difficult grade.

Joint Meetings. — Nevertheless, the two societies will naturally feel very closely akin, and occasional joint meetings may be held. Some workers go so far as to join the two societies in the monthly missionary meetings, business meetings, and socials. Others always appoint an Intermediate to lead the Junior consecration meetings. I should not adopt either plan, except as an occasional variation. If it is best to separate the Intermediates at all from the Juniors, it is best for both to consider them as distinct societies, allied only a little more closely than both are to the Young People's Society.

CHAPTER XXXIX.

JUNIOR UNIONS.

The Constitution. — The United Society of Christian Endeavor suggests the following constitution as suitable for a Junior union, subject, of course, to any modification that local needs may require : —

CONSTITUTION.

ARTICLE I. — *Name.*

This organization shall be known as the Junior Christian Endeavor Union of...

ARTICLE II. — *Object.*

The object of the union shall be to stimulate and encourage an interest in Junior Christian Endeavor work, to provide an opportunity for interchange of thought, and for improvement in methods among its leaders, to promote the growth of children in the Christian life, and to interest them in every branch of church and Sunday-school work.

ARTICLE III. — *Membership.*

Any Junior Society of Christian Endeavor connected with an evangelical church or mission, working upon Christian Endeavor principles, and having the Christian Endeavor pledge, may join this union upon its vote to do so, when such vote is approved by the pastor and Junior superintendent, and upon the society's application for admission to the executive committee of the union.

ARTICLE IV. — *Executive Committee.*

This union shall be controlled by an executive committee composed of the superintendents of the Junior societies belonging to the union, or of the chairmen of the Junior committees having the Junior societies in charge. This committee shall meet for consultation once a month, or upon the call of the president, and shall choose annually from among its members a president, vice-president, secretary, and treasurer, whose duties shall be those usually belonging to such officers.

The pastors and assistant superintendents of the societies belonging to the union shall constitute an advisory committee, which may meet for consultation with the executive committee, upon its request to do so.

If any society shall not have an assistant superintendent, the superintendent may appoint a member to act with the advisory committee.

ARTICLE V. — *Meetings.*

There shall be a rally or mass-meeting held quarterly, or as often as the executive committee deem advisable. Such meetings may be devotional, social, or otherwise, at the discretion of the executive committee.

ARTICLE VI. — *Quorum.*

Representatives from .... societies shall constitute a quorum for the transaction of business at any meeting of the executive committee.

ARTICLE VII. — *Honorary Members.*

All Christians not superintendents, but interested in the work among the children, may become honorary members of the union by paying the sum of .... annually or semi-annually, thereby signifying their willingness to do what is in their power to advance the interests of the union. Honorary members shall be members of the advisory committee.

ARTICLE VIII. — *Vote.*

Every member attending a rally or mass-meeting shall be entitled to vote upon any question that may be brought before such meeting.

ARTICLE IX. — *Finances.*

The expenditures of this union shall be met by voluntary semi-annual contributions from the different societies belonging to it, and by collections taken for this purpose at any of the mass-meetings or rallies.

ARTICLE X. — *Relation to the Christian Endeavor Union.*

Since the Junior Christian Endeavor work is closely allied to the work of the Young People's Society of Christian Endeavor, it is expected that the president of the Christian Endeavor Union shall have a voice in all the deliberations of the Junior Union, and the President of the Junior Union shall have the like privilege in all the deliberations of the Christian Endeavor Union, in order that the two unions may work in harmony and to the best interests of the Christian Endeavor cause in the city.

ARTICLE XI. — *Amendments.*

This constitution may be altered or amended by vote of............of the executive committee, when deemed advisable, at any session of the executive and advisory committees jointly convened for that purpose.

The Connection with the City Union. — The object of the Junior union is to bind together in bonds of friendly association and mutual interest all of the Junior societies of a city or district, to organize new societies, and to better the work of the old ones. A separate organization of the Junior societies is favored for the same reason that it is found best to organize each separate Junior society apart from the older Endeavorers. Union meetings must be prepared on somewhat different plans to interest Juniors and the older Endeavorers ; and besides, in most cities Endeavor societies are so numerous that no one set of officers could adequately manage both Junior and Young People's societies.

There should, however, be the closest possible connection between the Junior union and the city Christian Endeavor union, of which the Junior work should be considered merely a branch. The city superintendent of Junior work should be a member of the executive committee of the city union, and her report should be given at the annual meeting of that union. The work of the Juniors, moreover, should frequently be represented in the rallies of the larger body, in order that the claims of their younger brothers and sisters upon them may be brought home to the consciences of the older Endeavorers.

Another Way. — Another method of forming this connection is by constituting the officers of the Junior union a union Junior committee, with the president of the Junior union for the Junior superintendent of the city union. In this way the leading Junior workers are placed in authoritative contact with all the Endeavorers of the city. It is a good plan for these workers to district the city, appointing a leader over each district, urging him to come in contact with the superintendents in his section, to visit as many societies as possible, and to arrange for joint meetings and intervisitation.

The President. — The work of the president of the Junior union is limited only by her time and strength. She should visit as many of the societies in the union as possible, holding private talks with every superintendent, and inspiring the Juniors by bright and brief addresses. She will, of course, be the ruling spirit in the union lookout committee, guiding their work in the organization of new societies, and whenever possible be present to control the organization. She will have it among her duties to urge upon the older Endeavorers of the city the claims of Junior work, advising them to form Junior committees for the aid of their Junior superintendents.

The planning of the quarterly rallies of the union will largely fall to her share, as well as the management of the quarterly superintendents' meetings. Helped by the sub-committees of the executive committee, she will choose speakers, select topics, and do everything possible beforehand to make the meetings profitable and entertaining. She must keep posted upon all recent developments of Junior methods, and must not fail to keep up an acquaintance with the Junior workers of her city or district. In all of these tasks she will, of course, have most competent assistants, for Junior workers are proverbially ready and able.

President's Letters. — The Junior president will find it a pleasant as well as a profitable plan to issue during the year, at intervals, manifolded letters to the superintendents, and at other times to the Juniors themselves. These letters will contain questions the superintendents are to answer, plans the president wishes to bring before the societies either for their local work or for the work of the union, suggestions as to helpful books and pamphlets recently published, and praise for any especial progress that has been made in any direction. These letters will well repay the slight outlay of time and money that they render necessary.

Stimulating the Societies. — The president of the Junior union may do much to interest the Juniors throughout the union in certain lines of work by offering slight prizes for special excellence in certain directions. For example, the superintendent of the Topeka, Kan., Junior Union once offered a prize of a dollar to the Junior who would select the Bible verse which he liked best, and tell in a letter to the president of the union the reason for his preference. This little contest brought many interesting letters, which were read at a meeting of the union. In a similar way, a contest regarding the best committee reports might be held, or the best set of Bible verses to be used with flowers sent to the sick, or the best record of good-literature committee work, or the largest gifts to missions in proportion to the size of the society.

The Secretary. — The position of secretary of the Junior union is one of great importance. It is her task to send out notifications of the quarterly rallies and superintendents' meetings, informing the different superintendents what part, if any, they and their Juniors have in the programme, what is the theme of discussions at the superintendents' meetings, and what will be expected by way of participation from all who come. It will be her duty to correspond with whatever speakers from outside the society are obtained for the Junior rally. Especially it will be her task to collect the statistics of the union, the most important items of which I have enumerated in the following paragraph.

The Secretary's Report. — The annual report of the secretary of the Junior union should be printed either from type or by a manifolder. This report should show the names and membership, active and trial, of all societies in the union, the date of their organization, the names and addresses of their superintendents and assistant superintendents, and of the pastors of the churches with which they are connected. Additional facts which should be given are the number that have graduated from the society during the year, the number that have joined the church, the amount of money given to missions, the number of new members received during the year, active and trial being separated, and any other statistics that will be of general interest. Large space in the report should be given to accounts of any especially helpful plans that have been tried and proved throughout the union, as well as to suggestions for fresh endeavors.

The Executive Committee. — The executive committee of the Junior union consists of all the superintendents of the union, while an advisory body is at hand, consisting of the assistant superintendents and the pastors. Such a body is too large, in the great cities, to be effective; and it is best to subdivide it. Select from the members of the executive committee a Junior union lookout committee, whose duties it will be to preside over the organization of new societies, planting these new societies, as far as possible, in every church that does not yet contain a Junior organization. There should be also a rally committee, with the president of the union at the head, whose duty it would be to prepare the programme for the quarterly Junior rallies. Another committee should do the same thing for the quarterly meeting of the Junior superintendents, while another committee might act as an information committee, to report at the superintendents' meeting any interesting facts regarding the progress of the Junior work, and any helpful plans they have come across in their reading. In a similar way other sub-committees might be formed.

The Union Treasury. — The work of a Junior union cannot be carried on without money. The correspondence, the printing of the report, the circular letters, the car-fare of the speakers, the gifts of literature to those who are organizing new societies — all such things take money. The entire sum necessary, however, to do a large amount of good in the course of a year's Junior work, is very slight, and the Junior superintendents and societies will gladly contribute it.

Do not fail to hold to the Christian Endeavor principle of freewill contributions. Under no circumstances levy a tax upon the societies, and never drop a society from the roll because it does not contribute money to the support of the union. You may go so far as to announce to the societies what amount of money is required to conduct the affairs of the union in good shape; but let each society determine for itself, considering its numbers and resources, what is its own share of this sum.

Stock in It. — The Juniors will be glad to contribute their share of the expenses of the Junior union; and if this responsibility is placed upon them they will think far more of the work of the union, and feel a sense of proprietorship in it.

Superintendent Conferences. — In no better way can the Junior work of a city be improved and vivified than by frequent conferences of the Junior superintendents. Let these be made as homelike and familiar as possible. The Baltimore plan is the best I have seen.

Some superintendent sends to the secretary of the Junior

union an invitation, which is accepted by the appropriate committee. Cards are sent to all the superintendents, inviting them and their assistants to attend the conference, and giving a subject for the evening. As the meeting is held in a home, it is far more likely to be informal and helpful.

It is opened by a short, interesting paper on some topic relative to Junior work; and after this comes the main feature, — the question-box. When notices of the meeting are sent to the superintendents, each is asked to send to the secretary any question he desires answered and discussed. On receipt of these questions they are immediately sent to the different superintendents, that they may think them over and be ready to reply in the conference. When this answer comes from some one in the audience, the other persons in the company are encouraged to express their views, and so the discussion is started.

After the question-box, the receiving superintendent and her assistants serve light refreshments, and the rest of the evening is spent socially.

Topics for Superintendents' Meetings. — In most superintendents' meetings the problem will be what topics of burning interest to omit, rather than what to talk about. However, the following list of themes for discussion may prove useful and suggestive : —

The advantages of Intermediate societies.
Graduation : at what age? with what ceremonies?
How to promote regular attendance.
Your pet plan of Bible study.
How do you arouse interest in temperance?
How do you make sure the Juniors read the daily readings?
What is your way of teaching missions?
What committees are essential?
What novel committees have you found useful?
How to win and hold the boys.
How to get all to sing.
Teaching Juniors to pray.
Fresh modes of carrying on the consecration meeting.
How to keep the society treasury full.
The preservation of order in the meetings.
Interesting the parents in the society.

The good of Mothers' Societies of Christian Endeavor.

How to teach the Juniors to give.

How to influence the home life of Juniors.

What do your Juniors learn about their church?

Your brightest Junior social.

Shall our trial members have a pledge?

How get the Juniors from the trial to active membership?

What does the parents' pledge mean in your church?

How can we improve our union work?

What relief work may our Juniors undertake?

How does your pastor help your society?

How do you present to your Juniors the claims of Christ?

Object lessons for Juniors.

How much to do for the Juniors.

How do you get the older Endeavorers interested in your Juniors?

How do you emphasize the Junior pledge?

What does your society do for the Sunday school?

How do you receive new members?

How do you carry on your business meetings?

Where may new societies be organized?

Encouragements. — Begin your superintendents' meetings with a note of cheer and hope, after the fashion of one meeting of the Cleveland Junior Union. The first part of the evening was spent entirely in the recitation of "encouragements," each superintendent bringing forward some experience with her Juniors that had been an encouragement to her.

Cut Short the Business. — The business to be brought before the executive committee of the union at the monthly superintendents' meetings should be disposed of as promptly as possible, that the superintendents may get, as soon as may be, to the main work of the hour. Hold an introductory song and prayer service, not to last more than ten minutes, read the minutes of the last meeting, pass upon applications from new societies for entrance into the union, and as promptly as possible despatch whatever business may be necessary, and then take up the regular topic of the day.

The Rallies. — At the Junior rallies the best portion of the church should be set apart for the Juniors themselves. They should sit together as societies, and in order that enough space may be reserved, each superintendent should inform the president of the union beforehand how many Juniors may be expected from her society. The Juniors themselves should wear badges, and carry at the heads of their lines their society banners. As they enter they should sing their society marching songs.

As much as possible the entire exercises and management of the rally should be in the hands of the Juniors. They should largely compose the reception committee, to meet newcomers at the door or station. A Junior choir should chiefly furnish the music, and Junior ushers should escort the company to their seats. Indeed, it will not be impossible to find a Junior who can conduct with dignity and propriety the opening devotional exercises. The address of welcome should be made by a Junior from the society of the church, and the response be given by one of the visiting Juniors.

Throughout the programme, — and, by the way, the printed programmes should be as bright and attractive as possible, using gay colors, — let as much as possible be given to the Juniors to do. They should come with their memories stored with certain psalms or other Scripture passages to repeat in concert. For variety, they may be asked to learn the words of a hymn, to repeat in the same way. An interesting feature will be the singing of different hymns by each society, the societies having practised in their own churches. There should always be a roll-call of the societies, and this is one way of responding. At other times the societies will respond by the concert repetition of Scripture verses. Possibly not at every rally, but once or twice a year certainly, conclude the rally with a consecration service, the societies taking part as a whole in whatever way they see fit. At the close, repeat the pledge in concert.

Throughout the longer and more formal exercises, give the children something to do on every possible occasion. It will serve to hold their attention if you call upon them now and then to raise their hands in voting, to wave their handkerchiefs, to wave flags, or to rise all together. A concert exercise by the Juniors, especially one that will require a little costuming, short papers by Juniors upon different phases of the work, recitations by separate Juniors, Junior songs, either solos or choruses, — all of these will serve to make the young people feel that the meeting is their very own.

Many a Junior rally has been spoiled by a long harangue by some man or woman who has no sympathy with children, and no understanding of what will interest and help them. Let no consideration of so-called policy persuade you to place such a person upon the programme. Those who speak before Juniors at their rallies should be skilled with the chalk, or able to enforce a truth by the use of objects, in some such way as Mr. Sleeper at the Montreal Convention with his Junior in armor, or Mr. Tyndall at the New York Convention with his two balloons, one filled with heavy gas and the other with light, which he put through all sorts of fascinating evolutions illustrating the dangers of bad companionship.

Above all, see that the programme is not too long. This is the all but universal sin of Junior rallies. There is such an abundance of material, there are so many interesting things that may be done, that those who prepare the rallies are almost certain to fall into the temptation of adding just one thing more, until the effect of the whole is spoiled, the children are tired, and the parents displeased. Save some plans for the next time, and remember that one good speaker is the making of any programme.

A Motto Exercise. — A pleasant exercise for a Junior rally is a motto exercise. Some time beforehand instruct each superintendent to have her society choose some bright and helpful motto which they will repeat in concert at the rally. These mottoes should be sent to the one who is to have charge of the exercises; and he will prepare himself with a bright sentence or two after each motto is repeated, showing the Juniors something that is especially good to be remembered about each motto.

Topics For Rallies. — Here are some good topics for a Junior rally, the themes to be treated by the Juniors themselves: "What the Junior society has done for me." "What can Juniors do for missions?" "Why should we look forward to graduating into the older Endeavor society?" "How will our Junior training help us in the older society?" "The good I have gained from the Junior pledge." "What I like best in the work of each committee." "The hard things in Junior society work." "Bible Juniors, and what they teach me." "Why I love the Bible." "Stories about some famous hymns."

" What Juniors can do for temperance." " What Juniors can do for their country." " How to earn money for missions." " The Junior songs I like best, and why." " Some mistakes we Juniors make." " How we can help the Sunday-school." " What we can do for our pastors."

The Annual Meeting. — Whatever is done at the quarterly meetings of the union, be sure to make the annual meeting an especially noteworthy occasion. Decorate the church in which it is held. Prepare special music. Obtain, if possible, an attractive speaker from abroad. Advertise the meeting well in the churches and the newspapers, and especially endeavor to obtain a large company of the older Endeavorers, as of course the Juniors will come any way.

If your union has a large membership, it is a good plan to have two sessions, one in the afternoon and one in the evening, the former being devoted especially to the Junior superintendents and the children, and the latter serving to present the claims and the work of the Junior society to the older Endeavorers and to the grown-up Christians. A large number of Juniors, of course, will be present at this evening session; and so especial pains should be taken to bring the exercises to an early close.

A Prize Banner. — It is a good plan for the Junior union to present a prize banner, to be held by the society that reports the best work for six months.

A Circular Letter. — The Junior superintendents of the union will get much good from a circular letter. The president writes the first letter, giving methods that she has found useful. The first superintendent who receives this letter adds other methods, or tells her troubles, asking for assistance, and then sends it to the next superintendent on the list, who does the same.

So the letter goes the rounds among the superintendents, each reading all that has preceded it, and adding her own new plans, troubles, or suggestions for help in the troubles that the others have brought forward. The circular letter, thus greatly enlarged and enriched, returns to the president, who reads the whole, detaches her original letter, writes a new one, and sends the whole to the one who first received her original letter.

Thus it goes the rounds again, each superintendent detaching her own letter, and adding a new one.

Intervisitation. — Superintendents of Junior city unions will find it wise to plan an occasional visiting day or week for the Juniors. Two members, — good ones to send will be the president and the chairman of the prayer-meeting committee, — should go from each society of the union to visit some other society. The superintendent of the union should make the appointments, and should arrange that each society will send forth two members and have two visitors. The following Sunday each visiting committee should report to its own society any helpful suggestions or plans which they have gained by their observations.

Get Fresh Ideas. — In some way or other it should be made possible for the Junior superintendents also to pay occasional visits to other societies. This intervisitation is helpful in this as in no other work, with the exception of Sunday-school teaching. Where there are assistant superintendents the feat is easily accomplished; but if there are none, then some older Endeavorer might without harm be pressed into service as substitute superintendent for a single day.

An Entertainment Committee. — A union entertainment committee may do much to increase the interest in Junior socials. The chairman of this committee obtains from the Junior superintendents lists of the Juniors in each society who have special talents in the way of entertaining, whether as singers, declaimers, conductors of games, or anything of the sort. Whenever a Junior superintendent needs outside help for the management of any part of a proposed entertainment, she applies to this entertainment committee, and learns what Endeavorers of neighboring societies she can probably call in to her assistance. In this way the Junior socials are improved, and, bett than that, the Juniors of different societies get to know one another.

CHAPTER XL.

THE STATE JUNIOR SUPERINTENDENT.

The Office. — There are few State Christian Endeavor unions now without a State superintendent of Junior work; soon, I hope, all State unions will appoint such officers. They are greatly needed, especially now, while the Junior work is young; and they always will be needed, to inspire the workers, co-ordinate their efforts, and diffuse the best and newest methods.

The work gains so much from experience that it will always be best to retain a good worker in office for more than one year. Give her a generous share of the State funds and a liberal portion of the State convention's time; for her work is second in importance to that of no State officer, — not even the State president himself. I say *her* work, because most State superintendents thus far are women, though some of the most zealous and efficient are consecrated young men.

The Record. — One of the first duties a State superintendent must perform is to see to it that the list of Junior societies in the State is accurate. That is to be the basis of all her activities. If she is in doubt on that score, let her ask all district and county secretaries to make a thorough canvass, and report to her the result.

The State record should contain the name of the church with which each society is connected, the names of pastor and Junior superintendent, the date of organization, and the number of members, of each class, on the first of each year. Additional records, of only secondary importance, will tell how many Juniors are graduated each year, how many join the church, how much money is given to missions, what committees are used, and will give all other obtainable facts that will help to show the status of each society.

Organization. — Having these facts before her, the State superintendent will at once see in what districts few Junior societies are found, and will seek to stir up the district and county officers, and, these failing, the individual societies. She will send literature explaining the good the society may do, and how it may be organized. With each package of literature she will send a personal note, inviting correspondence.

Very soon the field will become individualized, separate churches and pastors emerging here and there as possible new Junior centres. Upon these she will concentrate her fire. Mr. Sleeper's pamphlet, "A Word to Busy Pastors About the Junior Society," published by the United Society, and sold for $1.00 a hundred copies, will prove useful in this bombardment. So will "Hints for Forming" ($1.50 a hundred), the Junior Constitution, and various other leaflets. If she knows any able Junior worker in the neighborhood, she will ask her to call on the pastor and talk up the society. If her own services are desired to organize the new venture, she should not hesitate to go and set the society on foot.

Deputies. — It will be better, however, if the State superintendent can interest some local worker to organize and watch over each society that is started. During the first months constant help and advice will be needed, and it will be far better for society and pastor if the organizer is close at hand besides saving the time and strength of the State superintendent for other purposes, and training the local workers to become Junior missionaries.

At Conventions. — Let the State superintendent plan to be present at as many local Christian Endeavor gatherings as possible in the course of the year, especially in those parts of the State where the Junior society is least flourishing. The officers of the conventions will be glad to give you an opportunity to speak, if you make arrangements long enough beforehand. Open a question-box at a later session. Preside throughout the convention at an information bureau, where you can distribute Junior literature, and answer questions in private. Remember that your chief work at these conventions is to set the Endeavorers themselves to organizing new Junior societies.

The Junior Hour. — One of the best plans for an interesting Junior hour at a State convention was once tried in Wisconsin. Twelve Juniors from as many different towns and cities were set to writing two-minute papers upon different phases of Junior work, — prayer-meeting work, Bible work, lookout work, social work, missionary work, sunshine work, temperance work, helping the pastor, etc. Some substitutes were provided, which proved to be wise. The topics were assigned among these representatives by the State superintendent, who knew which society had been doing the best work along each line, and the young speakers in every case confined themselves to practical experience, and so were both interesting and helpful to the large audience.

Junior Headquarters. — The State superintendent should establish Junior headquarters at the State convention. In this room the Junior workers should register and hold their conferences, as well as become acquainted with each other by social intercourse. In this room should also be arranged samples of all kinds of Junior literature and helps.

Inspiration and Information. — Another very important part of the State superintendent's work is the popularization of good Junior methods. In her correspondence she should constantly invite accounts of fresh ways of doing things in Junior societies. Once in a while she should send to every Junior superintendent in the State what may be termed "suggestion sheets." These are manifolded letters consisting of short and pointed paragraphs, say ten or a dozen, each containing suggestions for novel methods of work. These suggestions may be obtained from private correspondence with progressive workers, or culled from the best Christian Endeavor papers and pamphlets. These sheets should be printed from a duplicating machine. The various hints should be condensed as far as is consistent with clearness. Each "suggestion sheet" thus sent out should invite fresh suggestions.

The Report. — The State superintendent's annual report should be given wide circulation. It should contain an abstract of the statistics gathered, an account of the parts of the State yet needing to be roused to the importance of Junior work, an urging to missionary effort along this line, and suggestions regarding the most important methods of work. Every society in the State should receive a printed copy of this report, which should be read at some society meeting.

JUNIOR CHRISTIAN ENDEAVOR SUPPLIES

For Sale by

United Society of Christian Endeavor
BOSTON AND CHICAGO

Junior Badges.

	EACH
Gold	$1.00
Silver	.25
Corinthian Silver	.15
Gold and Enamel	1.00
Silver and Enamel	.30
Corinthian Silver and Enamel	.20
Celluloid Buttons	.05

Honor Roll.

The Junior Honor Roll is handsomely lithographed in seven colors, is 24 x 32 inches in size, and has spaces for the names of forty Juniors. The roll is mounted on linen tinned at the top and bottom to prevent tearing.

It can be used for several purposes at the discretion of the Junior Superintendent — either for keeping a record of perfect lessons, or for learning Bible verses, or for marking attendance. Every Junior society should have this Roll on the walls of their prayer-meeting room. Price, securely packed, 75 cents, post-paid.

Hymn-Books.

JUNIOR CAROLS. The best book for Juniors ever published. 157 hymns, besides responsive readings and special exercises. Durably bound.

Words and Music: In quantities, by express, at purchaser's expense, 25 cents each. Sample copy, 30 cents.

Words only Edition: Flexible cloth. In quantities, by express, at purchaser's expense, 10 cents. Single copy, by mail, 11 cents.

JUNIOR CHRISTIAN ENDEAVOR SONGS. Compiled by Ira D. Sankey, John Willis Baer, and William Shaw. The Responsive Readings will be found very helpful.

Words and Music: Board covers, in quantities, by express, at purchaser's expense, price, 25 cents; single copy, by mail, 30 cents.

Words Only Edition: In quantities, by express, at purchaser's expense, price, 10 cents; single copy by mail, 11 cents. Cash must be sent with all orders, or, if desired, they will be sent C. O. D.

THE KING'S PRAISES — A Collection of Junior Songs. — By Charles S. Brown. In heavy manila paper covers. Price, sample copy, 12 cents, post-paid; in quantities, 10 cents each, 50 for $4.50, or 100 for $8.00; express not prepaid.

It is confidently believed that this is the best small collection of hymns that has ever been compiled for Junior Christian Endeavor societies or for Primary Departments of Sabbath schools. The book contains the words and music of about 50 pieces, every one of which is a gem. Many of the songs have been written especially for this book, and are copyrighted property.

Cards.

Per hund.

Junior Membership Pledge. Handsomely lithographed.............. $ .50

Junior Lookout Committee Excuse Cards .... .30

Junior Optional Pledge 30

Junior Daily Record of Bible Reading. A pretty card with the C. E. monogram printed in gold and color. There are thirty-one dots on the monogram, one to be pricked out each day when the Bible verse is read . .50

Junior Missionary Offering. The card is about 7 x 5 inches. The face contains the pledge and other matter attractively printed in two colors. On the back are ten small envelopes. In these the Juniors are to put their pennies until each contains five cents, making a total, when all are filled, of fifty cents. The card is then returned to the superintendent, and the money sent to the missionary boards. Price, card and envelopes complete, post-paid 3.00

Junior Temperance Pledge 30

Junior Topic Cards (Topics for the year) 1.00

Junior Leaflets.

A Word to Busy Pastors. By Rev. W. W. Sleeper. Two cents each . 1.00

A Word to Junior Superintendents. By John Willis Baer. Two cents each 1.00

Catechisms in Junior Societies. By Rev. F. E. Clark. Three cents each, 1.50

Quiet Hour for Juniors. By Mrs. L. T. Sloan. Two cents each . . ∞

Helps and Hints for Junior Workers. By Mrs. Ella N. Wood. Five cents each 3.00

Junior Christian Endeavor; Its Field and Work. By Mrs. F. E. Clark and Miss Kate H. Haus. Five cents each 3.00

Junior Christian Endeavor Unions. By Kate H. Haus. Three cents each, 1.50

Junior Constitution and By-Laws. Two cents each 1.00

Junior Prayer-Meeting Topics and Daily Verse. The yearly prayer-meeting topics and a Scripture verse for every day in the year, bearing upon the topics. Three cents each 1.50

Junior Societies : What They Are ; How to Start Them ; Things to Remember. By Rev. F. E. Clark. Three cents each 2.00

Meetings for Juniors and How to Conduct Them. By Mrs. James L. Hill. Twelve cents each. (In quantities, ten cents.)

Missionary Plans for Junior Societies. By V. F. P. 2.00

Scripture Illustrated (Object-Lessons). By Mrs. Alice M. Scudder. Five cents each 3.00

Junior Catechisms.

Gospel Truth. By Rev. James W. Cooper, D.D. The great truths of the Bible answered in the exact words of Scripture. Five cents each ; $1.00 for twenty-five ; $3.00 a hundred.

Questions on the Books of the Old Testament. By Mrs. C. J. Buchanan. Consecutive Bible studies especially adapted to young people. Five cents each; $1.00 for twenty-five ; $3.00 a hundred.

Outline Study of the Life of Christ. By Rev. A. W. Spooner. For little learners. Five cents each ; $1.00 for twenty-five ; $3.00 a hundred.

Lessons on the Life of Jesus. By Rev. Geo. B. Stewart, D.D. Two courses of forty lessons each. The Saviour's life is considered chronologically in an interesting, winsome manner. Ten cents each ; $1.00 a dozen.

2

Junior Books.

Bible in Lesson and Story, The. By Ruth Mowry Brown. 7¼ x 5 inches, 254 pp. Handsomely illustrated with twelve full-page engravings. Bound in royal purple cloth, with illuminated title in gold, $1.25. Forty chapters upon as many Bible truths, each chapter written in a manner that will especially interest the children. In connection with each lesson is a delightful, illustrative story, together with a "Memory Gem" and an "Occupation," in which the children are given something to do that will help impress the truths that have been taught. It is equally adapted to Junior workers, primary teachers, or for use in the home.

Object-Lessons and Illustrated Talks. By Rev. George F. Kenngott. 76 pp. Heavy paper covers, 25 cents. Fifty-three different object-lessons and illustrated talks for the use of superintendents of Junior and Intermediate societies, together with an Order of Service, a word about stories, etc.

Junior Recitations. By Amos R. Wells. 6¾ x 4½ inches, 128 pp., cloth binding, with unique cover design in colors. Fifty cents. A book of children's Recitations, Dialogues, Exercises, etc., suitable for Anniversary, Missionary, Temperance Meetings, and other special occasions. The volume has one unique feature that will commend it to all practical workers: each piece is introduced with directions for its rendering, — gestures, costumes, if any, decorations, accessories of all sorts. In this way the working value of the book is doubled. A large part of the book consists of exercises by Professor Wells that have never before been published in any form.

Good Times with the Juniors. By Lillian M. Heath. Cloth, 50 cents. The latest and best book of the kind that has ever been published. It is filled to overflowing with suggestions for socials, entertainments, receptions, drills, etc., besides giving several character sketches or plays for little folks. The different holidays, such as Christmas, Thanksgiving, Independence Day, Washington's Birthday, Valentine Day, etc., are all remembered. Each programme is complete in itself, but the various games are indexed separately.

Social Evenings. By Amos R. Wells, Managing Editor of *The Christian Endeavor World*. Price, 35 cents. A book for Social Committees, and for all who appreciate pleasant and helpful amusements.

Social to Save. By Amos R. Wells. Cloth. Price, 35 cents. A companion volume to "Social Evenings." Everything is new and fresh. A mine of enjoyment for your society and home circle.

The Junior Manual. A Handbook for Junior Workers. By Amos R. Wells. This is the only full and complete manual for Junior workers ever published. It contains many times more matter than any other help for Junior superintendents ever written. It is practical. All its plans have been tried and proved. Hundreds of Junior superintendents, from all parts of the world, have contributed to it their brightest methods. It covers the ground. All phases of the subject are thoroughly treated. It is very concise. Into every paragraph is condensed a plan that might well be expanded into an article. Forty chapters; 300 pp.; 900 separate articles. Price, cloth-bound, $1.25, post-paid. Special edition, in board covers, 75 cents.

UNITED SOCIETY OF CHRISTIAN ENDEAVOR,

TREMONT TEMPLE, BOSTON, MASS.   155 LA SALLE ST., CHICAGO, ILL.

The King's Praises.

A Collection of Junior Songs. By Charles S. Brown. In heavy manila paper covers. Price, sample copy, 12 cents, post-paid; in quantities, 10 cents each, $4.50 for fifty, or $8.00 for one hundred; express not prepaid.

It is confidently believed that this is the best small collection of hymns that has ever been compiled for Junior Christian Endeavor societies or for Primary Departments of Sabbath Schools. The book contains the words and music of about fifty pieces, every one of which is a gem. Many of the songs have been written especially for this book, and are copyrighted property.

Junior Graduation Diplomas.

Junior workers have been calling for some time for an attractive but inexpensive diploma that could be given to the members of the Junior Society when they are graduated into the Young People's Society of Christian Endeavor. The United Society has met this demand by issuing a beautiful little diploma, 8 x 10 inches, lithographed in three colors. It has met with the unqualified approval of Junior leaders, and we feel sure that it will be greatly prized by the Junior graduates. Price, sample copy, 5 cents; 40 cents per dozen.

Intermediate Diplomas.

We also have diplomas same as above, but for Juniors who graduate into the Intermediate Society. Price, 5 cents each; 40 cents a dozen.

Bible Games.

Who Knows His Bible? Children and Young folks seek and must have amusement, and Christian parents have a duty to perform in that direction. They ought to make the home, fireside, and centre-table the brightest spots on earth. Pastime is lost time if profit to the individual is not part of the sport. All good qualities are combined in the new game. It combines three games, all useful and enjoyable. Price, 50 cents, post-paid.

Divided Wisdom. A game based on hymns and Bible proverbs. By "Pansy" (Mrs. G. R. Alden). There is probably no person living today who has exerted a more helpful influence over young people than the well-known author, "Pansy." To meet the needs of the children in their leisure moments and provide them with exercises that would be not only interesting but helpful and instructive led to the preparation of this game. Price, 50 cents, post-paid.

Bible Authors. A Bible game that is both entertaining and instructive, and that will, in the most interesting way, make the children familiar with a large number of Bible verses and characters. Price, 50 cents.

The Williston Game of Bible Queries. By Mrs. James L. Hill. Our latest game and one of the very best. There are two sets of cards, one of questions and the other of answers. Three or more entirely different games can be played. They are all exceedingly interesting and helpful. Just the thing for young people. Price, 35 cents, post-paid.

Junior Christian Endeavor Committee Report Blanks.

Every Junior worker will appreciate the importance of having some simple but suggestive form of report blank for the use of committees. The following blanks covering the work of the principal committees, have been prepared and have me the unqualified approval of many Junior superintendents who have examined them Every Junior Society should have a set.

No. 1. Lookout Committee Blank.
No. 2. Prayer-meeting Committee Blank.
No. 3. Social Committee Blank.
No. 4. Music Committee Blank.
No. 5. Missionary and Temperance Committee Blank.
No. 6. Sunday-school Committee Blank.
No. 7. Flower and Sunshine Committee Blank.

These blanks are printed in duplicate so the committee can retain one and giv the other to the secretary. They are bound in pamphlet form, each pamphlet con taining twenty-five blanks.

PRICE.

Any of the above Committee Blanks (each) 2
  (Complete set of seven for $1.50.)

Junior Pledge for Chapel Wall.

Trusting in the Lord Jesus Christ for strength, I promise Him that I will strive to do whatever He would like to have me do; that I will pray and read the Bible every day; and that, just so far as I know how, I will try to lead a Christian life. I will be present at every meeting of the society when I can, and will take some part in every meeting.

The accompany ing cut is a facsimile of our large Junior Wall Pledge. Size 28 × 36 inches printed on heavy paper in large, clear type that can be easily read across large vestry. It i suspended from rod with roll attached and does not requir framing. Price, post paid, 75 cents.

UNITED SOCIETY OF CHRISTIAN ENDEAVOR,

Tremont Temple,
BOSTON, MASS.

155 La Salle Street
CHICAGO, ILL.

THE JUNIOR CHRISTIAN ENDEAVOR WORLD.

In response to a wide-spread demand, THE JUNIOR CHRISTIAN ENDEAVOR WORLD was established in January, 1893. It at once reached a large circulation, and has been steadily growing in usefulness and popularity. The testimony of Junior workers all over the country is that this little paper is exceedingly valuable in interesting the Juniors and helping the superintendent in her difficult task. It is

. . . AN EIGHT-PAGE MONTHLY . . .

Each page 9 × 13 inches in size. It is printed on **excellent paper**, and is crowded with bright illustrations. It is edited by the editors of THE CHRISTIAN ENDEAVOR WORLD.

IT CONTAINS ALL THE HELPS

Needed by the Juniors for the proper management of their society work.

Delightful Stories and Sketches Among these writers are Sophie May, Rev. J. F. Cowan, Mrs. Fannie E. Newberry, Dr. F. E. Clark, Rev. Leander S. Keyser, Mrs. Mary E. Allbright, Amos R. Wells, Mrs. F. E. Clark, Mrs. Alice May Scudder, Mrs. Belle Kellogg Towne, and Sophie Swett.

Pansy will continue to contribute to every number one of her delightful and helpful stories. This of itself ought to win for the paper thousands of subscribers, for Pansy writes for no other paper in this way.

Bright Sayings To this page the Juniors contribute the comical and original remarks made by their younger brothers and sisters, as well as the bright sayings they have heard from their elders. It is wonderful how many of these are sent in, and how good they all are.

Golden Nuggets In this department the young people will continue to quote the most interesting bits from their reading. In " Bright Sayings " they will continue to tell the funniest stories they can find from their reading or experience.

The Prayer-Meeting Page is by Dr. John F. Cowan, and gives just the help needed by Junior leaders and Junior followers.

Uncle David's Easy Chair is the letter department, and gives interesting letters from the Juniors everywhere. Besides, every number has the picture of a Junior society.

Don't you think your society ought to have a large club for this paper? Don't you think it would give you better meetings, and make all your members more interested in their Junior work? Try it.

TERMS.

The Junior Christian Endeavor World is published once a month, is illustrated, and contains eight pages.

The Subscription Price is 35 cents a year when the paper is sent to an individual address, or only 25 cents a year when ten or more papers are sent in one package addressed to one person.

Payment for Subscriptions must be made in advance, and should be sent to

THE JUNIOR CHRISTIAN ENDEAVOR WORLD,

TREMONT TEMPLE, BOSTON, MASS.   *155 LA SALLE ST., CHICAGO, ILL.*

www.ingramcontent.com/pod-product-compliance
Lightning Source LLC
LaVergne TN
LVHW011343080426
835511LV00005B/117